# Health
## Focus on You®

**Linda Meeks-Mitchell, M.S.**
Associate Professor of Health Education
College of Education
The Ohio State University
Columbus, Ohio

**Philip Heit, Ed.D.**
Professor and Chairman of Health Education
Professor of Allied Medicine
College of Medicine     College of Education
The Ohio State University, Columbus, Ohio

## CONSULTANTS

Doris Bennett, M.D.
Chief of Pediatrics
Kenmore Center of Harvard
 Community Health Plan
Boston, Massachusetts

Todd F. Holzman, M.D.
Child Psychologist
Harvard Community Health Plan
Wellesley, Massachusetts

Mary Alice Beetham, M.S.P.A.
Health Education Consultant
Columbus, Ohio

Gus T. Dalis, Ed.D.
Consultant, Health Education
Los Angeles County Office
 of Education
Downey, California

Florence Fenton, Ed.D.
Supervisor, Health Services
Prince George's County Schools
Upper Marlboro, Maryland

Rick Kearns, M.S. Ed.
Director: Center for
 Fitness/Wellness
Idaho State University
Pocatello, Idaho

## MERRILL
### PUBLISHING COMPANY
A Bell & Howell Information Company
Columbus, Ohio
Toronto • London • Sydney

## A Merrill Health Program

**Health:** Focus on You, K Big Book (with TE)
**Health:** Focus on You, Student Editions, 1–8
**Health:** Focus on You, Teacher Editions, 1–8
**Health:** Focus on You, Teacher Resource Books, K–8 (Reproducible Masters)
Enrichment Booklets
Posters

**Linda Meeks-Mitchell and Philip Heit** are coauthors of *Health: Focus on You,* Merrill Publishing Company's K to 8 health program. Both authors conduct workshops in health science, curriculum design, and health methodology, in addition to the courses they teach at The Ohio State University. Both authors have taught health education in public schools and have individually written articles and texts. Mrs. Meeks-Mitchell is coauthor of *Toward a Healthy Lifestyle Through Elementary Health Education.* Mrs. Meeks-Mitchell and Dr. Heit are the coauthors of *Teaching Health in Middle and Secondary Schools.*

### Reviewers:

Louise Lilley Bell, *Camden Public Schools, Camden, New Jersey*
Gail Hallas, *R.N., C.N.A., Florida Health Education, St. Petersburg, Florida*
Sylvia M. Kennedy, *Lafayette Parish School Board, Lafayette, Louisiana*
Carroll Knutson, *Trimpe Junior High School, Bethalto, Illinois*
Veronica Maschio-Skerker, *Canton High School, Collinsville, Connecticut*
Frank T. Mondi, *Margate Middle School, Margate, Florida*
Donna L. Osness, *Mohawk Instructional Center, Shawnee Mission, Kansas*
Millicent C. Rhodes, *Coordinator of Health Education, Nashville, Tennessee*
Debra D. Rich, *Beaumont Junior High School, Lexington, Kentucky*

### Consultant for Substance Abuse:

Stuart L. Weibel, Ph.D., *OCLC Office of Research, Dublin, Ohio*

*Series Editor:* Mary Baker; *Editor:* Nerma C. Henderson; *Project Designer:* Patrick J. McCarthy; *Project Artist:* Dennis L. Smith; *Illustrators:* Nancy A. Heim, Charles Passerelli; *Photo Editor:* Lindsay Gerard; *Production Editor:* Annette Hoffman

### Cover Photo Description and Credit:

Making sure that a kite will fly after making it is a very satisfying experience.
**Cover Photo:** George Anderson

ISBN 0-675-06246-2

Published by
**Merrill Publishing Company**
**A Bell & Howell Company**
**Columbus, Ohio 43216**

Printed in the United States of America

# Preface

Have you ever hit a tennis ball with a tennis racket? Have you ever hit a baseball with a bat? If you have, you had to focus on or pay attention to the moving ball. When you hit the ball and followed through with your swing, you were successful. You had a good feeling about yourself.

To have a successful life, you need to focus on or pay attention to your health. You need to learn how to be healthy. *Health: Focus On You*® provides factual information about the ten major areas of health—Mental Health, Family and Social Health, Growth and Development, Nutrition, Exercise and Fitness, Drugs, Diseases and Disorders, Consumer and Personal Health, Safety and First Aid, and Community and Environmental Health. This factual information helps you develop skills that promote your health, the health of others, and the quality of the environment. These skills will help you manage your life now and in the future. Life management skills are listed at the end of each chapter.

*Health: Focus On You*® teaches you a responsible decision-making model to assist you with the many decisions you will make. The decisions you make will have an impact on you, others, and the environment. These decisions should be healthful, safe, and legal. They should promote self-respect and respect for others. These decisions should follow parental guidelines.

*Health: Focus On You*® provides an enjoyable approach to learning. As you focus or pay attention to health, you learn that a healthful lifestyle provides more enjoyment to you and others than does a lifestyle filled with harmful habits and decisions. A healthful lifestyle adds years to your life and life to your years.

# TABLE OF CONTENTS

**Health and Your Life** . . . . . . . . . . . .viii

**Unit**

**1**  Growing Up Healthy . . . . . .2

**Chapter**

**1**  **Learning to Be Healthy** . . . . . .4

1:1  What Is Health?. . . . . . . . . . . . . . . . . .5
1:2  The Importance of
Health Knowledge . . . . . . . . . . . . . .6
1:3  Making Decisions About Health. . . . . .8
1:4  How to Gain Health Knowledge . . . . .9

Life Management Skills . . . . . . . . .13

**Chapter**

**2**  **Relating to Others** . . . . . . . . .14

2:1  What Is a Friend? . . . . . . . . . . . . .15
2:2  Who Are Your Friends? . . . . . . . . .17
2:3  The Importance of Communication . .19
2:4  Sharing with Your Family . . . . . . . .20
2:5  Being Grateful . . . . . . . . . . . . . . .21

Health Highlights
Divorce and Dissolution . . . . . . . . .22

Life Management Skills . . . . . . . . . .25

**Chapter**

**3**  **Growth and Development** . . .26

3:1  Hormones and Adolescence . . . . . .27
3:2  Physical Growth
During Adolescence . . . . . . . . . . . .28
3:3  Emotional Growth
During Adolescence . . . . . . . . . . . .29
3:4  Social Growth During Adolescence . .32
3:5  What Is Stress? . . . . . . . . . . . . . .33
3:6  Kinds of Stress . . . . . . . . . . . . . .34
3:7  What to Do About Distress . . . . . . .36

Health Highlights
Aging Healthfully . . . . . . . . . . . . . .38

Life Management Skills . . . . . . . . .41

**Unit**

**2**  Taking Care of
Your Body . . . . . . . . . . . . . .42

**Chapter**

**4**  **Physical Exercise and
Physical Fitness** . . . . . . . . . . .44

4:1  What Is Physical Fitness?. . . . . . . .45
4:2  What Makes You Physically Fit? . . . .46
4:3  Exercises That Make
You Physically Fit. . . . . . . . . . . . . .48
4:4  How Physical Fitness
Helps You to Be at Your Best . . . . .50
4:5  How to Begin Your
Physical Fitness Program . . . . . . . .52

Life Management Skills . . . . . . . . .57

**Chapter**

**5**  **Dental Health** . . . . . . . . . . . . .58

5:1  A Tooth Has Different Parts . . . . . .59
5:2  Different Teeth Do
Different Things . . . . . . . . . . . . . . .60
5:3  Tooth Decay . . . . . . . . . . . . . . . .62
5:4  Periodontal Disease . . . . . . . . . . .63
5:5  How to Brush Your Teeth . . . . . . . .64
5:6  How to Floss Your Teeth . . . . . . . .65
5:7  How Fluorides Work. . . . . . . . . . . .66
5:8  What About Sugar? . . . . . . . . . . . .67

Health Highlights
What About Braces? . . . . . . . . . . .68

Life Management Skills . . . . . . . . .71

**Chapter**

**6     Nutrition and Your Habits . . . 72**

6:1     Nutrients . . . . . . . . . . . . . . . . . . . . . **73**
6:2     The Food Groups—The Best Habit . . **75**
6:3     The Overeating Habit. . . . . . . . . . . **77**
6:4     The Breakfast Habit . . . . . . . . . . . . **78**
6:5     The Vending Machine
        and Fast Food Habit. . . . . . . . . . . . **79**
6:6     The Habits of Athletes . . . . . . . . . . **80**

        Health Hightlights
        Seven Diet Goals. . . . . . . . . . . . . **82**

        Life Management Skills . . . . . . . . . **85**

**Unit**

**3     How Your
        Body Works . . . . . . . . . . . . . . 86**

**Chapter**

**7     Your Five Senses . . . . . . . . . . 88**

7:1     Your Sense of Sight . . . . . . . . . . . . **89**
7:2     Protecting Your Sight . . . . . . . . . . . **91**
7:3     Your Sense of Hearing . . . . . . . . . . **93**
7:4     Signs of Hearing Loss . . . . . . . . . **93**
7:5     Protecting Your Hearing . . . . . . . . **94**
7:6     Your Sense of Taste. . . . . . . . . . . . **95**
7:7     Your Sense of Smell . . . . . . . . . . . **96**
7:8     Your Sense of Touch . . . . . . . . . . . **97**

        Health Highlights
        The TV Habit—Good or Bad?. . . . . **98**

        Life Management Skills. . . . . . . . **101**

**Chapter**

**8     Your Body Systems . . . . . . . 102**

8:1     The Nervous System . . . . . . . . . . **103**
8:2     The Muscular-Skeletal Systems . . . **104**
8:3     The Circulatory system. . . . . . . . . **105**
8:4     The Respiratory System . . . . . . . . **107**
8:5     The Digestive System. . . . . . . . . . **108**
8:6     The Urinary System . . . . . . . . . . . **110**

8:7     The Endocrine System . . . . . . . . . **110**
8:8     The Reproductive System. . . . . . . **112**

        Life Management Skills. . . . . . . . **115**

**Chapter**

**9     Having a Disability
        or a Handicap . . . . . . . . . . . . 116**

9:1     What Are Disabilities
        and Handicaps? . . . . . . . . . . . . . **117**
9:2     Being at Your Best . . . . . . . . . . . . **118**
9:3     Being Blind . . . . . . . . . . . . **121**
9:4     Being Deaf . . . . . . . . . . . . **123**
9:5     Having a Brain
        or Nerve Disorder . . . . . . . . . . . **125**
9:6     Other Types of Handicaps . . . . . . **127**

        Health Highlights
        "The Kids on the Block" . . . . . . . **128**

        Life Management Skills. . . . . . . . **131**

**Unit**

**4     Consumer Health . . . . . . 132**

**Chapter**

**10     The Wise Consumer . . . . . . 134**

10:1     Who Is a Health Consumer? . . . . . **135**
10:2     Health Products for
         Physical Health . . . . . . . . . . . . . **136**
10:3     Health Products for
         Mental Health . . . . . . . . . . . . . **137**
10:4     Health Products for
         Social Health . . . . . . . . . . . . . **138**
10:5     Health Services . . . . . . . . . . . . . **138**
10:6     Health Service for
         Physical Health . . . . . . . . . . . . . **140**
10:7     Health Services for
         Mental Health . . . . . . . . . . . . . **142**
10:8     Health Services for
         Social Health . . . . . . . . . . . . . **142**
10:9     Making Wise Choices. . . . . . . . . . **143**

         Health Highlights
         UPC in the Supermarket. . . . . . . **144**

         Life Management Skills. . . . . . . . **147**

**Chapter**

**11    The Physical Examination** . .**148**

11:1    The Importance of a
        Physical Examination . . . . . . . . .**149**
11:2    Health History . . . . . . . . . . . . . . .**150**
11:3    Weight and Height . . . . . . . . . . .**151**
11:4    Temperature . . . . . . . . . . . . . . .**152**
11:5    Eyes and Ears. . . . . . . . . . . . . .**153**
11:6    Nose. . . . . . . . . . . . . . . . . . . . .**154**
11:7    Mouth and Throat. . . . . . . . . . . .**154**
11:8    Reflex Tests. . . . . . . . . . . . . . . .**155**
11:9    Palpation or Feeling . . . . . . . . . .**156**
11:10   Percussion or Tapping . . . . . . . .**156**
11:11   Ausculation or Listening . . . . . . .**157**
11:12   Blood Pressure and Pulse . . . . . .**158**
11:13   Blood Sample . . . . . . . . . . . . . .**159**

        Health Highlights
        Disease Prevention . . . . . . . . . .**160**

        Life Management Skills. . . . . . . .**163**

**Chapter**

**12    Doctors and Hospitals** . . . . .**164**

12:1    What Is a Hospital? . . . . . . . . . .**165**
12:2    Types of Doctors at
        the Hospital. . . . . . . . . . . . . . . .**167**
12:3    People Who Work at
        the Hospital. . . . . . . . . . . . . . . .**168**
12:4    A Day at the Hospital . . . . . . . . .**169**
12:5    The Operating Room . . . . . . . . .**172**
12:6    The Emergency Room . . . . . . . .**172**

        Life Management Skills. . . . . . . .**175**

**Unit**

**5    Drugs, Alcohol,
      and Tobacco** . . . . . . . . . . . .**176**

**Chapter**

**13    Some Facts About Drugs** . . .**178**

13:1    What Is a Drug?. . . . . . . . . . . . .**179**
13:2    Depressants . . . . . . . . . . . . . . .**180**
13:3    Stimulants . . . . . . . . . . . . . . . . .**182**
13:4    Hallucinogens . . . . . . . . . . . . . .**184**

13:5    Marijuana . . . . . . . . . . . . . . . . .**184**
13:6    Prescription Drugs . . . . . . . . . . .**185**
13:7    Over-the-Counter Drugs . . . . . . .**186**

        Health Highlights
        Tamper-Resistant
        Drug Packaging . . . . . . . . . . . . .**188**

        Life Management Skills. . . . . . . .**191**

**Chapter**

**14    Alcohol and Tobacco** . . . . . .**192**

14:1    What Is Alcohol? . . . . . . . . . . . .**193**
14:2    What Alcohol Does
        in the Body . . . . . . . . . . . . . . . .**194**
14:3    How Others' Drinking
        Can Affect You. . . . . . . . . . . . . .**196**
14:4    Protecting Yourself. . . . . . . . . . .**196**
14:5    Cigarette Smoking:
        Your Concern. . . . . . . . . . . . . . .**197**
14:6    Tobacco and Your Health . . . . . .**198**
14:7    Sidestream Smoke. . . . . . . . . . .**200**
14:8    Smokeless Tobacco . . . . . . . . . .**200**

        Life Management Skills. . . . . . . .**203**

**Chapter**

**15    Making Responsible
      Choices** . . . . . . . . . . . . . . . .**204**

15:1    Decision Making. . . . . . . . . . . . .**205**
15:2    Factors That Influence Decisions. . .**206**
15:3    How You Make a Decision . . . . . .**210**
15:4    How to Be Drug-Free . . . . . . . . .**212**

        Health Highlights
        Crack and Designer Drugs . . . . . .**214**

        Life Management Skills. . . . . . . .**217**

**Unit**

**6    First Aid and Safety** . . . . .**218**

**Chapter**

**16    Medical Emergencies** . . . . .**220**

16:1    What Is a Medical Emergency?. . . .**221**
16:2    General Rules for
        Emergency Care . . . . . . . . . . . .**222**
16:3    First Aid for Heart Attacks. . . . . .**223**

16:4  First Aid for Strokes . . . . . . . . . . . **225**
16:5  First Aid for Asthma . . . . . . . . . **226**
16:6  Appendicitis . . . . . . . . . . . . . . . **226**
16:7  Diabetic Coma . . . . . . . . . . . . . **228**
16:8  Insulin Shock . . . . . . . . . . . . . . **229**

Health Highlights
Sports Specialists . . . . . . . . **230**

Life Management Skills . . . . . . . . **233**

Chapter
**17    Dealing with
Heat and Cold** . . . . . . . . . . . **234**

17:1  Heat Cramps . . . . . . . . . . . . . . . **235**
17:2  Heat Exhaustion . . . . . . . . . . . . **237**
17:3  Heatstroke . . . . . . . . . . . . . . . . **237**
17:4  Prickly Heat . . . . . . . . . . . . . . . **239**
17:5  Sunburn . . . . . . . . . . . . . . . . . . **239**
17:6  Frostbite . . . . . . . . . . . . . . . . . **241**
17:7  Hypothermia . . . . . . . . . . . . . . **243**

Health Highlights
Deep-Freeze Surgery . . . . . . . . . . **244**

Life Management Skills . . . . . . . . **247**

Chapter
**18    Sports and
Play Injuries** . . . . . . . . . . . . . **248**

18:1  Scrapes . . . . . . . . . . . . . . . . . . **249**
18:2  Cuts . . . . . . . . . . . . . . . . . . . . **250**
18:3  Sore Muscles . . . . . . . . . . . . . . **251**
18:4  Dislocations . . . . . . . . . . . . . . . **253**
18:5  Safety in Running . . . . . . . . . . . **254**
18:6  Safety in Team Sports . . . . . . . . **256**

Life Management Skills . . . . . . . . **259**

Unit
**7    Your Environment** . . . . . . **260**

Chapter
**19    Types of Pollution** . . . . . . . . **262**

19:1  Air Pollution . . . . . . . . . . . . . . . **263**
19:2  Pesticides . . . . . . . . . . . . . . . . **265**
19:3  Water Pollution . . . . . . . . . . . . . **266**

19:4  Noise Pollution . . . . . . . . . . . . . **268**
19:5  Radiation . . . . . . . . . . . . . . . . . **269**
19:6  Solid Wastes . . . . . . . . . . . . . . **270**

Health Highlights
The Silent Destroyer . . . . . . . . . . **271**

Life Management Skills . . . . . . . . **273**

Chapter
**20    Pollution and
Your Health** . . . . . . . . . . . . . **274**

20:1  Air Pollution and Your Breathing . . . **275**
20:2  Air Pollution and Illness . . . . . . . . **276**
20:3  Air Pollution and the Body Parts . . . **277**
20:4  Noise Pollution and
Your Hearing . . . . . . . . . . . . . . **279**
20:5  Noise Pollution and Your Body . . . . **280**
20:6  Pesticides and Your Health . . . . . . **281**
20:7  Water Pollution and
Your Health . . . . . . . . . . . . . . . **282**
20:8  Radiation and Your Health . . . . . . **282**

Health Highlights
The Chernobyl Incident . . . . . . . . . **283**

Life Management Skills . . . . . . . . **285**

Chapter
**21    Controlling Pollution** . . . . . **286**

21:1  Controlling Air Pollution
Through Laws . . . . . . . . . . . . . **287**
21:2  Your Role in Air Pollution . . . . . . . **288**
21:3  Avoiding Air Pollution . . . . . . . . . **289**
21:4  Noise Pollution and the Law . . . . . **290**
21:5  Noise Pollution Indoors . . . . . . . . **290**
21:6  Avoiding Pesticide Pollution . . . . . **291**
21:7  Controlling Water Pollution . . . . . . **292**
21:8  Getting Rid of Solid Wastes . . . . . **293**
21:9  Recycling . . . . . . . . . . . . . . . . . **294**
21:10  Avoiding Lead Poisoning . . . . . . . **295**

Life Management Skills . . . . . . . . **298**

Glossary . . . . . . . . . . . . . . . . . . . **299**

Index . . . . . . . . . . . . . . . . . . . **307**

# Health and Your Life

**Health** is the quality of life that includes your physical, mental, and social well-being. **Wellness** is another way to describe the quality of life that includes physical, mental, and social health. Look at the Health Triangle. The Health Triangle has three points — physical, mental, and social. **Physical Health** is the condition of the body. **Mental health** is the condition of the mind and the emotions. **Social health** is the way you relate to others. Each of these three kinds of health contributes to a balanced lifestyle.

Inside the Health Triangle is a wheel. The wheel is composed of ten components, or parts, that relate to health and wellness: **(1)** Mental Health, **(2)** Family and Social Health, **(3)** Growth and Development, **(4)** Nutrition, **(5)** Exercise and Fitness, **(6)** Drugs, **(7)** Diseases and Disorders, **(8)** Consumer and Personal Health, **(9)** Safety and First Aid, and **(10)** Community and Environmental Health. Every day you choose healthful or harmful behaviors in each of these ten components. The wheel is called a **Behavior Wheel.**

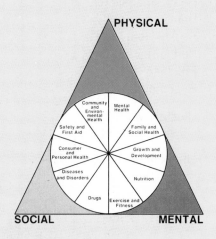

Your health fluctuates or changes daily depending on the choices you make. Your health status is the combination of the healthful and harmful behaviors you select. Look at the double pointed arrow. When you choose healthful behaviors, you move toward a higher level of wellness and optimum health. When you choose harmful behaviors, you move toward a lower level of health. You threaten your health.

There are ways you can take responsibility and have a high level of wellness or health. First, you need to have health knowledge. **Health Knowledge** is an awareness of facts about each of the ten components of health. You will gain knowledge about all ten components as you read this book. Then you will need to use your knowledge to select healthful behaviors. **Life Management Skills** are healthful behaviors that promote

LIFE
SKILLS

a quality lifestyle for you and others. Life management skills make you more effective in your relationships and in managing your environment. At the end of each chapter in this book, life management skills are listed. You are encouraged to make a health behavior contract for each life management skill. A **Health Behavior Contract** is a plan you follow to be healthy.

Your knowledge and your skills must be combined with responsible decision making to achieve the highest level of health. A **Responsible Decision-Making Model** includes steps you can use to make responsible decisions. The steps are:

- Identify the problem.
- Identify ways to deal with the problem.
- Think about the possible results of each action. A responsible action is one that is (1) healthful, (2) safe, (3) legal, (4) respectful of self and others, and (5) follows parents' or guardian's guidelines.
- Make a responsible decision.
- Evaluate that decision.

Sometimes the most responsible decision is to say no. **Refusal skills** are ways to reinforce a decision to say no to behaviors that are harmful for you, others, or the environment. Refusal skills may include (1) giving reasons for your refusal, (2) using behavior to reinforce your refusal, (3) showing you care about the person, (4) providing alternatives, and (5) taking definite action.

Remember, your health is your responsibility. You can strive for optimum health by focusing on health knowledge, life management skills, health behavior contracts, responsible decision making, and refusal skills.

# Growing Up Healthy

Alan Benoit

# Unit 1

Why do you need to be at your best?

How do you relate with family and friends?

How will you change as you grow?

# Learning to Be Healthy

Gerard Photography

*If you were asked to describe yourself, what would you say? The reflection of the boy shows how he looks. The reflection does not reveal what he is thinking or how he relates to others. When you see your reflection how do you see yourself?*

Always give your best efforts in what you do and the best will return to you.
Maybe you have heard a saying like this before. What does it mean to you? What does it have to do with your health? What does it mean to be at your best?

**GOAL:** *You will study ways of gaining knowledge about your physical, mental, and social health and how to use this knowledge to make decisions about your health.*

**Section**

## What Is Health?

**1:1**

When you are **healthy,** you are living your life at your very best. You have good physical, mental, and social health. Take out a sheet of paper. List three things that describe you when you are at your best. What are you like at your best? How do you feel?

*What is health?*

What three ways did you choose to describe yourself? Others in your class most likely wrote different things about themselves. Although you are like others in some ways, no one is just like you. Being healthy involves three areas of your life—physical, mental, and social health.

Your **physical health** has to do with your body. You may have a cold or you may feel tired. If so, your body is not working at its best. You are not at your best. You do not have good physical health. At other times, your body works the best that it can. You have good physical health and you are at your best.

*Define physical health.*

*Define mental health.*

Your **mental health** includes how you think and feel and how you deal with your problems. You may feel very hurt or angry. If you do not know what to do about your feelings, it may affect your mental health. At other times you think clearly. You feel good about yourself. You can deal with your feelings and with problems you face. You can be at your best.

*Define social health.*

Your **social health** has to do with the way you relate to others. You may not get along with others. You may not know how to share. If so, you are not at your best. You do not have good social health. At other times, you are friendly and helpful. Others enjoy being with you. You have good social health and you are at your best.

## Section

## 1:2 The Importance of Health Knowledge

*What is health knowledge?*

As you grow, you learn many ways in which you can be at your best. You gain health knowledge. **Health knowledge** is an awareness of facts which affect your health. For example, you learned that brushing your teeth makes your teeth feel and look good.

**FIGURE 1–1.** You can gain health knowledge about giving first aid to another person.

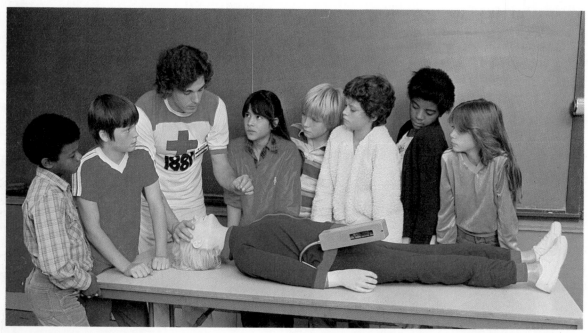

Hickson-Bender Photography/Courtesy Red Cross, Marion, Ohio

Some students your age tell how health knowledge helps them to be at their best.

Bill should wear his glasses in school, but he thinks they spoil his appearance. In school, Bill is making more mistakes than he should in his schoolwork. He learns that glasses affect his physical health. He decides to wear his glasses to be at his best.

Dave had difficulty with his math assignment. He worried about his grades and could not sleep. Then Dave learned something about mental health at school. He learned that he will think and feel better if he discusses his concerns with his teacher. Dave uses this knowledge and talks with his teacher. He feels better and he can sleep. Once again, he can be at his best.

Sally does not listen while others are talking. She does not have many friends. Sally gains knowledge about social health at school. She learns that people who listen make better friends. Sally begins to listen while others are talking. Sally's social health will improve.

## Think About It

1. Why do you need health knowledge?
2. How does health knowledge help you to be at your best?
3. How did knowledge of social health help Sally to be at her best?

Section

# 1:3 Making Decisions About Health

*What is a decision?*

A **decision** is the act of choosing or making up your mind. Having health knowledge will help you make a decision. You can make choices to improve your health.

> Mary learns that she will be able to think more clearly at school if she eats breakfast. Mary has a health decision to make. If she has breakfast, Mary has to get up early. She can sleep later if she skips breakfast. Mary decides to sleep later.
>
> Pedro learns that he will feel better if he gets enough sleep. If he watches television, Pedro will stay up late. Pedro has a health decision to make. Pedro decides to get a good night's sleep.

Mary did not use her health knowledge. On the other hand, Pedro used his knowledge to make a decision that will make him healthy. Many people have the health knowledge to make good decisions. However, they do not always choose to be healthy. Others use their health knowledge to make good health decisions.

You have learned two very important facts about health knowledge.

*What are two important things you have learned about health knowledge and health decisions?*

- You need health knowledge to know how to be at your best.
- You need to use your health knowledge to make good health decisions.

## Activity

### *How do you use health knowledge?*

Make a list of five things that you do to be healthy. Describe each of these. Select one and describe how this health behavior helps you to be at your best.

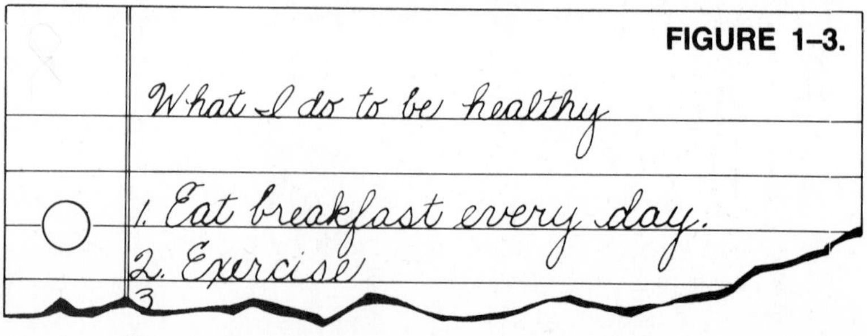

What I do to be healthy
1. Eat breakfast every day.
2. Exercise
3


FIGURE 1–3.

# How to Gain Health Knowledge

Can you name at least three places where you have gained health knowledge? Your family has most likely taught you many things about health. Your mother or your father may have told you not to run between parked cars. You gained knowledge about safety. Your parents and your dentist may have taught you when and how to brush your teeth. Do you brush them when you awake, after you eat, and before you go to bed? You gained knowledge about dental health.

You also gain health knowledge from what others say and do. A favorite teacher exercises every day. You ask why. Your teacher tells you that exercise is helpful for a person's heart. You gain health knowledge.

You may learn health knowledge by reading a magazine, book, or newspaper. It may be very cold outside. In the newspaper, it may suggest that you wear more clothes than usual to keep warm. You gain health knowledge when you read ways to take care of your health.

*Name ways that you gain health knowledge.*

**FIGURE 1–4.** You gain health knowledge when you have your teeth examined (a) and when you spend time with a favorite person (b).

Larry Hamill

Doug Martin

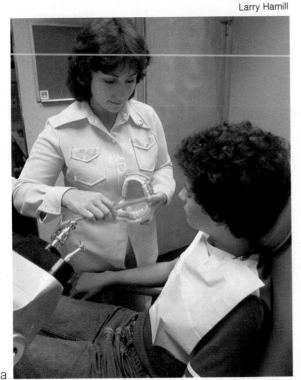

a

b

You may gain health knowledge from watching television or listening to the radio. Sometimes there are special TV shows about health care. You might see what your lungs will look like if you smoke cigarettes. On the radio you might hear news about the weather. You learn that there is going to be a tornado. You are instructed about what you should do. You gain health knowledge.

At school, you gain health knowledge in your health education class. Your teacher may write health facts on the chalkboard or show you a movie. You are reading this textbook. This textbook contains many facts. It will help you gain health knowledge.

Some people who are healthy think they know all there is to know about health. This is not true. There is always more health knowledge to gain to make healthy decisions. When you have health knowledge and make healthy decisions, you will be at your best.

*When will you be at your best?*

## Activity

### *Can You Learn New Health Facts?*

Obtain a newspaper. Clip out articles that contain health knowledge. Underline health facts with a red pen or pencil. Make a health knowledge bulletin board. Read the articles that other students place on the bulletin board. Make a list of new health facts that you have learned.

**FIGURE 1–5.** Information about health is available in many booklets.

# Review

## Summary

1. To be at your best, you need to have good physical, mental, and social health.  *1:1*
2. Health knowledge is an awareness of facts that helps you to be at your best.  *1:2*
3. Health knowledge helps you to make choices that will make you healthy.  *1:3*
4. You gain health knowledge from your family, other persons, magazines, newspapers, radio, television, and classes at school.  *1:4*

## Words for Health

*Below are vocabulary words and incomplete sentences. Complete each sentence with the correct vocabulary word. DO NOT WRITE IN THIS BOOK.*

decision           mental health
health knowledge   physical health
healthy            social health

1. When you make wise choices about your body, you have good _____.
2. When you are living your life at your best, you are _____.
3. When you make a choice, you have made a _____.
4. If you relate well with others, you have good _____.
5. If you are not happy with yourself, you have poor _____.
6. _____ can be learned at home and at school.

## Look at Your Health

1. What three kinds of health do you need to be healthy?
2. What is physical health?
3. What traits describe you when you have good mental health?
4. What traits describe you when you have good social health?
5. What is the most important reason for having health knowledge?
6. What do you do when you make a decision about health?
7. What are two important facts about health knowledge?
8. Where can you gain health knowledge by reading?

# Review

9. Where can you gain health knowledge by listening?
10. Why do people who are healthy always need more health knowledge?

## Actions for Health

*Think about the following situations. Then respond to the questions that follow.*

*Situation:* Today it is very cold outside. While you are eating breakfast, you listen to the radio. The weather report says the temperature outside is very low. Snow is forecast. Your mother suggests that you wear boots. You do not like boots.

1. What are your choices?
2. How does health knowledge influence your choice?
3. What would you do? Give a reason for your decision.

*Situation:* Today you learned from your dentist how to brush your teeth correctly. When you get home, you cannot remember how to hold the toothbrush.

1. What choices do you have?
2. What are some ways that you could learn how to hold the toothbrush?
3. What would you do? Give a reason for your decision.

*Situation:* Your parents have set your bedtime for 9:30 P.M. You are watching a TV program that will not be over until 10:00 P.M. Your parents are at a meeting. Your aunt is with you, but she does not know what time your bedtime is.

1. What choices do you have?
2. How does health knowledge influence your choice?
3. What would you do? Give a reason for your decision.

*Situation:* Mike does not eat breakfast. He is usually tired and grumpy at school in the morning. You sit next to him. You tell your parents that it is difficult for you to relate to Mike. Your parents suggest that Mike may be tired because he skips breakfast. They show you a book that says breakfast is an important meal. They convince you that Mike would feel better if he had breakfast every morning.

1. Would you share this health knowledge with Mike? Why or why not?
2. How might you share this health knowledge with Mike?
3. What happens when you do not have health knowledge?

## Individual Research

1. Make a list of magazines that contain health knowledge.
2. Make a list of ten health facts that are important for your family. Discuss these with family members.
3. Write a report about the training necessary before a person can teach first aid classes.
4. Copy the health triangle below on a sheet of paper. Make each side of the triangle equal. Find the word "balance" in a dictionary. Why do you need to have a balance of physical, mental, and social health?

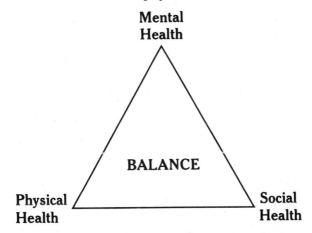

**Mental Health**

BALANCE

**Physical Health**

**Social Health**

# LIFE MANAGEMENT SKILLS

- Take care of your body.
- Use your mind to think clearly.
- Be friendly and helpful and relate well with others.
- Gather health knowledge from parents, books, and school.
- Make responsible decisions that are healthful, safe, and legal, that show respect for self and others, and that follow parents' guidelines.

# Relating to Others

Hickson-Bender Photography

*The dog will lead the boy safely across the street. The boy depends on the dog. They trust each other. How do they communicate? Are there people you depend on for safety and protection? Can others depend on you, and trust you?*

Some people say that a dog is a person's best friend. Why do you think some people believe this? What are some of your needs that might be met by having a dog or another pet? What are some of your needs that might be met by having a friend?

**GOAL:** *You will consider how to communicate, share, and express gratitude in your relationships with your family and friends.*

## What Is a Friend?

People your age were asked to describe some of the needs that were met by their animal "friend." Here are some of the things they said.

I feel safe when I am with my dog. She protects me.

My cat cuddles up next to me. This gives me a feeling of being close.

My dog waits for me at the door after school. He makes me feel important.

I like to play with my cat. We play with a ball of yarn. We have fun together.

No matter what happens, my dog likes me. She accepts me as I am.

When I am sad, my cat will come and sit next to me. She understands how I feel.

My dog licks my face first thing in the morning. He lets me know that it is going to be a great day. I feel happy.

*Why are animal "friends" special?*

Sometimes I sit in my bedroom and talk to my cat. She always seems to listen to everything that I say.

I can trust my dog. He will never let me down.

My cat is like one of the family. She belongs with us. She even sits at my feet at the dinner table.

*Who is a friend?*

What is a friend? A **friend** is someone whom you know well and like. Just like a pet, a friend is someone who meets some of your needs. Look at the chart "WHAT IS A FRIEND?" When you read this chart, you will see why a dog or pet is sometimes called a person's best friend.

**FIGURE 2–1.**

WHAT IS A FRIEND?

1. A friend is someone who makes me feel safe and secure.

2. A friend is someone with whom I feel close.

3. A friend is someone who helps me to feel important.

4. A friend is someone with whom I have fun.

5. A friend is someone who likes and accepts me as I am.

6. A friend is someone who tries to understand how I feel.

7. A friend is someone who makes me happy.

8. A friend is someone who listens to what I am saying.

9. A friend is someone whom I can trust.

10. A friend is someone with whom I feel I belong.

**FIGURE 2–2.** Everyone needs a friend.

## Activity
### *Are You A Friend?*

Make a list of your friends. Look at the chart "WHAT IS A FRIEND?" When you are with your friends, do you act as a friend? Write a note to one of your friends. Tell your friend why you like him or her.

## Think About It

**1.** Why is a dog sometimes called a person's best friend?

**2.** How are animal friends or pets similar to other friends?

# Who Are Your Friends?

Some people have many friends and some people have only a few. Some people do not know who their friends are. Who are your friends?

There is a special saying about friends. It is "make new friends but keep the old, one is silver and the other gold." What does this mean?

It is important to make new friends and to keep old friends. Friends you have known for awhile know you well. You can count on them when you need someone. They can count on you too. You have shared many things and good times. You feel comfortable with one another.

*Why are friends you have known for a while special?*

**FIGURE 2–3.** Friends share good times together.

*Why is making a new friend important?*

You will want to make new friends too. When you make a new friend, you have another person on whom you can count. This person is another person with whom you can share. Each of you can learn new things.

Maria has two friends with whom she spends much of her time. She trusts her friends and they trust her. They have fun together. A new girl moves into the house next to Maria's. One day both of Maria's friends are busy. The new girl asks her to go bowling. Maria has never been bowling. She decides to go because her two friends are busy. She has a lot of fun. She has learned something new. And she has a new friend.

*Why is it good to have more than one friend?*

It is good to have more than one friend. You can share different interests. You will learn more about others. You will learn more about yourself.

 **Activity**

### Can You Make a New Friend?

Ask a new person to do something with you. Set a time. Discuss two or three things you can do. After spending time with this person, write down two things you learned.

# The Importance of Communication

The sharing of what you think and feel with another person is called **communication.** Learning to communicate with others is very important. When you have clear communication, you relate well with your friends. You are able to share what you think and feel with your family.

There are three important rules that will help you develop good communication with others.

1. Listen carefully when someone is talking to you.

2. Do not repeat things to others that someone tells you in confidence.

3. Do not judge others or make fun of them when they tell you something.

Here are some examples which show that these three rules are important.

Joyce and Jill are talking. Joyce tells Jill that she is disappointed because she did not make the soccer team. Jill starts to talk about something else. Joyce does not feel that Jill is listening to her.

Miguel is talking to Juan about his family. Miguel is worried because his younger sister is doing poorly in school. Juan tells Joe, another friend, that Miguel's sister is not very smart. Miguel is hurt. He thought that Juan would not repeat what he had been told.

Bill and Martin are talking. Bill says that he did not understand the math homework. Martin says, "It was easy. You must not be very smart." Bill feels that Martin is judging him.

In each of these examples, one of the communication rules was broken. When you break one of these rules, you will not relate well with others.

## Think About It

**3.** What happens when one of the rules for good communication is broken?

**FIGURE 2–4.** Friends share what they think and feel.

*List three rules for good communication.*

# Sharing with Your Family

*How does a family member differ from a friend?*

How many people are in your family? People in a family have special feelings about each other. A family member is someone you know well and like just as a friend is. But there is a special closeness and sharing that comes from belonging to the same family.

Donna belongs to a family. She lives with her brother, mother, and grandmother. They spend time having fun together and sharing work around the house. On weekends, Donna goes to her father's house. She likes to tell him about her week.

Mike belongs to a very large family. He has three sisters and four brothers. He lives with them and with his parents and his grandparents. They live on a farm. Each has a job to do on the farm. They share the work.

Dave lives alone with his father. Last year his mother was killed in a car accident. Dave and his father miss his mother very much. They can talk about their sad feelings. It helps to have someone in your family with whom you can share all your feelings.

Molly and Meg are twins who live with their brother, Mike, and their mother and father. Mike has to use a wheelchair. The family has become very close working together to help Mike. This year Mike learned to play basketball. After he shoots, Molly and Meg get the ball for him so that he can shoot again.

How do you help members of your family? Can you think of some new ways to help one another?

**FIGURE 2–5.**

30

**FIGURE 2–6.** Writing a thank-you note is one way of showing that you are grateful.

## Being Grateful

If you are **grateful,** you are thankful for what you have. You appreciate others, and you feel good when others do things for you. You want to do nice things for others. You share your good feelings with persons that are around you. Then others know that you are grateful.

*What does it mean to be grateful?*

Denise's parents bought her a new bicycle. She knows her parents worked hard to earn the money to buy her the bicycle. Denise takes special care of her bicycle. If you are grateful, you take special care of gifts.

Just as Bob got on the school bus, he remembered his lunch money. The bus driver said she would wait while he ran home to get his money. Bob smiled and said "thank you." If you are grateful, you remember to thank others when they do nice things for you.

Mary and Jill are very good friends. Jill has a good sense of humor. Mary smiles and laughs when she is with Jill. Mary tells Jill how pleased she is to have her for a friend. If you are grateful, you tell others what you like about them.

## Think About It

4. How does being grateful help you to relate well to others?

## Divorce and Dissolution

Janet Adams

Sometimes changes occur in a family. A family may move. Someone may come to live with a family. A family member may die. There is another kind of change that may happen too. Parents may get a divorce or dissolution (dis uh LEW shun). A divorce and a dissolution are two legal ways to end a marriage. More than twelve million children under the age of 18 have parents who are no longer married to each other.

Research shows that these children and their parents have many adjustments to make. An adjustment is a change to make something better. It also means getting used to a change. Usually the first adjustment has to do with feelings. Studies show that children of divorced parents have many different feelings. Some feel guilty. They think that they may have caused their parents' breakup. They try to think of ways to help their parents get back together. But children do not cause their parents' breakup. And usually they cannot help them become happily married again. The children must adjust to the divorce rather than dream about their parents' marriage being renewed.

Children may also feel angry. They may think "Why did this happen to me?" Parents can help their children with these feelings. Parents know that it is a difficult time for the children. They do not want their children to be unhappy.

Children may also become afraid. They may think "What will happen to me next?" They may worry that they will not see one of their parents as often. They may wonder where they will live. They may have to adjust to a new school. When children have fears, they need to talk with their parents. Their parents can assure them and calm their fears.

Children may need to adjust to stepparents. A stepmother is someone who marries a person's father. A stepfather is someone who marries a person's mother. It takes time to become close to stepparents. There may be new rules in the family that must be observed. The family may do things in new ways.

There also might be new children in the family. A stepbrother is the son of a person's stepmother or stepfather. A stepsister is the daughter of a person's stepmother or stepfather.

Most young people need time to make an adjustment to the end of their parents' marriage. One research finding is especially important. Young people who talk about their feelings are more likely to make a healthy adjustment to the changes. They have many long talks with their parents. Their parents help with the many adjustments that must be made.

## Chapter 2
## Review

## Summary

1. A friend is someone who meets many of your needs.    2:1
2. It is important to make new friends and to keep old friends.    2:2
3. When you follow the communication rules, you will relate well with others.    2:3
4. There is a special closeness and sharing that comes from belonging to the same family.    2:4
5. Being grateful helps you to relate well with others.    2:5

## Words for Health

*Below are vocabulary words and incomplete sentences. Complete each sentence with the correct vocabulary word. DO NOT WRITE IN THIS BOOK.*

    communication
    friend
    grateful

1. When you are thankful and appreciate others, you are _____.
2. Someone whom you know well and like is a _____.
3. If you have good _____, you can share what you think and feel.

## Look at Your Health

1. What are some of the traits that describe a good friend?
2. Why is it important to keep old friends?
3. Why is it important to make new friends?
4. Why should you have more than one friend?
5. What are three rules for good communication?
6. What are some ways that family members are close?
7. What does a grateful person do after receiving a gift?
8. What does a grateful person do when another person is helpful?
9. What does a grateful person do when someone far away does something nice?
10. If another person has a really nice trait, how would you show that you appreciate that person?

## Actions for Health

*Think about the following situations. Then respond to the questions that follow.*

*Situation:* Your friend has just told you a secret. Another friend asks you to repeat the secret.

**1.** What are your choices?

**2.** What is the best thing for you to do? Why?

*Situation:* You had difficulty with your homework. Your teacher says, "I'll stay after school to help you." You spend time going over the homework. You feel a lot better. You finally understand. You are grateful.

**1.** What might you do to share your grateful feelings with your teacher?

**2.** What would you do?

**3.** Why is it important to share your grateful feelings?

*Situation:* You and your best friend usually do things together on Saturday mornings. Then your friend moves away. You received a new game for your birthday. The new game needs two people to play. You wish your friend still lived near.

**1.** What are some things you could do to play the game?

**2.** Which would you decide to do? Why?

## Individual Research

**1.** Read a book about friendship. Make a report.

**2.** Copy the following chart on a sheet of paper. Complete the chart. What have you learned about yourself? What have you learned about your friends?

| Sharing My Interests | |
| --- | --- |
| **My Interests** | **My Friend Who Shares This Interest** |
| 1.<br>2.<br>3.<br>4.<br>5.<br>6.<br>7.<br>8. | |

3. Write a want ad for a friend. Include all the responsibilities and qualities you would expect of a friend. Then answer the question, "Would you hire yourself?"

4. Find out what kinds of careers involve communications. Interview someone who has a communications job. What do they think of the three rules that you learned? Would this person add an additional rule about communicating?

5. It is important to be thankful or grateful and to appreciate members of your family. Copy the chart below on a sheet of poster paper. Share it with the members of your family. Put it in your home where it will be seen by all family members. Have family members write on your poster.

| We Are Grateful for Our Family | |
|---|---|
| **Name** | **Something for Which I Am Grateful** |
| | |
| | |
| | |
| | |

6. Copy the three communication rules on a sheet of paper. Share these rules with members of your family. Ask each family member to think of another rule for communication. Add these rules to your list.

7. Write a report about a guidance counselor. What does a guidance counselor do? Why is this an important career?

# LIFE MANAGEMENT SKILLS

- Make an effort to form new friendships.
- Work to keep the friendships you have.
- Follow rules for effective communication.
- Share special feelings with family members.
- Be grateful or thankful for what you have.
- Make adjustments if there are changes in your family relationships.

# Growth and Development

Hickson-Bender Photography

*Changes are a part of life. Do you remember when you were three years old? If your family has kept photos over the years, you can see yourself as you were. How have you changed? Have you thought about how you will look when you are an adult?*

All living things grow and develop. A seed is planted in the ground. Soon, the seed sprouts. The plant grows larger and larger. With proper care, it blossoms. Your body goes through many changes also. This chapter describes some of the physical, emotional, and social changes you will experience.

**GOAL:** *You will learn about the physical, emotional, and social changes and stresses that are a part of your growth and development.*

## Hormones and Adolescence

**Adolescence** (ad ul ES unts) is the time in your life when your body changes from that of a child to that of an adult. During this time, you are called an **adolescent.** As an adolescent, you begin to experience new emotions or feelings. Why do these changes occur?

*Define adolescence and adolescent.*

There are organs in your body that are called glands. **Glands** secrete hormones into your bloodstream. A **hormone** is a chemical messenger that controls and regulates your growth and development. Hormones are active during adolescence.

*What is the relationship between glands and hormones?*

The pituitary (puh TEW uh ter ee) gland is in your brain. This gland is about the size of a pea. The **pituitary gland** secretes a growth hormone into your bloodstream. **Growth hormone** causes your bones and muscles to grow. You begin a growth spurt. Your arms and legs become longer.

*What is a function of the pituitary gland?*

*What is the function of the hormone secreted by the thyroid gland?*

*Why do boys and girls grow and develop at different rates?*

*When does adolescence usually start?*

The **thyroid** (THI royd) **gland** is in your neck. It secretes a hormone that controls how fast you will grow. Your body cells depend on food and oxygen to grow. This hormone works by controlling how much food and oxygen the cells use.

## Think About It

1. What body changes are caused by hormones?

## Section

## 3:2

**FIGURE 3–1.**

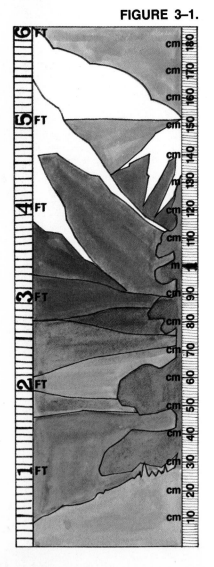

## Physical Growth During Adolescence

Not all boys and girls your age grow and develop at the same rate. This is because you are not exactly like any other person. Your glands may not begin to produce hormones at the same time as your friend who is the same age. You may start adolescence sooner or later than your friend.

Girls usually begin adolescence between the ages of 11 and 13. Boys usually begin adolescence between the ages of 12 and 14. This is why many girls are taller and more developed than boys when they are 11 to 14 years of age.

Diane and Dave are twins. They just had their twelfth birthday. They measure their growth on a chart like Figure 3-1. Diane is much taller than Dave. Dave is uncomfortable because his twin sister is bigger than he is. However, Dave will probably have a growth spurt soon.

What are some other physical changes that happen during adolescence? A girl will grow taller. Her hips will widen. Fat will deposit in certain areas of her body. Her voice may lower some, but it usually remains at a higher pitch than a boy's voice.

A boy's voice will deepen in pitch. Sometimes his voice will crack while he is talking. This is a normal part of maturing. The muscles in his legs and arms will grow larger and his shoulders will broaden. Hair grows on his face.

## Think About It

2. Why do girls grow and develop sooner than boys during adolescence?

**FIGURE 3–2.** How many emotions can you identify?

## Emotional Growth During Adolescence

**Emotions** are feelings that you have inside you. Some examples of the many different emotions you have are shown above. During adolescence, you may begin to experience many rapid changes in your emotions.

*What are emotions?*

Alice is feeling very cheerful and happy. Suddenly she feels very sad. These rapid changes in emotions confuse her.

Bob gets angry very easily. Sometimes he does not know why he is angry. He even yells at others for no reason. Later, he feels bad that he expressed so much anger.

Growing up involves many changes in your emotions. **Emotional growth** is learning to control your emotions. A young child may break a toy during a temper tantrum to express anger. Should someone your age behave in this way? As you grow up, you learn better ways to deal with your emotions.

*What is emotional growth?*

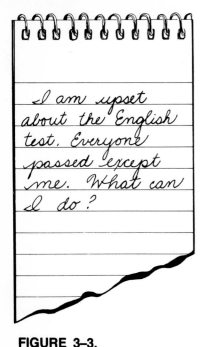

**FIGURE 3–3.**

*What can you do to learn to control your emotions?*

Here are some helpful hints for learning to control your emotions.

- When you have strong feelings, ask yourself why are you feeling this way.
- Write down three ways that you might express your feelings.
- What would happen if you did each of these three things?

Which is the best way to handle your emotions? Let us see how Susan can learn to control her emotions.

Susan is growing very rapidly. She is taller than other girls her age. Some of the boys at school call her "giant" for a nickname. Susan feels very angry.

Why is Susan feeling angry? Susan is angry because the boys tease her. She feels uncomfortable with these new changes in her body. She wishes that the boys would not call attention to these changes. What could Susan do about her angry feelings? She could say something nasty to the boys. She could explain that she is growing faster than others. Soon they will grow taller. She could speak with her parents or her teacher.

What will happen if Susan does each of these things? If Susan says something nasty to the boys, they may still

**FIGURE 3–4.** Some adolescents are taller than others of the same age.

Hickson-Bender Photography

tease her. Most likely, this will not be helpful. If Susan explains why she is tall, the boys will have more health knowledge. Many people do not tease others when they have knowledge and understanding. If Susan talks to her parents and teacher, they can reassure her. This may be the best way for Susan to handle her emotions. Although the boys are wrong in their teasing, Susan must also accept changes in her body.

## Activity
### *How Can You Deal With Emotions?*

Form groups of four with your classmates. Make an "Emotion Wheel" out of cardboard like the one below. Use a paper fastener to attach an arrow. Write the names of different emotions in the blank spaces. Take turns spinning the arrow. When the arrow stops on the name of an emotion, give an example of something that might cause a person to experience this emotion. Describe ways the person might deal with this emotion. Discuss some of these ways.

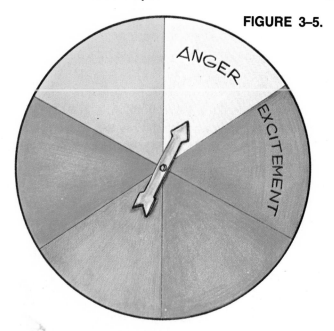

**FIGURE 3–5.**

## Think About It

3. Why is it important to learn to control your emotions?

**FIGURE 3–6.** Clogging is a kind of folk dance. Cloggers have fun together.

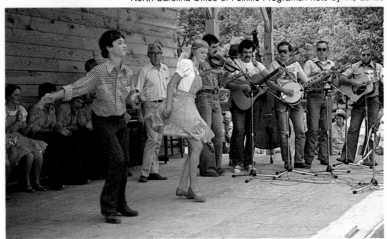

## Section

## 3:4

*Define social growth.*

*What are some hints for relating well with a member of the opposite sex?*

# Social Growth During Adolescence

Your **social growth** has to do with the progress you make in relating with other people. You already have some special relationships with others. These are your friendships. Your friends are most likely the same sex as you are. However, you can have friends of either sex.

During adolescence, you will become more interested in the opposite sex. If you are a girl, you may find yourself thinking about boys. You may want to spend time talking to boys. Boys feel the same way about girls, too. They begin to notice how they dress and what they say. Here are some helpful hints for learning to relate well to persons of the opposite sex.

- Always use good manners. Remember that people relate well to persons who say "please," "thank you," "excuse me," and "I am sorry" when these words are needed.
- Listen carefully when someone is talking to you.
- Remember to say something nice about someone else or to say nothing at all. Do not say something that might hurt another person.
- Select interests or hobbies to share with one another.
- When you are with someone of the opposite sex, try to learn two things about that person.

# What Is Stress?

**Stress** is the body's reaction to any demand made upon it. The demand may be physical or mental. Here are some things which may produce stress:

*What is stress?*

- giving a speech in front of your classmates
- being very ill
- having a disagreement with a friend
- not eating breakfast or lunch
- being in a room filled with loud noises
- doing something for the first time
- worrying about a test

Each of these kinds of stress will produce changes in your body. Your heart may beat faster. Your breathing may increase. Your glands are also affected. Your **adrenal** (uh DREEN ul) **glands** increase the production of a hormone called adrenaline (uh DREN ul un). **Adrenaline** causes your liver to release sugar into the bloodstream. This results in your having more energy.

*What body changes might result from stress?*

Other changes happen when you experience stress. More blood will flow to your muscles. Less blood will go to your stomach. Your mouth may become dry. Your hands may become moist. Your muscles may feel tight or tense.

Doug Martin

**FIGURE 3–7.** There are many situations which might cause a person stress.

**FIGURE 3–8.** Is the feeling of "butterflies" before a race a sign of eustress or distress?

## Section

## 3:6

*What is the difference between eustress and distress?*

# Kinds of Stress

Sometimes the changes in your body that result from stress are healthy. Stress that improves how your body works is called **eustress** (YOO stress). At other times, stress may produce changes in your body that are harmful. Stress that harms the body is called **distress.** Let us take a close look at the difference between eustress and distress.

Today Jeff is going to be in a bicycle race. He is very excited. His heart beats very fast and he takes many deep breaths. His liver releases sugar into his bloodstream. Blood flows to the muscles in his arms and legs. The extra energy from the sugar and the increased blood to his muscles will help Jeff. Jeff will use these during the race. After the race his body will return to normal.

In this case, Jeff has eustress. The stress will help him perform at his best. Have you ever had eustress when you were about to do something?

Now let us look at distress—stress that may harm the body. Jeff does not get along well with his family. They have many disagreements. As soon as Jeff gets home, he feels the effects of stress. His hands get moist. His mouth becomes dry. His heart beats fast. He takes quicker breaths. Extra sugar goes into his bloodstream. More blood goes to his muscles and less blood goes to his stomach.

At the dinner table, Jeff continues to feel this stress. He has difficulty eating. When he eats, stress affects the digestion of food in his stomach. A sore may form in the stomach lining. The sore is called an ulcer (UL sur).

*What is an ulcer?*

When Jeff goes to bed, he has a hard time getting to sleep. Normally Jeff's heartbeat rate would have been slow at night. But Jeff's heart still beats fast. Jeff will most likely be tired in the morning.

Jeff is experiencing distress. Can you describe the difference between eustress and distress? Eustress produces body changes that help you get ready for something. You will take advantage of the increased blood flow. Your body will use the extra sugar. Then your body will return to normal.

**FIGURE 3–9.** Distress affects everything a person does.

During distress your body does not need extra sugar or the increased blood flow to the muscles. The decreased flow of blood to the stomach and the extra sugar in the blood may harm your body. This is even more likely if the distress lasts a long time.

## Think About It

**4.** When is stress helpful?

**5.** What is the difference between eustress and distress?

## What to Do About Distress

If you want to be at your best, you will want to prevent or avoid distress. Here are some things you can do.

- Do not try to do too many things at one time.
- When you have too much on your mind, you worry about getting everything done.
- Plan your day. Decide what things you have to do.
- Plan a time to relax and to rest.

*List things you can do to prevent or avoid distress.*

**FIGURE 3–10.** Physical exercise often helps to relieve distress.

Doug Martin

- Keep your body healthy. Get plenty of sleep and eat good foods. Then if you have distress it will do less harm to your body.
- When you have a problem, think of three or four possible solutions. Decide which of these would be the best choice. Try it.
- When you have distress and do not know what to do, talk with someone at home or at your school.

Physical exercise will be very helpful to you in dealing with distress. When you exercise you use up extra sugar. The blood in the muscles of the arms and legs is needed. Your body will return to normal after you finish exercising.

 ## Activity
### *How Can I Deal With Distress?*

One of the best ways to deal with distress is to plan your day. Copy the following chart. Decide what things you have to do and plan a time to do them. Plan a time to rest and relax. After you make your plan, follow it for the day. What two things have you learned?

| MY PLAN FOR TODAY: | | |
|---|---|---|
| | **What I Will Do** | **(  ) I Did It** |
| 6 AM | | |
| 7 AM | | |
| 8 AM | | |
| 9 AM | | |
| 10 AM | | |
| 11 AM | | |
| 12 N | | |
| 1 PM | | |
| 2 PM | | |
| 3 PM | | |
| 4 PM | | |
| 5 PM | | |
| 6 PM | | |
| 7 PM | | |
| 8 PM | | |
| 9 PM | | |

## Aging Healthfully

There is a famous saying. It states, "Today is the first day of the rest of your life." What does this saying mean to you? What are you doing today that will help you be healthy tomorrow?

Some people are concerned about aging. Aging is the period in life after physical growth ends. Aging begins to take place when a person reaches the age of 20 or 21.

Why aging begins is not known. One theory states that after birth the body will continue to reproduce cells only a certain number of times. After that, the rate of cell reproduction is slowed. These researchers believe this slowdown causes aging.

Another theory of aging states that damage occurs to genes in the cells. Genes are the part of a cell that contain a person's traits. Once a gene is damaged, it reproduces another damaged gene. The reproduction of these damaged genes is thought by some to cause aging.

The true cause or causes of aging are not known. However, aging does not have to be an experience filled with sickness and despair. In fact, people in the United States are living healthier today than ever before. Many people are feeling healthier at ages 40 and 50 than they did at age 30. There are many reasons for this.

Research shows that your future is determined by what you do now. If you follow healthy habits now, you probably will be healthy as you age. If you follow poor health habits now, chances increase that you will have more health problems as you age.

How can you age healthfully? Here are some ways you can begin now.

- Do not smoke.
- Plan a schedule of physical exercise.
- Eat a well-balanced diet.
- Learn to deal with stress.
- Have regular physical checkups.

Your future is influenced by the health habits you now have. What are you doing so that you will age healthfully?

Joseph DiChello, Jr.

# Review

## Summary

1. During adolescence, hormones control and regulate your growth and development.  *3:1*
2. Boys and girls experience many physical changes during adolescence.  *3:2*
3. An adolescent experiences many rapid changes in emotion.  *3:3*
4. During adolescence, you become more interested in members of the opposite sex.  *3:4*
5. Stress produces changes in your body.  *3:5*
6. Body changes caused by stress can be healthy or unhealthy.  *3:6*
7. A healthy person makes a plan to deal with distress.  *3:7*

## Words for Health

*Below are vocabulary words and incomplete sentences. Complete each sentence with the correct vocabulary word. DO NOT WRITE IN THIS BOOK.*

adrenal glands          glands
adrenaline              growth hormone
adolescence             hormone
adolescent              pituitary gland
distress                social growth
emotional growth        stress
emotions                thyroid gland
eustress

1. The _____ is a gland the size of a pea that secretes growth hormone.
2. The progress you make in relating to others is your _____.
3. The _____ secretes a hormone that controls how fast you grow.
4. _____ is a physical or mental demand on the body.
5. _____ secrete hormones into your bloodstream.
6. The feelings that you have inside you are _____.
7. Learning to control your emotions is _____.
8. _____ is a hormone that causes your liver to release sugar into your bloodstream.

# Review

9. Glands that produce a hormone that results in your having more energy are the _____.
10. Stress that improves how your body works is _____.
11. Your body changes from that of a child to an adult during _____.
12. A(n) _____ is a chemical messenger that controls and regulates growth and development.
13. _____ causes your bones and muscles to grow.
14. _____ is stress that may harm the body.
15. You are a(n) _____ when your body changes from that of a child to an adult.

## Look at Your Health

1. What happens to a person's body during adolescence?
2. What gland secretes growth hormone?
3. How does the thyroid gland influence adolescence?
4. Why do boys and girls grow at different rates?
5. When do girls begin adolescence? Boys?
6. What physical changes occur in adolescent girls?
7. What physical changes occur in adolescent boys?
8. What should you do to learn to control your emotions?
9. What are some helpful hints for relating well with members of the opposite sex?
10. What is the difference between eustress and distress?

## Actions for Health

*Think about the following situations. Then respond to the questions that follow.*

*Situation:* You have a test in school tomorrow. Now it is bedtime. You have not finished studying.

1. What choices do you have?
2. Describe each choice as a eustress or a distress. Give reasons for your answer.
3. What choice would you make? Why?

*Situation:* At school, you sit next to a member of the opposite sex. You like this person. You would like to get to know this person better.

1. Make a list of interests or hobbies you could share.
2. How will you ask this person to spend time with you?
3. What will you do if this person says no? Yes?

*Situation:* You are going to give a speech at school tomorrow. You have practiced several times. You know the speech well. You are excited and nervous. You have difficulty sleeping.

1. Are you experiencing eustress? distress? both?
2. Give a reason for your answer.
3. What health action might you take?

## Individual Research

1. Make a list of ten manners to remember.
2. Write a report on two different ways to handle stress.
3. Explore the importance of relaxation. Research the kinds of exercise, such as yoga, that will help you relax.
4. Write a report about a person who is trained to teach other people to use biofeedback. What kind of training does this person need? How does this person help others?
5. Find out about a career as an endocrinologist. Why does this career require many years of education?
6. Interview a pediatrician to learn more about this important health career.

# LIFE MANAGEMENT SKILLS

- Recognize and accept the changes in your body that accompany adolescence.
- Learn to control your emotions.
- Express your emotions in healthful ways.
- Always use good manners.
- Listen carefully when others speak to you.
- Share interests and hobbies with opposite sex friends.
- Have a plan to reduce stress.

# Taking Care of Your Body

How can you be physically fit?

Why is dental health important?

How do eating habits affect your health?

George Anderson

# Physical Exercise and Physical Fitness

Alpha

*His health is excellent. His gymnastics form is perfect. The light has recorded every move he made and has created a beautiful pattern. Could you learn to do the same exercise? What kinds of exercises do you do? Are you physically fit?*

What choices do each of the following situations present?

- You want to go to your friend's house but you have to wait for one of your parents to drive you there.
- You miss the bus and you worry about how you will get home.
- You are in a long line in a store waiting to take an elevator up to the second floor.

Unless you cannot walk for some reason, you might have walked to your friend's house rather than be driven. You might have walked home since the bus was gone. You might have walked up the stairs to the second floor of the store. Besides getting you where you needed to go, walking is a form of physical exercise. Physical exercise helps you to look and feel your best.

**GOAL:** *You will learn about different components of fitness, the types of exercises to gain fitness, and the resulting health benefits.*

**Section**

## What Is Physical Fitness?

**4:1**

**Physical fitness** involves exercises that get your body in the best physical condition for you. It is so important that there is a special President's Council on Physical Fitness. The people on this Council met and wrote a description of physical fitness. It said, in part, that when you are physically fit, your body is in excellent condition for you.

*What is physical fitness?*

**FIGURE 4–1.** Physical work is good exercise.

What does this mean? It means that you are able to do normal work without feeling tired. For example, you might sit for two hours and do your homework. After you finish your work, you would still have enough energy to enjoy other types of activities. You would think clearly and your body would feel good. If you had an unexpected problem, you would even have enough energy to do something about it.

## Think About It

**1.** Why is it important for you to be physically fit?

## Section

## 4:2

## What Makes You Physically Fit?

*What does physical fitness include?*

You need physical exercise to become physically fit. It is important to learn what kinds of physical exercise you need. Many people think they only need to do one kind of exercise to be physically fit. Because Jane rides her bike each day, she thinks she is physically fit. But physical fitness includes five different areas: (1) muscular strength, (2) muscular endurance, (3) flexibility (flek suh BIHL ut ee), (4) agility (uh JIHL ut ee), and (5) cardio-respiratory (KARD ee oh · RES pruh tor ee) fitness.

You have **muscular strength** when your muscles are strong. Your muscles help you lift, pull and push. John can lift weights that weigh half his body weight above his head. John has muscular strength.

**Muscular endurance** is your ability to last or to continue using muscular strength. When John lifts a weight above his head, he uses muscular strength. If John holds the weight above his head until he counts to fifteen, he has muscular endurance. John can continue to use his strength for a period of time.

**Flexibility** is your ability to be flexible, to bend and to move in different ways. To be flexible you need to exercise every part of your body. Sally is flexible. Each day Sally does exercises that stretch the muscles in her legs, arms, thighs, back, waist, and neck.

**Agility** is the ability to be agile (AJ ul), to make quick and easy movements with your body. You are agile when your brain learns to coordinate (koh ORD un ayt) the movements of your muscles. To coordinate means to work together. If you play tennis, your brain must coordinate your eyes and your hands. You have to watch the ball, but you also have to swing the racquet. You need to be agile to kick a ball. You also need to be agile to ride your bicycle.

**Cardio-respiratory fitness** involves the physical condition of your heart, blood vessels, and lungs. You do exercises which move your whole body for a certain amount of time. Your heart and lungs become stronger. They are able to deliver oxygen to your body tissues and to remove waste more easily. You can develop cardio-respiratory fitness by exercises such as swimming or running long distances.

**FIGURE 4–2.**

What Makes You Physically Fit? **47**

## Think About It

2. What is the relationship between physical exercise and physical fitness?
3. Why would it be difficult to be physically fit if you only did one kind of exercise?

## Exercises That Make You Physically Fit

*What is an isometric exercise?*

There are different types of exercises that make you physically fit. In an **isometric** (i suh MET rihk) **exercise** you tighten your muscles without making any movement. You keep your muscles tight for five to eight seconds. Make a tight fist and hold it for five seconds. You are doing an isometric exercise. Isometric exercise makes the muscles attached to your bones larger and stronger.

*What is an isotonic exercise?*

When you do an **isotonic** (i suh TAHN ihk) **exercise** you contract your muscles to produce a movement. Lifting weights is an example of an isotonic exercise. Most people do isotonic exercises to gain muscular strength. Their muscles become firm and strong. Isotonic exercises are usually done for a short period of time. They do not strengthen your heart muscle or improve cardio-respiratory fitness.

**FIGURE 4–3.** Isometric exercise (a), isotonic exercise (b).

a

Gerard Photography

b

Larry Hamill

a

b

**FIGURE 4–4.** Anaerobic exercise (a), aerobic exercise (b).

*What is an anaerobic exercise?*

An **anaerobic** (an uh ROH bihk) **exercise** is done for a short time and uses a lot of oxygen. Anaerobic means "without air." Have you ever run as fast as you could to the other side of the playground? Afterward you needed to stop and catch your breath. Your body did not have enough oxygen. You used a sudden burst of energy when you ran so fast. Your muscles required more energy than your breathing rate could supply. If you run like this you are doing an anaerobic exercise. Anaerobic exercises help you build up speed. They do not develop overall fitness because they cannot be maintained very long.

*What is an aerobic exercise?*

An **aerobic** (er ROH bihk) **exercise** uses a lot of oxygen and is continued for an extended length of time. Aerobic means "with air." You breathe in the same amount of air your body uses. For example, you may ride your bicycle half an hour three days a week. When you do this regularly, your body condition will improve. Your heart and lungs will become stronger. Some other examples of aerobic exercises are long-distance running and swimming, or walking for an extended period of time. To improve your physical fitness, you must do these for a certain length of time at least three to four days a week. Many people run for 20 minutes at least three days a week.

## Think About It

4. How is an isometric exercise different from an isotonic exercise?

5. How is an anaerobic exercise different from an aerobic exercise?

Exercises That Make You Physically Fit **49**

## Activity

### *What Kinds of Exercises Do I Do?*

Copy the chart on a sheet of paper. Column 1 tells the name of a type of fitness. Think of an exercise you might do that develops this kind of fitness. Write it in column 2. Then in column 3 write what type of exercise it is—isometric, isotonic, anaerobic, or aerobic. The first example is done for you.

| 1. TYPE of FITNESS | 2. EXAMPLE | 3. TYPE of EXERCISE |
|---|---|---|
| Muscular Strength | lift weights | isotonic |
| Muscular Endurance | | |
| Flexibility | | |
| Agility | | |
| Cardio-Respiratory Fitness | | |

**FIGURE 4–5.**

## Section

## 4:4

# How Physical Fitness Helps You to Be at Your Best

*Why is it important to be physically fit?*

Why is physical fitness important? How does being physically fit help you to be at your best? You need to be physically fit for two very important reasons. First, physical fitness may help lengthen your life. Second, physical fitness can improve your health. Here are ten of the reasons why these statements are true.

*Why is it important to have a strong heart muscle?*

1. Physical fitness improves the health of your heart and blood vessels. When you exercise, your heart muscle becomes stronger. A strong heartbeat pushes out more blood. When your heart muscle is strong, it will beat less often each minute than a weak heart muscle. This in turn will cause less wear on your blood vessels and your heart.

2. Physical fitness improves the health of your lungs. When you exercise, your lungs expand. The muscles that help your lungs expand get stronger. Each time you breathe you can take in more air. Breathing in more air means that your blood has more oxygen to deliver to your cells. Your cells need oxygen to do work.

3. Physical fitness improves the health of your bones. Weak and brittle bones are common in many people over 40 years of age who do not exercise. When you exercise, your bones become more dense. You are less likely to get hurt if you fall or are in an accident.

4. Physical fitness can help you deal with stress. In Chapter 3, you learned that stress is the body's reaction to any demand made upon it. The demand may be physical or mental. It may be helpful or harmful. If stress is harmful it may affect your health. A research study at the University of Southern California found that a 15–minute walk reduces harmful stress more than taking a pill to relax the body.

5. Physical fitness may improve the way you look. When you exercise, your body uses the energy from the foods you eat. You are more likely to weigh the right amount for your body build. Your skin will be healthy and clear. Your muscles will look and feel firm.

6. Physical fitness may improve your grades in school. Exercise improves the circulation of your blood. Exercise increases the amount of oxygen available to your body organs. Exercise helps you to think more clearly. It helps all your muscles—even the ones you use to sit at your desk. You can sit and think for longer periods of time after exercising.

7. Physical fitness promotes sleep. It is important to feel relaxed before you can sleep. Some people are restless and do not sleep well. They wake up feeling tired. When you exercise, you can relax and you sleep better. You are not restless. You wake up feeling fresh.

8. Physical fitness may help you recover sooner from an illness. When you do not feel good, there may be something wrong inside your body. If you are in good physical condition, it is easier for your body to return to normal good health.

**FIGURE 4–6.**

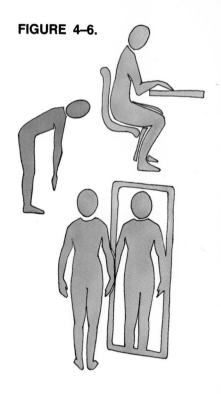

*How might exercise improve your looks?*

**FIGURE 4–7.** Exercise helps people of all ages to look and feel their best.

*Why is exercise an anti-aging pill?*

9. Physical fitness slows the signs of aging. Dr. Alexander Leaf of the Harvard Medical School says, "Exercise is the closest thing to an anti-aging pill." You learned that your heart and lungs become stronger when you exercise. Other parts of your body become stronger too. Exercise can help your body to remain healthy for more years.

10. Physical fitness helps you to feel good about yourself. When you plan a program of exercise and stick to it, you are doing something to make yourself a better person. You are meeting your goals. This produces a good feeling.

## Section

## 4:5

# How to Begin Your Physical Fitness Program

Most people admit that physical fitness helps them to be at their best. However, many of these same people do not exercise. They think of reasons or excuses not to exercise. Some persons your age were asked why they do not exercise. Here are some of their answers.

*What are some reasons people use for not exercising?*

- I think exercise is boring.
- I'm not good at sports and others might laugh at me.
- I want to seem weak so others will take care of me.
- I look all right the way I am.
- I am too busy with other activities.
- I do not have time to fit exercise into my day.

Do you make excuses for not getting enough exercise to be physically fit? If so, write your reasons on a sheet of paper. Ask yourself, "Are these good enough reasons not to look and feel my best?" Hopefully, your answer will be no.

## Getting Started

Many people your age do not make a plan for physical fitness. They think that they do not need one if they ride a bike, swim, walk, or run. But remember, to be physically fit you need to work on the five fitness areas. The areas are muscular strength, muscular endurance, flexibility, agility, and cardio-respiratory fitness. Most people who do not make an exercise plan will not be fit in each of these physical fitness areas. Here are some tips for planning to be physically fit.

- Make a list of exercises for each of the five fitness areas.
- Select one exercise you want to do for each area.
- Plan a time during the day when you can exercise.
- Make a list of clothing or equipment you will need.
- If you want company, find others who want to join your exercise plan.
- Make a chart or checklist to keep track of your plan. This will help you to see if you are meeting your plan.

*List tips for beginning an exercise program.*

Doug Martin

**FIGURE 4–8.** Exercises should be done correctly if they are to benefit a person.

Gerard Photography

**FIGURE 4–9.** Warming-up and cooling-down exercises help your body to get the best results from an exercise program.

*Why is warming up important?*

*Why is cooling down important?*

## Warming Up

Before you begin your exercises, you will want to warm up. **Warming up** gets your muscles ready to do more work. Warming up will help prevent injury and soreness to your muscles. You should warm up for 10 to 20 minutes before doing more difficult exercises. One of these exercises is shown above.

## Cooling Down

After exercise, you should cool down for about 10 minutes. **Cooling down** gives your heart a chance to slow down. Your body temperature becomes lower or cooler. If you do not give your body time to cool down, you may feel dizzy or faint. Some people walk while they are cooling down. Others do stretching exercises. If you take a bath or shower after exercising, use lukewarm water.

 **Activity**
### Are You Doing the Right Exercises?
Make a list of the exercises you are presently doing. Tell how each exercise is making you physically fit.

# Review

## Summary

1. When you are physically fit, you can do many things because your body is in good condition.      *4:1*
2. Physical fitness includes muscular strength, muscular endurance, flexibility, agility, and cardio-respiratory fitness.      *4:2*
3. There are different kinds of exercises that make you physically fit: isometric, isotonic, anaerobic, and aerobic exercises.      *4:3*
4. Physical fitness may help lengthen your life and improve your health.      *4:4*
5. It is important to make a plan that includes the five fitness areas and exercises for warming up and cooling down.      *4:5*

## Words for Health

*Below are vocabulary words and incomplete sentences. Complete each sentence with the correct vocabulary word. DO NOT WRITE IN THIS BOOK.*

| | |
|---|---|
| aerobic exercise | isometric exercise |
| agility | isotonic exercise |
| anaerobic exercise | muscular endurance |
| cardio-respiratory fitness | muscular strength |
| cooling down | physical fitness |
| flexibility | warming up |

1. _____ gives your heart a chance to slow down and your body temperature becomes lower and cooler.
2. When you contract your muscles to make a movement, you are doing a(n) _____.
3. A(n) _____ uses a lot of oxygen and is continued for an extended length of time.
4. _____ involves exercises that get your body in the best possible physical condition for you.
5. When you do exercises that stretch and bend your body, you will increase your _____.
6. If you do _____ exercises, you may prevent injury and soreness to your muscles.
7. When you have strong muscles to help you lift, pull, and push, you have _____.

# Review

8. When you swim or run a long distance several times a week, you develop _____.
9. A(n) _____ is one where you tighten your muscles for five to eight seconds.
10. When you can continue to use muscular strength for a period of time, you have _____.
11. You are increasing your _____ when you coordinate the movements of different muscles while playing tennis.
12. A(n) _____ helps develop speed but does not contribute to overall fitness.

## Look at Your Health

1. What are some things you are able to do when you are physically fit?
2. What five different areas are included in physical fitness?
3. What is the difference between muscular strength and muscular endurance?
4. How can you develop a flexible body?
5. What are four kinds of exercises that make you physically fit?
6. Give three facts about aerobic exercises.
7. What are two important reasons why you should be physically fit?
8. Name ten ways that physical fitness can improve your health.
9. Why is it important to do warming-up exercises?
10. What happens to your body as you cool down for ten minutes after exercising?

## Actions for Health

*Think about the following situations. Then respond to the questions that follow.*

*Situation:* Last week, your best friend began an exercise program to improve cardio-respiratory fitness. Today your friend's legs feel very sore. You ask your friend about the exercise program. Your friend says, "After school, I have a snack. Then I change clothes and run a mile and a half. I take a hot shower as soon as I finish running, but something is wrong with my program!"

1. Name three possible reasons that your friend might feel sore.
2. How can your friend make a better exercise plan?

*Situation:* Today you tried to touch your toes during a gym class exercise. It has been a while since you have exercised. The backs of your legs hurt while you are touching your toes.

1. What kind of fitness are you lacking?
2. What types of exercises might you do to improve this kind of fitness?

## Individual Research

1. Write a report on the exercises that a person in a wheelchair might do to be physically fit.
2. Write a report on the President's Council on Physical Fitness.
3. Write a report that describes a PAR COURSE. What types of exercises are included at each station (isometric, isotonic, anaerobic, aerobic)?
4. Find out about a career as a physical education teacher. Write to the American Alliance of Health, Physical Education, Recreation, and Dance at 1900 Association Drive, Reston, Virginia, 22091.
5. Talk with someone who works at a park or other recreational facility. Write a report about the field of recreation as a career.

# LIFE MANAGEMENT SKILLS

- Participate in exercises that improve muscular strength.
- Participate in exercises that improve muscular endurance.
- Participate in exercises that improve flexibility.
- Participate in exercises that improve agility.
- Participate in exercises that improve cardio-respiratory fitness.
- Plan a time during the day to exercise.
- Warm up before exercising.
- Cool down after exercising.

# Dental Health

*You eat a variety of foods. Some foods have smooth surfaces, others have rough surfaces. Some foods are soft, others are hard. You have different kinds of teeth. How do they help you enjoy the different kinds of food? Which foods are your favorites?*

C an you give reasons why dental health is an important part of your general health? Here are three reasons why you need to have healthy teeth to be at your best.

- Your teeth help you chew food so that you can digest it properly.
- Your teeth help you speak clearly.
- Your teeth are an important part of your appearance.

**GOAL:** *You will learn about your teeth and gums and how to care for them.*

---

## A Tooth Has Different Parts

**Section**

**5:1**

A tooth has many parts. Learning about these parts will make it easier to understand how your teeth help you. You will learn how you can care for them. Look at the diagrams of a tooth on page 60 as you learn more about each part.

- The **root** of a tooth holds it in the jawbone.
- The **crown** is the part that you can see in your mouth.
- The **cusp** is the pointed part of the crown of the tooth.
- The **enamel** is the very hard tissue that covers the crown.
- The **dentin** is the hard tissue that forms the body of the tooth.
- The **pulp** is in the center of the tooth. The pulp contains nerves and blood vessels. These enter the tooth through an opening at the tip of the root.
- The **cementum** (sih MENT um) is a bonelike tissue that covers the root.
- The **periodontal** (per ee oh DAHNT ul) **membrane** is the layer of tissue between the cementum and the jawbone. It helps to hold the tooth in place.

*Name eight different parts of a tooth.*

A Tooth Has Different Parts **59**

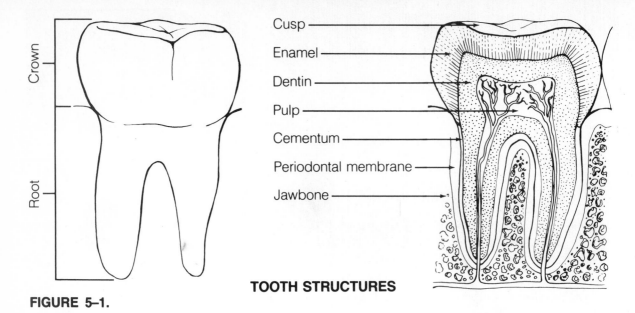

**TOOTH STRUCTURES**

**FIGURE 5–1.**

Look at the picture of the tooth again. Now describe what each part of the tooth does.

**Activity**

***Tooth Structure***

Draw a tooth. Label each of the following parts: root, crown, cusp, enamel, dentin, pulp, cementum, periodontal membrane. Know the function of each tooth part.

## Section

## 5:2

## Different Teeth Do Different Things

*How do your teeth help you?*

You have already learned how your teeth help you. Do you remember the three ways? Teeth help you chew your food. Teeth help you speak clearly. Teeth help you look nice when you smile.

Look at the picture of teeth on page 61. Notice that all teeth do not look alike. This is because different teeth do different things.

*Name four different kinds of teeth. Describe what each kind does.*

**Incisors** (ihn SI zurz) are the teeth in the front and center of your mouth. They have a flat, sharp edge. The incisors cut the food that you eat.

## ADULT SET OF TEETH

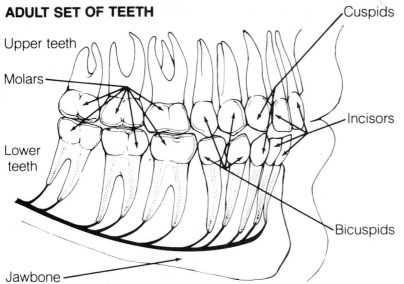

FIGURE 5–2. An adult normally has 32 teeth.

**Cuspids** (KUS pudz) are the teeth in the corners of your mouth. They have a long, heavy root. The crown of the cuspids has a very pointed cusp. The cuspids are used to tear food.

**Bicuspids** (bi KUS pudz) are the teeth in back of your cuspids. They have two cusps. They have one or two roots. The bicuspids are used to tear and crush the food you eat.

The **molars** are the teeth in the back of your mouth. They have several cusps and two or three roots. The molars are used to grind food.

## Think About It

**1.** Why do different teeth do different tasks?

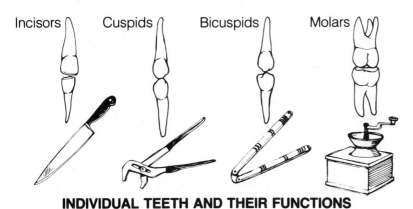

**INDIVIDUAL TEETH AND THEIR FUNCTIONS**          FIGURE 5–3.

# Tooth Decay

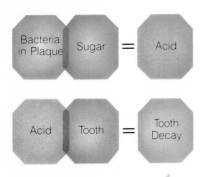

**FIGURE 5–4.**

*Define plaque.*

*What is calculus?*

*How is acid formed on teeth?*

*What is a cavity?*

*What is a filling?*

**FIGURE 5–5.**

**STAGES OF TOOTH DECAY**

Tooth decay is nearly as common as the common cold. Around 98 percent of all Americans will have tooth decay at some time during their lives. Let us look at how your teeth may decay.

A sticky substance called **plaque** (PLAK) is always forming on your teeth. Plaque forms near the gumline and between your teeth. It tends to stick to the grooves and curves on your teeth. Plaque contains bacteria.

You need to remove the plaque from your teeth each day. If the plaque is not removed, it becomes hard. When plaque becomes hard it is called **calculus** (KAL kyuh lus). You cannot remove calculus by yourself. This is why you go to the dentist to have your teeth cleaned. The dentist or dental hygienist (HI jeen ust) will remove the calculus.

Let us see what happens when you do not remove the plaque and calculus on your teeth. We can learn how this may cause tooth decay.

When you eat foods that contain sugar, the sugar and the bacteria in plaque form an acid.

The sticky plaque will hold this acid on your tooth. This acid may make holes called **cavities** in the enamel that covers your tooth.

Sometimes you go to the dentist and learn that you have a cavity in the enamel of a tooth. A dentist is the only one who can repair a cavity. The dentist will put in a filling. A **filling** is material that repairs the cavity in a tooth.

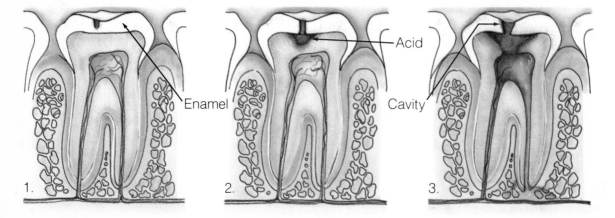

But what happens if you do not go to the dentist right away? Bacteria from plaque may get into the dentin. Remember that the dentin is the hard tissue that forms the body of your tooth. The bacteria can then destroy your whole tooth structure. What do you suppose would happen next if you do not get a filling? You may have guessed. The bacteria may get into the root of the tooth and cause a very bad dental disease.

## Think About It

2. Why do you need to have your teeth cleaned regularly by a dentist or a dental hygienist?
3. Why is it important to have a dentist fill a cavity as soon as possible after it forms?

**Section**

**5:4**

## Periodontal Disease

**Periodontal** (per ee oh DAHNT ul) **disease** is a disease of the gums and other tissues that support your teeth. It is very common in adults. However, periodontal disease may begin at your age. To be at your best, you will want to know how you can keep from having this disease. Let us learn how it begins and what you can do to prevent it.

Plaque is the major cause of periodontal disease. Plaque may form around your gums and make them sore. If this happens, your gums will bleed easily. When your gums are sore and bleed easily, you may have **gingivitis** (jihn juh VITE us). If you have gingivitis, your dentist can tell you what to do to make your gums healthy again.

Suppose that you do not do anything about the plaque on your teeth and that calculus forms. What happens if you do not get the calculus removed? More plaque will form on top of the calculus. Your gums will slowly separate from your teeth and make spaces or pockets. These pockets become filled with bacteria. This is periodontal disease.

If you do not go to the dentist to get help, this disease will destroy the bones that support your teeth. Even if your teeth are healthy, they will become loose. They may even fall out.

*What are signs of gingivitis?*

**FIGURE 5–6.** X-ray photos of teeth will indicate the presence of cavities and fillings.

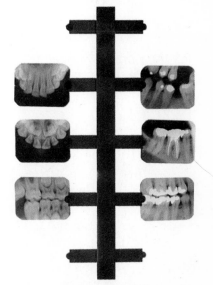

Gerard Photography

Periodontal Disease **63**

The best way to prevent periodontal disease is to remove the plaque on your teeth each day. This also helps to keep you from having tooth decay.

## Think About It

4. Why should you learn ways to stop periodontal disease at your age when most people who have this disease are much older than you?

*Why is it important to brush your teeth?*

# How to Brush Your Teeth

**FIGURE 5–7.**

**STEPS OF TOOTH BRUSHING**

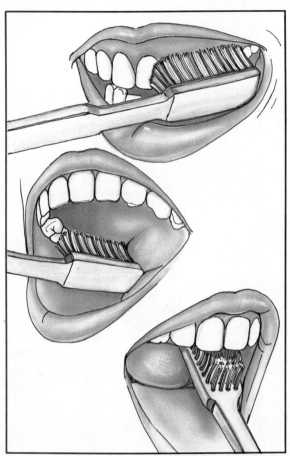

**Toothbrushing** removes plaque from the exposed surfaces of your teeth. There are several different ways to brush your teeth. The following way to remove plaque is recommended by the American Dental Association (ADA).

1. Place the head of your toothbrush beside your teeth with the bristle tips at an angle to your gums.
2. Move the brush back and forth. Use short strokes about a half-tooth wide. Stroke several times. You will be gently scrubbing your teeth.
3. Brush the outer surfaces of each tooth. Brush the upper and lower teeth. Remember to keep the bristles of your toothbrush at an angle to your gums.
4. Now do the same thing on the inside surface of each tooth. Keep the strokes short. Stroke several times. Again, you are gently scrubbing your teeth.
5. Scrub the chewing surface of each tooth.
6. For the front teeth, you will turn your toothbrush a different way. Stroke up and down several times. Go over your gums too.
7. The last thing you will do is brush your tongue. This keeps your mouth clean and it freshens your breath.

# How to Floss Your Teeth

**Flossing** removes plaque and bits of food from between the teeth. It also helps to remove the plaque and food near the gumline. It is important to clean between the teeth and near the gums with floss because a toothbrush cannot get to these hard-to-reach places. Floss is the stringlike material that you place between your teeth. These places are where tooth decay and gum disease usually begin.

You will need to learn how to floss the right way. Then you will have to practice. Here are the steps for flossing as suggested by the American Dental Association.

*Why is it important to floss your teeth?*

**FIGURE 5–8.**

**STEPS OF TOOTH FLOSSING**

1. Break off about 40 centimeters of floss. Wind most of it around one of your middle fingers.

2. Wind the rest of it around the same finger of the opposite hand. This finger can "take up" the floss as you use it.

3. Use your thumbs and forefingers with 2 to 3 centimeters of floss between them to guide the floss between your teeth.

4. Hold the floss tightly. Use a gentle sawing motion to insert the floss between your teeth. Never snap or push the floss into your gums. When the floss reaches your gum line, curve it into a C-shape against one tooth. Gently slide it into the space between the gum and the tooth but do not force it too hard.

5. While holding the floss tightly against the tooth, move the floss away from the gum by scraping the side of the tooth.

6. Without removing the floss, curve it around the other tooth and scrape it too. Scrape floss down on upper teeth and up on bottom teeth.

7. Repeat this method on the rest of your teeth.

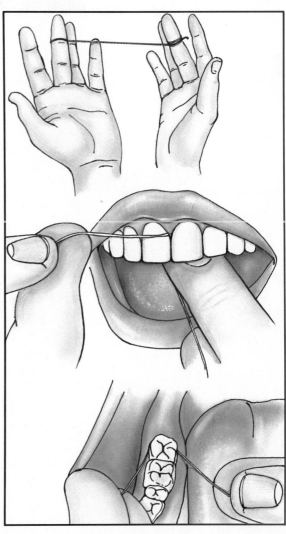

**FIGURE 5–9.** Fluoride treatments are given by many dentists.

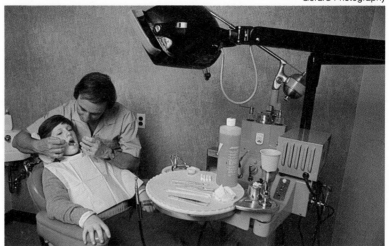

## Section

### 5:7

# How Fluorides Work

Research shows that fluoride (FLOOR ide), a chemical, helps to prevent tooth decay. For this reason many people believe that you need to get fluoride in some way. The American Dental Association agrees.

Fluoride makes tooth enamel to be hard. When your teeth were being formed during childhood, you may have gotten fluoride in different ways. You may have had fluoride in water supplies or food. You may have taken a fluoride pill or tablet.

*How does fluoride help to prevent tooth decay?*

This fluoride got into your bloodstream. It was carried in your blood to your teeth. At this time, your body was making the enamel for your teeth. The fluoride mixed with the other things that made up the enamel. The enamel became very hard. This hard enamel helps to protect your teeth from the bacteria and acids that cause tooth decay.

*Name four ways you can get fluoride.*

There is another way that fluoride can help to prevent tooth decay. Your dentist may put fluoride on your teeth. You can put fluoride on the outside of your teeth. You may use a fluoride toothpaste or a fluoride rinse. The fluoride becomes part of the outer surface of the tooth. It helps make your teeth more resistant to decay.

Fluorides are available to you in many different forms. While they do not prevent all tooth decay, they are helpful.

## Think About It

5. Why is it important to have fluoride in your body when your teeth are being formed?

6. What is the easiest way for children to get fluoride in their bodies?

## What About Sugar?

You have learned that good dental health includes brushing and flossing your teeth to remove plaque. But there is something else that is very important. You should be careful about how much sugar you eat. Sugar and the bacteria in plaque combine to form the acid which makes cavities in your teeth.

What can you do about sugar? You can cut down on the amount of sugar that you eat. When you get hungry for sugar, eat something without sugar. Eat an apple instead of a piece of cake. Do not eat sweet snacks that stick to your teeth. If you do eat sugar, eat it only at mealtimes. Then, always brush your teeth after meals to remove the sugar from your teeth.

*What can you do about sugar?*

## Activity

### Healthy Snacks

Form groups of four with your classmates. You will have five minutes to make a list of health snacks for after school. Choose snacks that do not contain sugar. Share your list with other groups. Combine the lists into one long list to share with your parents or guardians. How many of these snacks are available in your home?

Larry Hamill

**FIGURE 5–10.** Choose healthy snacks.

## What About Braces?

Wendy's first appointment with Dr. Feldman went smoothly. Dr. Feldman is an orthodontist (or thuh DAHNT ust). An orthodontist is a dentist who is trained to fit braces on people's teeth. Dr. Feldman examined Wendy's teeth, jawbones, and face muscles. After the short exam, Dr. Feldman told Wendy and her parents that she needed braces. He said that Wendy had an overbite that needed to be corrected. An overbite means the upper front teeth stick out over the lower front teeth when the mouth is closed.

Wendy's second appointment involved further examinations. Dr. Feldman completely examined Wendy's teeth. He also checked to see if the size of her jawbones were big enough to hold all of her teeth. Often, two or more teeth are removed to prevent them from crowding each other. Dr. Feldman then took several X rays of Wendy's teeth and face bones. He used the examination to help him decide what kind of braces to put on Wendy.

Wendy asked Dr. Feldman how long she would have to wear braces. He said she would need to wear them for two years. And after the braces were removed she would have to wear a retainer for about two years. A retainer is a plastic device that keeps the teeth from moving back to their original place.

"Will I need an injection?" Wendy asked. "No," Dr. Feldman said, "usually, it is not necessary to numb your gums and teeth while fitting the braces."

Finally, Wendy asked, "Is it going to hurt when you put my braces on?" Dr. Feldman said, "That's what most young people want to know before I put their braces on. Let me explain what I'm going to do."

He showed Wendy the plastic arches called separators. Separators fit between and separate the teeth so the braces can be fitted properly. When the separators are in place, a person will feel as if something is wedged between the teeth. After a few hours the teeth will become tender. This will last a couple days. Rinsing the mouth with warm salt water and taking aspirin will relieve the discomfort.

Dr. Feldman showed Wendy the braces. They are small shiny bands of metal. They fit around the teeth like a ring fits around a finger.

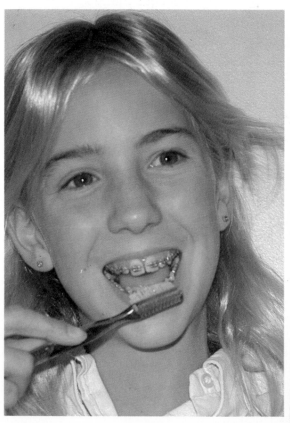

Dr. Randall Feldman

# Review

## Summary

1. A tooth has many parts: root, crown, cusp, enamel, dentin, pulp, cementum, periodontal membrane. — 5:1
2. Different teeth—incisors, cuspids, bicuspids, molars—do different tasks. — 5:2
3. When you do not remove plaque and calculus from your teeth, you may get a cavity. — 5:3
4. If you remove plaque from your teeth each day, you will prevent periodontal disease. — 5:4
5. Toothbrushing every day removes plaque from the exposed surfaces of the teeth. — 5:5
6. Flossing between your teeth removes the plaque and bits of food that are not reached with your toothbrush. — 5:6
7. Many people believe that you need to get fluoride in some way to help prevent tooth decay. — 5:7
8. You are less likely to get tooth decay if you decrease the amount of sugar you eat. — 5:8

## Words for Health

*Below are vocabulary words and incomplete sentences. Complete each sentence with the correct vocabulary word. DO NOT WRITE IN THIS BOOK.*

| | |
|---|---|
| bicuspids | flossing |
| calculus | gingivitis |
| cavities | incisors |
| cementum | molars |
| crown | periodontal disease |
| cusp | periodontal membrane |
| cuspids | plaque |
| dentin | pulp |
| enamel | root |
| filling | toothbrushing |

1. You can see the _____ of each tooth when you look at your mouth in a mirror.
2. In the corner of your mouth are the pointed _____ that tear food.

# Review

3. _____ is a sticky substance that forms on your teeth.
4. The _____ have two cusps that are used to tear and crush food.
5. When plaque hardens it is called _____.
6. You can remove plaque and bits of food from between your teeth by _____.
7. A(n) _____ is a material that repairs a cavity in a tooth.
8. The _____ of the tooth holds it in the jawbone.
9. The hard tissue that forms the body of the tooth is the _____.
10. You may have _____ if your gums are sore and bleed easily.
11. The teeth in the front of your mouth that cut up the food you eat are _____.
12. _____ removes plaque from the exposed surfaces of your teeth.
13. The pointed part of the crown of the tooth is the _____.
14. The _____ of the tooth contains nerves and blood vessels.
15. _____ affects the gums and other tissues that support your teeth.
16. Holes in the enamel that covers your teeth are called _____.
17. The _____ are used to grind food.
18. The hard tissue that covers the crown of the tooth is the _____.
19. The bonelike tissue that covers the root of the tooth is the _____.
20. The _____ is the layer of tissue between the cementum and the jawbone.

# Look at Your Health

1. Name eight parts of a tooth.
2. Name three ways that teeth help you.
3. Name four different kinds of teeth and tell what they do.
4. How is calculus removed from your teeth?
5. What forms on your teeth when you eat sugar?
6. What is periodontal disease?
7. What are three structures inside your mouth that should be brushed?
8. Why is it important to floss between your teeth?
9. What are four ways that you can get fluoride?
10. How can you cut down on the amount of sugar that you eat?

## Actions for Health

*Think about the following situations. Then respond to the questions that follow.*

*Situation:* You are having some of your friends over to your house Friday after school. You and your friends have just finished reading this chapter on dental health. You all agree to reduce the amount of sugar you eat. You plan to serve your friends a snack.

1. List snack foods that are usually served when you get together with your friends.
2. List snack foods that you could serve that are low in sugar.
3. Select a snack for your friends from this list.

*Situation:* You have just visited your dentist for a checkup. Your dentist thinks you should brush your teeth more often and floss each day. You decide to improve your dental health.

1. When do you plan to brush and floss your teeth each day?
2. What might keep you from brushing and flossing your teeth?
3. How can you change your schedule to be certain that you have good dental health habits?

## Individual Research

1. Write a report on the American Dental Association.
2. Interview a dentist and dental hygienist. Write a report about these careers.
3. Some persons are against adding fluoride to water. Find out their reasons.
4. Write a report about mouth protectors. How do they prevent injury to the mouth and teeth? In what sports are they usually worn?

## LIFE MANAGEMENT SKILLS

- Brush your teeth and gums daily to remove calculus.
- Floss your teeth daily to remove plaque and food.
- Use toothpaste with fluoride and/or have your dentist apply fluoride to your teeth.
- Have regular dental checkups.
- Reduce sweet snacks that stick to your teeth.
- Select a diet that contains vitamins A and D for strong teeth and vitamin C for healthy gums.

# Nutrition and Your Habits

Eric Hoffhines

*The apples have been growing and getting ripe in the summer sun. Now, the beautiful color is a sign that they are ready to be picked and eaten. Have you ever picked apples? Your body needs the stored energy in foods like apples. How can you be sure to choose the right foods to eat?*

E ach of the following examples has something in common. Do you have any habits that are similar to these?

**GOAL:** *You will study the food groups and the nutrients necessary for your good health. You will learn the seven dietary goals.*

- Ricardo stops at the store on the way home from school each day to buy a candy bar.
- John is overweight. He eats potato chips and enjoys sugar-filled drinks.
- Mabel enjoys ballet. She needs a lot of energy. She is careful to eat healthy foods at each meal. She avoids snacks.

**Section**

**6:1**

## Nutrients

Ricardo, John, and Mabel have developed certain eating habits. A **habit** is a usual way of doing things. Your eating habits may be healthy or unhealthy. **Nutrition** (new TRIHSH un) is the study of what you eat, your habits, and how these affect your health.

Your body has certain needs. You eat many different foods to meet these needs. **Nutrients** (NEW tree unts) are substances in foods that are needed by your body to grow. You also need nutrients to repair your body cells and to supply energy.

*What are nutrients?*

Your body needs six main kinds of nutrients. When you have these each day, you will look and feel your best. What foods provide these important nutrients?

*Why do you need proteins?*

**Proteins** are nutrients that are needed for growth and repair of your body's cells. Your muscles, skin, nails, and hair are made of proteins. Foods which contain protein are fish, chicken, turkey, meat, eggs, milk, wheat germ, peanuts, cheese, and beans.

*Why do you need fats?*

**Fats** are nutrients that provide your body with energy. They also help your body store vitamins. Do you know what foods contain fats? There is fat in butter, meat, whole milk, and ice cream.

*Why do you need carbohydrates?*

**Carbohydrates** are the nutrients which are the main sources of energy for your body. Sugars and starches are carbohydrates. There are many foods which you can choose that contain carbohydrates. They include cereal, rice, potatoes, bread, noodles, fruit, candy, and soft drinks. Which of these foods are better for you?

*Why are vitamins necessary?*

**Vitamins** are nutrients which help your body use proteins, fats, and carbohydrates. There are many different vitamins. Some important vitamins are listed in the chart. Do you eat the foods which provide these vitamins?

*How do minerals function in your body?*

**Minerals** are nutrients that are involved in many of the activities in your body. You need minerals to make your muscles and nerves work and to build bones and teeth. Some important minerals that your body needs are in the chart. Do you eat foods which contain the minerals that your body needs?

**FIGURE 6–1.**

| SOME VITAMINS | | |
|---|---|---|
| | **Some Functions** | **Some Sources** |
| **Vitamin A** | Keeps eyes, skin, and hair healthy | Butter, cheese, egg yolk, green, leafy vegetables |
| **Vitamin D** | Necessary for formation of bones and teeth | Dairy products, fish-liver oils |
| **Vitamin K** | Necessary for normal blood clotting | Green, leafy vegetables, liver |
| **Vitamin $B_1$** | Necessary for function of nerves | Whole grain cereals, poultry, eggs |
| **Vitamin $B_{12}$** | Necessary for formation of red blood cells | Red meats, milk, eggs, cheese |
| **Vitamin C** | Necessary for strong bones | Citrus fruits, green vegetables |

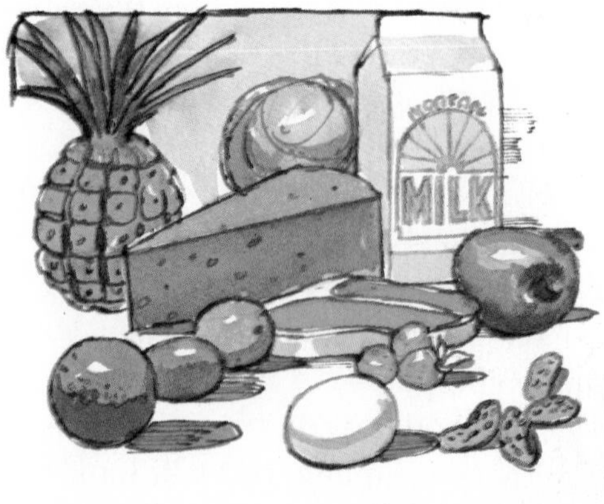

| SOME MINERALS | | |
|---|---|---|
| | Some Functions | Some Sources |
| Calcium | Makes up bones and teeth | Milk, cheese, clams, oysters |
| Iron | Makes up blood cells | Liver, lean meats, green, leafy vegetables, shellfish, molasses |
| Phosphorus | Makes up bones and teeth with calcium | Milk, whole grain cereals |
| Potassium | Keeps fluids balanced within cells | Fruits, milk, meat, cereals, vegetables |
| Copper | Necessary for production of hemoglobin in red blood cells | Liver, shellfish, whole grains, poultry, nuts |
| Iodine | Necessary for production of the thyroid gland hormone | Iodized salt, clams, lobsters, oysters |

**FIGURE 6–2.**

What else does your body need for you to be at your best? You may have guessed—water. **Water** helps your body do many things. It is a necessary part of all the cells in your body. It helps you digest your food. It is a part of blood and urine. There are many ways that you get the water your body needs. You may drink water or other beverages. You also get water in soup, fruits, and vegetables.

*Why do you need water?*

## Think About It

1. How do nutrients keep your body healthy?
2. Why can you not live without water?

**Section**

## The Food Groups—The Best Habit

**6:2**

The best eating habit you can have is to eat the six nutrients every day. Foods that contain the same nutrients belong to a **food group**. There are five food groups. The food groups and numbers of servings you need each day are the

*What is a food group?*

- milk group (4 servings)
- meat group (2 servings)
- fruit and vegetable group (4 servings)
- grain group (4 servings)
- combination group

The combination group contains ingredients from more than one food group and supplies the same nutrients as the foods they contain.

Some foods are not in any of the five healthful food groups. These foods make up a category called the "others" group. Foods in the "others" group are usually high in calories and contain few vitamins and minerals. They are mostly sugars and fats. Cookies, cakes, pies, salad dressings, and soda pop are examples of these foods. It is best to avoid eating these foods.

**FIGURE 6–3.** The healthful food groups.

| MILK | MEAT | FRUIT-VEGETABLE | GRAIN | COMBINATION |
|---|---|---|---|---|
| Supplies these key nutrients:<br>■ calcium<br>■ riboflavin (vitamin B$_2$)<br>■ protein<br>for strong bones and teeth, healthy skin and good vision | Supplies these key nutrients:<br>■ protein<br>■ niacin<br>■ iron<br>■ thiamin (vitamin B$_1$)<br>for muscle, bone, and blood cells and healthy skin and nerves | Supplies these key nutrients:<br>■ vitamin A<br>■ vitamin C<br>for night vision and to help resist infections and heal wounds | Supplies these key nutrients:<br>■ carbohydrate<br>■ thiamin (vitamin B$_1$)<br>■ iron<br>■ niacin<br>for energy and a healthy nervous system | Combination foods contain ingredients from more than one food group, and supply the same nutrients as the foods they contain. |

A serving is:

| MILK | | MEAT | | FRUIT-VEGETABLE | | GRAIN | | COMBINATION | |
|---|---|---|---|---|---|---|---|---|---|
| 1 cup | Milk | 2 oz | Cooked, lean meat, fish, poultry | ½ cup | Juice | 1 slice | Bread | 1 cup | Soup |
| 1 cup | Yogurt | 2 | Eggs | ½ cup | Cooked vegetable or fruit | 1 cup | Ready-to-eat-cereal | 1 cup | Pasta dish (macaroni and cheese, lasagna)** |
| 1½ oz | Cheese (1½ slices) | 2 oz | Cheese | 1 cup | Raw vegetable or fruit | ½ cup | Cooked cereal | | |
| 1 cup | Pudding | 1 cup | Dried peas or beans | | | ½ cup | Pasta | 1 cup | Main course (stew, chili, casseroles) |
| 2 cups | Cottage cheese | 4 tbsp | Peanut butter | Medium | Apple, banana, or orange | ½ cup | Rice | ¼ 14'' | Pizza (thin crust) |
| 1¾ cups | Ice cream | | | ½ | Grapefruit | ½ cup | Grits | 1 | Taco, sandwich |
| | | | | ¼ | Cantaloupe | | | | |

Number of Servings

| MILK | MEAT | FRUIT-VEGETABLE | GRAIN | COMBINATION |
|---|---|---|---|---|
| 4 | 2 | 4 | 4 | These count as servings (or partial servings) from the food groups from which they are made. |

Eric Hoffhines

**FIGURE 6–4.** Eating habits are difficult to change.

## The Overeating Habit

Nutrition would not be a problem if you ate only the amount of nutrients that your body needs. But some people eat for other reasons. These persons eat more food than they need. Eating more food does not mean that they are eating the right kinds of food. They may not be getting enough of the six nutrients.

Phil eats when he is bored. When he cannot decide what he wants to do, he eats a dish of ice cream. Many people overeat because they are bored.

*List reasons some people eat too much.*

Doris eats when she is frustrated. She finds it difficult to do her math homework. She eats pretzels and drinks soda pop while she studies. Many people overeat because they are frustrated.

Pedro likes to eat candy bars that he sees advertised on TV. They look good to him even though he is not hungry. Many people overeat because they see foods on television or at the store. They are tempted to eat even when they are not hungry.

Do you eat because your body needs nutrients? Do you eat because you are bored, frustrated, lonely, or depressed? Think carefully about your eating habits.

**FIGURE 6–5.** Many restaurants offer a variety of breakfast choices.

Eric Hoffhines

# The Breakfast Habit

*Why is it important to eat protein for breakfast?*

*What happens when you skip breakfast?*

Are you in the habit of eating breakfast every day? Breakfast is the most important meal of the day. A healthy breakfast includes protein. When you begin the day with protein, you have energy for the morning. You will not feel tired or hungry. You will think clearly at school.

Young people your age who do not eat breakfast may get hungry at school. They may feel dizzy or faint. They may not get along well with others. Some people may think they will lose weight if they skip breakfast. This is not true. People who skip breakfast usually eat more food during the rest of the day.

What foods do you like to eat for breakfast? Some people eat foods like eggs, cereal, or bacon. But others eat different foods. Dafney eats cottage cheese. Roberto eats a cheese sandwich. Edward likes peanut butter and crackers. Each of these foods contains protein. If you do not like the usual breakfast foods, choose foods that you like that contain protein.

## Think About It

**3.** How can eating a good breakfast help you learn more and get better grades in school?

# The Vending Machine and Fast Food Habit

Are you a steady customer at a drive-in restaurant? Do you like to stop at an ice cream store for a milkshake? Do you stop at a donut shop before or after school? If you do, you are eating fast foods. A **fast food** is a food that is ready to eat when you buy it. Fast foods make up about one-third of the foods Americans eat each day.

*What is a fast food?*

Many fast foods are sold in vending machines. Perhaps you have taken a trip in a car with your parents and you stopped for gasoline. You were so hungry you bought a candy bar from a vending machine. Perhaps there is a vending machine in your school. During your lunch break, you might buy a pastry or a sugar-filled drink.

It is best not to get into the habit of buying fast foods that contain very few nutrients or too much sugar. Such foods help cause tooth decay. They do not help you grow. They do not repair body cells. Fast foods that contain no nutrients may make you less hungry. Then you will not eat the foods that your body needs. If you have the fast food habit, you will want to make wise choices.

**FIGURE 6–6.** Complete meals are available from some vending machines.

**Activity**

*My Eating Habits*

Copy the following chart on a sheet of paper. Complete the chart. What have you learned about your eating habits?

| FAST FOODS I EAT | FOOD GROUP TO WHICH IT BELONGS |
|---|---|
| 1. 2. 3. 4. 5. | |

FIGURE 6–7.

## Think About It

**4.** Why do Americans eat so many fast foods?

**5.** How could you break the fast food habit?

## Section

## 6:6

## The Habits of Athletes

Do you enjoy watching an athletic event on TV? Do you have a favorite athlete? You may have heard an athlete talk about foods. Perhaps you have heard an athlete tell about a favorite food. What foods should an athlete eat? Do athletes have special needs?

*What is the best diet for an athlete?*

Athletes need to eat the correct number of servings from the five food groups. Everyone needs to eat the six nutrients. If you exercise often, you usually do not need to make any changes in your eating habits. However, there are some things about eating habits and exercise that may interest you.

Some persons believe that those who exercise regularly need to eat more protein. This is not necessary. Did you know that persons who run a marathon race often eat more carbohydrates? The week before the race they may begin to eat foods like bread and spaghetti. The night before the race they may have a dinner with extra carbohydrates. This is called carbohydrate loading. **Carbohydrate loading** makes the body ready for exercise that requires endurance.

*What is carbohydrate loading?*

Some researchers believe that persons who exercise often need more vitamin B and C. You may want to ask your coach or doctor about the vitamins you need. Most likely you get all the vitamins you need by eating foods from the four food groups.

Can you think of anything else that is needed when you exercise often? When you exercise in hot weather, you perspire. Your perspiration cools your body. Have you ever smelled or tasted perspiration? It is salty. Your body loses salt when you perspire. After exercising in hot weather, you need to replace salt. You can put small amounts of salt on your food. This lessens the chance of getting muscle cramps.

Many people ask questions about the special drinks advertised for people who exercise. Are these special drinks necessary? Can you obtain the same health benefits by drinking water or fruit juice? You may be surprised to learn that there are no health benefits obtained from these special drinks. After you exercise a great deal, drink plenty of water or fruit juice. If you perspired, you would usually get the amounts of salt you need from a balanced diet. You do not need to spend money for special drinks.

Steve Lissau

**FIGURE 6–8.** Exercise during hot weather causes a person to perspire more.

## Seven Diet Goals

The United States Department of Agriculture and the Department of Health and Human Services have prepared a list of seven diet goals to promote good health.

Goal 1: *Eat a variety of foods.* You need about 50 different nutrients each day. You need 4 servings from the milk group, 2 servings from the meat group, 4 servings from the fruit and vegetable group, and 4 servings from the grain group each day.

Goal 2: *Be at the best weight for you.* Your best weight is the weight at which you look best, feel best, and are in the best health. Being overweight increases the risk of high blood pressure, diabetes, heart attack, stroke, and cancer. Overweight persons can plan to lose weight by cutting down on Calories, increasing physical activity, eating slowly, eating smaller amounts, and eating fewer fats and sweets.

Goal 3: *Eat fewer fatty foods.* There are two kinds of fats. *Unsaturated fats* are usually of vegetable origin. Vegetable cooking oils such as corn, olive, soybean, and peanut oils are unsaturated. Chicken, turkey, and fish also have unsaturated fats. These are healthier than foods with saturated fats.

*Saturated fats* are usually of animal origin. Steak, pork, liver, ham, and dairy products contain saturated fats. Saturated fats can clog artery walls, causing atherosclerosis (ath uh roh skluh ROH sus), a kind of heart disease.

Goal 4: *Eat foods that contain fiber.* Fiber is a natural material found in foods from plants. Fruits and grains often contain fiber. Fiber helps you have a daily bowel movement, lowering the risk of colon cancer.

Goal 5: *Eat and drink fewer foods and beverages that contain sugar.* Foods high in sugar are high in Calories, but low in vitamins and minerals. They cause weight gain and increase chances of tooth decay and heart disease.

Goal 6: *Eat less salt.* Too much salt is related to headaches and high blood pressure. You need only one teaspoon of salt daily. Many prepared foods contain the salt you need. Avoid adding salt to foods, and cut down on salty foods.

Goal 7: *Do not drink alcohol.* Alcohol harms body cells and destroys the liver. Drinking alcohol increases the chance of cancer of the stomach, and liver.

Latent Image

# Chapter 6

## Review

## Summary

1. Your body needs six kinds of nutrients: proteins, fats, carbohydrates, vitamins, minerals, and water. *6:1*

2. A healthy habit is to eat the correct number of servings from the five food groups each day. *6:2*

3. Persons who are overweight do not eat the correct amounts of nutrients needed by their body. *6:3*

4. A breakfast with protein will provide you with the energy you need all morning. *6:4*

5. Many persons buy fast foods that contain nutrients out of vending machines. *6:5*

6. Athletes and other persons who exercise need to eat the correct number of servings from each food group. *6:6*

## Words for Health

*Below are vocabulary words and incomplete sentences. Complete each sentence with the correct vocabulary word. DO NOT WRITE IN THIS BOOK.*

| | |
|---|---|
| carbohydrate loading | minerals |
| carbohydrates | nutrients |
| fast food | nutrition |
| fats | protein |
| food group | vitamins |
| habit | water |

1. _____ makes the body ready for exercise that requires endurance.
2. _____ are substances in foods that your body needs for growth, repair, and energy.
3. You need _____ to help your body use proteins, fats, and carbohydrates.
4. If you do things in a usual way, you have a _____.
5. _____ helps you digest food and makes up blood and urine.
6. _____ are nutrients needed for growth and repair of your body's cells.
7. _____ are nutrients that direct activities in your body.
8. Nutrients that help your body store energy are _____.

# Review

9. Foods that contain the same nutrients belong to a _____.
10. _____ are used as your body's main source of energy.
11. A food that you buy that is ready to be eaten is a _____.
12. The study of what you eat, your habits, and how these affect your health is _____.

## Look at Your Health

1. How are nutrients used by your body?
2. What are the six main kinds of nutrients that your body needs?
3. What are the five main food groups?
4. What are some reasons that people eat too much?
5. Why should you eat a breakfast that is high in protein?
6. What are some sources of protein that people eat for breakfast?
7. What are some examples of fast foods?
8. Why is it best not to make a habit of eating fast foods that are high in sugar?
9. What is carbohydrate loading?
10. Why might you need small amounts of salt after you exercise in hot weather?

## Actions for Health

*Think about the following situations. Then respond to the questions that follow.*

*Situation:* Tomorrow you have a big test at school. You want to get enough sleep and you need to study for the test. You also plan to get a good breakfast. It is 9 PM and you are tired. Should you study another hour right now or should you skip breakfast to study?

1. What are some good reasons for staying up another hour?
2. What are some reasons for studying in the morning?
3. Which choice will help you think more clearly on your test? Give reasons for your choice.

*Situation:* You forgot to pack your lunch today. You go to the vending machine where fast foods are sold. Here are your choices:

Foods—hot dog     peanut butter and crackers     donut
Drinks—orange juice     diet cola     orange drink

You have enough money to buy three things.

1. What three things would you consider in making your food selections?
2. What is the most important factor? Why?
3. What foods would you select? Give reasons for your answer.

## Individual Research

1. Interview a dietitian. Learn about the different diets that persons your age follow to lose weight. Write a report called "The best diet."
2. Write a report that discusses what a person who is underweight can do to gain weight.
3. Write a report about the breakfast habits of people in one of the following countries: Brazil, India, England, Japan, Mexico, France, Nigeria.
4. Write a research report about salt. Your report should discuss:
   (a) How much salt do people need?
   (b) What health problems may occur from too little salt in your diet?
   (c) What health problems may occur from too much salt in your diet?
5. Write to the National Dairy Council, Rosemont, Illinois, 60018. Find out about health careers in nutrition education.
6. Write a report about a dietitian who works at a hospital. What training does this person need?

# LIFE MANAGEMENT SKILLS

- Eat a variety of foods.
- Maintain your desirable weight.
- Eat foods with starch and fiber.
- Avoid foods high in fat, sugar, and sodium sold as fast foods or from vending machines.
- Avoid the use of alcohol.
- Select the correct number of servings from the food groups each day.
- Do not overeat.

# How Your Body Works

How do your senses affect your health?

How do your body systems work together?

How do people adjust to handicaps and disabilities?

Tony Gonzales/fpg

# Your Five Senses

Florence Barbanera/Alpha

*Where did I come in? How do I get out? A "House of Mirrors" is fun when you are at a fair. It would not be fun to be confused like that all the time. Your body senses usually tell you where you are and what you are seeing or hearing. Taking care of your sense organs and protecting them are important to your health.*

**S**uppose your ear is injured and you cannot hear sounds. Or, perhaps an illness affects your eyes and you cannot see. Hearing and seeing are two examples of your body's senses. Your body has three other senses. These are taste, smell, and touch.

Your body's senses tell you what is going on around you. They help to protect you. They help you enjoy things. If something happened to any of your body's senses, your life might change. This chapter describes how each of your sense organs works and how you can protect each sense organ.

**GOAL:** *You will gain an understanding of the importance of the five senses to your health.*

*Name the five senses.*

## Your Sense of Sight

Your eyes are like a camera in that they take pictures. But unlike a camera, your eyes send messages to a "computer." This "computer" is your brain. Your brain interprets what it is you are seeing. For example, you might see a funny picture. This picture will not really seem funny to you until it reaches your brain. When the picture reaches your brain, it is interpreted as being funny. You begin to laugh. If you did not see this picture, you would not laugh.

*How are your eyes like a camera?*

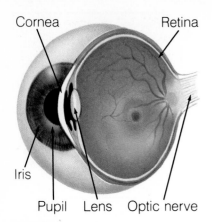

Cornea    Retina

Iris

Pupil    Lens    Optic nerve

**STRUCTURES OF THE EYE**

**FIGURE 7–1.**

*What happens to your pupils in light and dark areas?*

*What is the function of the lens?*

Let us see how a picture reaches your brain. The light from an object passes through the pupil of your eye. The **pupil** is the small dark hole that looks like a circle in the middle of your eye. The size of the pupil changes to control the amount of light that enters your eye. In a dark area, your pupil is open wide so that light can enter. If you are in an area with bright light, your pupil is small. Less light will enter. The size of the pupil is controlled by the iris. The **iris** contains muscles that control the size of the pupil. Your eye is protected in this way from too much light.

## Activity

### How Does Your Pupil Change?

You can see how your pupil reacts to light and darkness. Stay in a dark room for two minutes. Then enter a lighted area and immediately look at your pupils in a mirror. How do the pupils appear? How do they appear after 30 seconds?

Light goes through your lens after passing through the pupil. The **lens** causes the light rays to bend and focus on the retina (RET nuh). The **retina** is the inner lining of your eye. It has many nerves that are sensitive to light. These nerves change light to nerve messages. The **optic nerve** carries these messages from the retina to your brain. When the messages reach your brain, you see the objects.

## Think About It

1. How would your vision be affected if your iris became injured?

**HOW A PICTURE REACHES YOUR BRAIN**

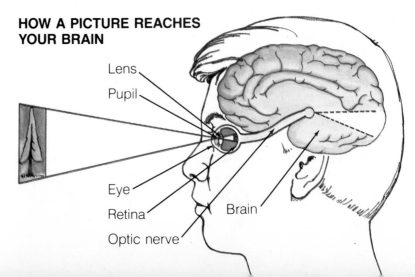

Lens
Pupil

Eye
Retina
Optic nerve

Brain

**FIGURE 7–2.**

**FIGURE 7–3.** Always use protective safety glasses when necessary.

## Protecting Your Sight

Think about the many activities you do each day. How would these activities be affected if you lost your sight? How might your life be affected if you could no longer do these activities?

Every day young people your age do things that can harm their sense of sight. Some may not wear protective eyeguards when they should. Some may strain their eyes by reading or doing homework without enough light. Many of these young people do not know they are harming their eyes. Sight can be affected very slowly. When something happens slowly, it is often not noticed. Others may have injuries or illnesses which affect their eyes. They may lose their sight quickly.

*Why might some people be unaware they are losing their sight?*

Your eyesight is important to your health. You can make choices that will protect your sight. Half of all cases of blindness can be prevented. Here are some things you can do to protect your sight.

- Use enough light. When doing homework, use a table light in addition to an overhead light. This will help prevent eyestrain.

- Avoid looking at the sun. If you look directly at the sun, nerve cells in your eyes can be damaged. Sunglasses will not protect your eyes if you look directly at the sun.
- Wear safety glasses. When using certain tools, bits of materials may get into your eyes. Wearing safety glasses can prevent this.
- Wear shatterproof eyeglasses when playing. If you need to wear eyeglasses, the shatterproof ones will not break into small pieces upon impact.
- Do not rub your eyes. When you rub your eyes, germs can enter them from your fingers. Never rub your eyes if something gets in them.
- Have eye examinations. Your eyes should be checked at least once each year by a doctor or school nurse. If any eye problem is detected in a checkup proper care can begin.
- Be careful at play. Accidents at play can injure your eyes. Always wear the proper equipment. Many accidents can happen because of carelessness.

## Think About It

2. Why do people who play in contact sports wear shatterproof glasses?
3. Why is an eye checkup needed once each year?

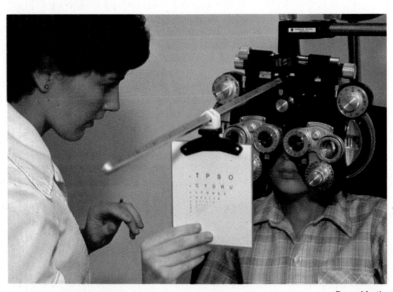

**FIGURE 7–4.** Regular eye checkups are important to good health.

Doug Martin

# Your Sense of Hearing

Your ears are the sense organs for hearing. You hear because sound waves travel through the parts of your ear to your brain. Let us follow the path that sound takes through your ears.

When a sound is made, sound waves move through the air. These sound waves enter a narrow tube in your ear. In your ear, they hit against a thin membrane called the **eardrum**. The eardrum vibrates. These vibrations cause tiny bones in the ear to vibrate. The vibrations then move through a spiral-shaped tube that contains nerve cells and is filled with a liquid. The vibrations cause the liquid to move. At this point, the vibrations send messages through the nerve cells to your brain. Your brain interprets these messages and you hear sound.

## Think About It

4. What would happen to your sense of hearing if your eardrums were injured?

**STRUCTURES OF THE EAR**

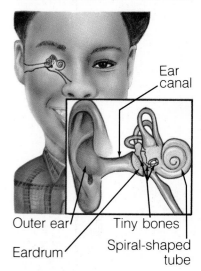

Ear canal

Outer ear

Tiny bones

Eardrum

Spiral-shaped tube

**FIGURE 7–5.**

*What path do sound waves follow in your ear?*

# Signs of Hearing Loss

Hearing loss usually occurs very slowly. For this reason, a person may not be aware of a hearing loss. Here are some signs that will warn of a possible hearing loss.

- Pain in one or both ears.
- Being told by others that you are talking louder than usual.
- Playing a TV, radio, or stereo louder than most people do.
- A buzzing or ringing in your ears after you hear a loud sound.
- Straining to hear a normal conversation.
- Often misunderstanding a teacher's directions in class.
- Asking people to repeat what they have said to you.
- Asking people to speak louder.

**FIGURE 7–6.** Musical instruments are sources of familiar sounds.

Larry Hamill

Ted Rice

**FIGURE 7–7.** Would a TV program be interesting if there were no sound?

## Section

## 7:5

*What is one important function of sound?*

*Name five things you can do to protect your hearing.*

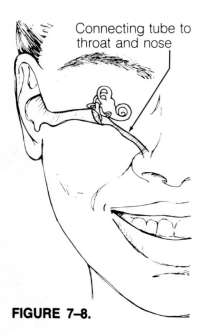

Connecting tube to throat and nose

**FIGURE 7–8.**

## Protecting Your Hearing

Pretend you are watching a movie. The sound suddenly stops but the picture continues. Would you be able to understand the rest of the movie? Would you be annoyed?

Perhaps something similar has happened to you. At times like this, you become aware of the importance of sound. Sound helps you enjoy things. Also, sound can warn you of danger. In what other ways is sound important?

Many people do things that harm their ability to hear. Many of the things that cause hearing loss can be prevented. Here are some hints for protecting your hearing.

- Wash your ears with soap and water every day.
- Do not insert cotton-tipped sticks or other objects into your ears. You can harm your eardrum.
- Blow your nose gently when you must blow it.
- Keep your nostrils open when sneezing. This will stop germs in your nose from entering your ears through the connecting tube. See Figure 7-8.
- Avoid loud sounds. Chapter 20 describes the effects of noise on your body.
- Have a doctor remove excess wax when it is necessary.

## Think About It

5. Why is it important to protect your hearing?

# Your Sense of Taste

Most people do not enjoy eating food when they have a cold. When you have a cold, your nose gets clogged. At this point, you may wonder what your nose has to do with eating. Your nose detects odors or smells. You taste food with your tongue. Your senses of smell and taste often work together. These senses send messages from your tongue and nose to your brain at the same time. When your nose is clogged, you cannot smell food. You do not enjoy the taste of food fully when you cannot smell it.

Your tongue is an important muscle in your body. This muscle helps you talk. It also helps you swallow. Your tongue is very sensitive. It is so sensitive that you know when even a hair is in your mouth.

Your tongue is an important sense organ. It has many tiny bumps called taste buds that contain nerve cells. Four different types of taste buds are on your tongue. Each type is located on a different section. Each type can detect a different chemical or taste. The four different tastes are sour, salt, sweet, and bitter. See Figure 7-9. Each food you eat has at least one of the four tastes. Your tongue sends messages about the tastes of foods to your brain. Your brain interprets what you are tasting.

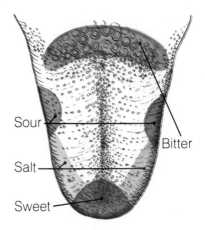

Sour

Bitter

Salt

Sweet

**FIGURE 7–9.**

*What is an important function of your nose?*

*Name the four kinds of taste.*

## Think About It

6. Why might some people eat less when they have a cold?
7. What might happen to your appetite if you had no taste buds?

Russ Lappa

**FIGURE 7–10.** The sight and smell of food when it is being cooked add to your enjoyment when you eat it.

**FIGURE 7–11.** The smell of the campfire may affect the taste of the roasted marshmallows.

**Section**

**7:7**

## Your Sense of Smell

Inside the upper part of your nose are special nerve cells. These nerve cells detect chemicals or smells when you breathe in or inhale.

Some people lose their sense of smell. Cigarette smoke and other drugs may damage nerve cells in the nose. Some people as they grow older also lose this sense. Partial or complete loss of smell is called **anosmia** (a NAHZ mee uh).

*What is anosmia?*

Many people do not realize the importance of smell. This sense can help protect you. For example, your sense of smell could warn you of fire. You would smell the smoke. What are other ways your sense of smell might protect you?

*Why is your sense of smell important?*

### Activity

***Taste and Smell***

Conduct the following experiment at home with a family member. (1) Select five different foods. (2) Blindfold the other person. Have this person also pinch his/her nose. There should be no breathing through the nose. (3) Have this person taste and identify each food. (4) How many foods were identified correctly? Now, repeat this experiment. This time do not pinch the nose. How many foods were identified correctly this time? What have you learned about your senses of taste and smell?

## Your Sense of Touch

Your skin is a sense organ. It can help you become aware of what is around you. There are five different types of nerve cells in your skin. These nerve cells are sensitive to pain, pressure, touch, heat, and cold.

*What are five types of nerve cells in your skin?*

Skin on different parts of your body may have different amounts and kinds of nerve cells. The tips of your fingers have fewer nerve cells that detect pain than does a similar area on your arm. This is one reason a doctor or nurse sticks the tip of your finger with a special instrument to get blood to determine your blood type.

As it was with your other senses, your brain is important to your sense of touch. When you touch something, messages pass to your brain. Your brain interprets the messages as pain, pressure, touch, heat, or cold.

*What is the role of your brain in your sense of touch?*

The sense of touch can help people with special needs. A person who cannot see can learn to read by touching raised dots that represent letters of the alphabet. This method of reading raised dots is called the Braille system. What other ways can the sense of touch help someone?

## Think About It

8. How might your life be affected if you could not feel with your fingers?

9. How does your sense of touch help protect you?

© Robert Lee II

**FIGURE 7–12.** Nerve cells in fingers that are sensitive to pressure aid in reading Braille.

## The TV Habit— Good or Bad?

How much TV do you watch every day? Many Americans your age spend at least four hours a day watching TV. You might want to determine how much time you spend watching TV. You could start counting the minutes. How many half-hour programs do you watch and how many hour-long ones?

Let us pretend that the electricity is shut off for some reason in your neighborhood. There would be no TV. What would you do?

- ride your bike?
- roller skate?
- go swimming?
- go running?
- fly a kite?
- read a book?
- play your musical instrument?
- twirl your baton?
- tell your parents about the good day you had in school?
- work on your hobby?
- give your dog a bath?
- build a tree house?

Watching less TV might give you time to do some of these activities. Which of these would appeal to you? Which would you do?

If you are in the habit of watching TV a lot, you may be missing out on some important activities. Many people believe that watching too much TV will interfere with your ability to play, think, and learn.

Have you ever noticed that when you watch TV with other people that there is not much communicating? Communication involves talking and listening. If you cannot communicate well, you will find it difficult to ask or answer a question in class. Could you give a good book report to your class?

What about being physically fit? You do not exercise your muscles when you are sitting in front of a TV. If you are not physically fit you would find it difficult to try out for cheerleading, or for a sports team, or for the band.

Communication and physical fitness require skills that need to be exercised. Talking and listening with your parents and friends are an important part of your mental and social health. Exercising your muscles is important to your physical health.

Do you think you should do something about your TV watching habits?

Dan McCoy/Rainbow

# Review

## Summary

| | |
|---|---|
| 1. Your eyes have many parts that work together to enable you to see. | 7:1 |
| 2. It is important for you to protect your eyes from injury and illness. | 7:2 |
| 3. Sound waves travel through the parts of your ears. | 7:3 |
| 4. Since hearing loss can occur slowly, you should be aware of its signs. | 7:4 |
| 5. There are many ways you can help to protect your hearing. | 7:5 |
| 6. Your senses of taste and smell work closely together. | 7:6 |
| 7. Your tongue has four different types of nerve cells that help you tell the difference between sour, salt, sweet, and bitter. | 7:7 |
| 8. The nerve cells in your skin are sensitive to pain, pressure, touch, heat, and cold. | 7:8 |

## Words for Health

*Below are vocabulary words and incomplete sentences. Complete each sentence with the correct vocabulary word. DO NOT WRITE IN THIS BOOK.*

| | |
|---|---|
| anosmia | optic nerve |
| eardrum | pupil |
| iris | retina |
| lens | |

1. A small, dark hole in the center of the eye is called the _____.
2. The _____ controls the size of the pupil.
3. _____ is the partial or complete loss of smell.
4. Messages are carried from the retina to the brain by the _____.
5. Light is focused on the back of the eye by the _____.
6. A thin membrane in the ear which vibrates when hit by sound waves is the _____.
7. The inner lining in the back of the eye is called the _____.

## Look at Your Health

1. What are the names of the five body senses?
2. In what way do your eyes differ from a camera?
3. How is the amount of light that enters your pupil controlled?
4. What are three things you can do to protect your sight?

# Review

5. How do you hear sounds?
6. What are three signs of hearing loss?
7. What are three things you can do to protect your hearing?
8. What role does your nose play in the sense of taste?
9. What is one thing that may cause a loss of your sense of smell?
10. What are the five types of nerve cells in your skin?

## Actions for Health

*Think about the following situations. Then respond to the questions that follow.*

*Situation:* You and your friends are at baseball practice. One of your friends decides to play catcher. Your friend refuses to wear a catcher's mask.

1. What could happen to your friend if a catcher's mask is not worn?
2. What could you do to convince your friend to wear a catcher's mask?
3. What could you do if your friend still refuses to wear a catcher's mask?

*Situation:* Over the past several months, you find that you have to speak very loud to be heard by your grandmother. You also notice that your grandmother has the volume on her radio turned on more than previously.

1. What do you suspect may be a problem for your grandmother?
2. What can you do to help your grandmother?

## Individual Research

1. Many people suffer hearing loss because they are around loud noises. Make a list of ten loud noises you hear each week. Describe how you might avoid each of these noises.
2. Contact your local Society for the Prevention of Blindness and gather free materials about eyesight.
3. Your senses help protect you. In a chart similar to the following one, list each sense. In the column next to each sense, describe one way in which this sense can help protect you.

| Senses | How Your Senses Protect You |
|--------|------------------------------|
| sight | |
| hearing | |
| smell | |
| taste | |
| touch | |

**4.** Copy the following table which lists each of the five senses. In the second column, describe how each sense can be harmed. In the third column, describe how you can protect each sense from each particular injury.

| Sense | How It Can Be Harmed | How It Can Be Protected |
|-------|----------------------|--------------------------|
| sight | | |
| hearing | | |
| smell | | |
| taste | | |
| touch | | |

**5.** An optometrist cares for people's eyes. Write a report about the job of an optometrist.

# LIFE MANAGEMENT SKILLS

- Be sure you use enough light when reading and writing.
- Avoid staring directly at the sun.
- Wear safety glasses when they are needed.
- Do not rub your eyes.
- Have regular eye examinations.
- Do not pinch your nostrils when you sneeze.
- Do not insert objects in your ears.

# Your Body Systems

George Hunter/Alpha

*Planes land and take off 24 hours each day. There is a pattern to the entire process. The pattern is a result of many systems working together. People in the control tower direct the pilots when to take off and land. Travelers buy tickets and board planes. What other activities go on at the same time? Your body also has systems which work together to influence your health. How are your body systems controlled?*

Chapter

**8**

This chapter describes the major body systems and how each one works. When you know how your body systems work, you will know how to take care of them. Healthy body systems make a healthier you.

**GOAL:** *You will study the major body systems and how they work together to influence your health.*

## The Nervous System

The organs of the body that act as a message center make up the **nervous system.** These organs are composed of nerve cells. The **spinal cord** and the **brain** are important parts of the nervous system. **Nerve cells** form fibers in the body that carry messages. These messages go to the spinal cord and brain. Nerve fibers also carry messages from the spinal cord and brain to other parts of the body. The brain is the mass of nerve cells inside the skull. Among other things, the brain controls thinking, creating, and remembering. The spinal cord is nerve tissue that extends from the brain down through most of the backbone. Nerves branching from the spinal cord go to all parts of the body.

Suppose someone throws a ball to you. Nerve cells in your eyes send a message to your brain. Your brain interprets this message. At this point you actually see the ball. Your brain responds to this message by telling you to catch the ball. To actually catch the ball, other parts of your body need to react also. Your brain will send messages to muscles. These muscles will move your arms, hands, and entire body into a position to catch the ball.

*What are two parts of the nervous system?*

*What is controlled by your brain?*

*How do the brain and muscles work together?*

**FIGURE 8–1.** Your nervous system coordinates many body activities.

The nervous system controls many body activities. In the ball-catching example, you saw how the nervous system affects your muscles. If your nervous system were injured, your muscles might not be able to do their work. A healthy nervous system helps your body coordinate well.

## Think About It

1. Why might you have no feeling in your legs if your spinal cord were injured?
2. How can a damaged brain affect a person's ability to catch a ball?
3. What is the relationship between the brain and muscles?

## Section

## 8:2

## The Muscular-Skeletal Systems

In building a new house, a wood frame is one of the first things built. A wood frame supports the walls, floors, and ceilings. If a house did not have a frame, there would be nothing to hold all of its parts together.

*What is your body frame?*

The body also has a frame. The body's frame is called a **skeleton.** The skeleton is composed of all the bones in the body. The skeleton makes up the **skeletal system.**

*Name two functions of the skeletal system.*

The skeletal system has at least two main purposes. One purpose is to hold the body together. This makes it possible for you to move. If you had no bones, you would not be able to stand, sit, or walk.

**FIGURE 8–2.** Ribs protect vital organs. Many bones and muscles work together just to hold a Ping-Pong paddle.

Another purpose of the skeletal system is to protect many of the organs inside your body. Your skull bones protect your brain. Your ribs protect your heart and lungs.

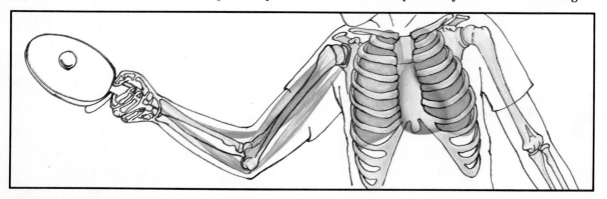

**FIGURE 8–3.** Bones work with muscles to produce motion.

Think about the injuries you could suffer if you had no skull or ribs. If you had no skull, you would suffer a major injury from a minor blow to your head. What other parts of your body are protected by bone?

Your **muscular system** is composed of muscle cells which have the ability to stretch. Some muscles are attached to bones. Others form parts of internal organs. Muscles attached to bones often work in pairs. As one muscle relaxes, the other tightens. This action causes movement of the skeleton.

## Think About It

4. What could happen to your lungs if you had no ribs?

**Section**

**8:3**

## The Circulatory System

The **circulatory system** is a transport system made up of blood, blood vessels, and the heart.

**Blood** is composed of a liquid called plasma (PLAZ muh) and cells. Blood has several functions. One function is to circulate nutrients and oxygen to your body cells. **Red blood cells** carry oxygen from the air in your lungs to all cells in your body. The cells in your body use the oxygen and in the process, waste materials are produced.

*Name the parts of the circulatory system.*

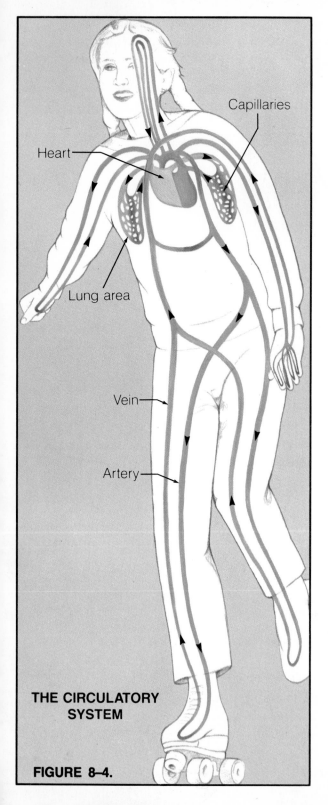

Heart

Capillaries

Lung area

Vein

Artery

**THE CIRCULATORY SYSTEM**

**FIGURE 8–4.**

Red blood cells carry these wastes away from your body cells. Oxygen is delivered to all cells, and wastes are removed by the red cells. Your blood also has **white blood cells** which help protect you from germs. **Platelets** (PLAYT luts) are cells in the blood which help to form clots. A person could suffer serious blood loss from a cut or wound if blood did not clot.

Blood circulates in your body through tubes called **blood vessels.** There are three types of blood vessels—capillaries (KAP uh ler eez), veins, and arteries.

**Capillaries** are tiny vessels that connect arteries to veins. Nutrients enter the bloodstream through the capillaries in the small intestine. Oxygen enters the bloodstream through the capillaries in the lungs. Nutrients and oxygen enter the body cells from the capillaries as blood circulates around the cells.

Blood returns to the heart from all parts of the body in **veins.** This blood contains waste products and very little oxygen. Veins may look like blue lines near the surface of your skin because they are seen through the color of your skin.

**Arteries** are the largest blood vessels. Because they carry blood away from the heart, artery walls are very muscular. Arteries which lead to the lungs contain blood with little oxygen. After blood circulates in the lungs and picks up oxygen, it returns to the heart. It is then pumped out through arteries to your body cells.

The **heart** is a muscle. Because the heart pumps blood through your body, it works harder than any other muscle in your body. Each day, the heart pumps about 10 000 liters of blood and beats over 100 000 times.

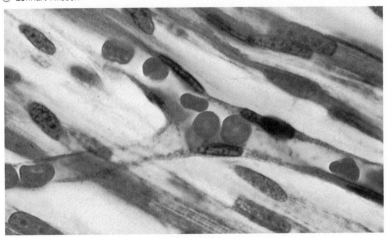

**FIGURE 8–5.** Red blood cells must move one-by-one through the tiny capillaries.

*What are platelets?*

*What are capillaries?*

If your heart does not work well, your body will suffer. A damaged heart may not be able to pump enough blood. Your body cells will not get enough nutrients and oxygen. This can make you feel weak. When you have a healthy heart, the rest of your body functions better. You can help to keep your heart healthy by eating a balanced diet, exercising, and not smoking.

*What are some ways to keep your heart healthy?*

## Think About It

**5.** What might happen to you if you had no white blood cells?

**6.** How is blood in veins different than blood in arteries?

**Section**

**8:4**

## The Respiratory System

The **respiratory system** functions in the exchange of gases between the air you breathe and your body. The air you breathe in, or inhale, contains many gases. One important gas in air is oxygen. As you inhale, air moves through your trachea (TRAY kee uh), or windpipe, to your lungs. Your **lungs** contain many tiny air sacs called **alveoli** (al VEE uh li). As blood circulates in capillaries through the alveoli, oxygen enters the blood. At the same time, a gas which is a waste product leaves the blood and enters the air sacs. You rid your body of the waste gas when you breathe out, or exhale. The waste gas is carbon dioxide.

*What are alveoli?*

The alveoli are important in breathing. If the alveoli become damaged, your body cannot get the oxygen it needs. This may cause extra strain on the heart. The heart must pump harder to get as much oxygen as possible to your body cells. Alveoli can be damaged by air pollution and cigarette smoking. Cigarette smoking is one of the leading causes of lung damage.

## Activity
### *Breathing Rate*
Record the following information on a sheet of paper. (1) Count the number of breaths you take in one minute while you are resting. (2) Run slowly in place for 30 seconds. Record the number of breaths for one minute. (3) Run fast in place for 30 seconds. Again record the number of breaths you take in one minute. (4) What was the difference in your breathing rate for each of the three times you counted?

## Think About It

**7.** Why is it important for your body to have healthy alveoli?

## Section
## 8:5

## The Digestive System

*What happens to food in your mouth?*

The **digestive system** includes the parts of your body that make food usable to your body. From the time food enters your mouth, it is changed, or digested. Food is chewed and softened in your mouth. It then moves from your mouth to your stomach. Food remains in your stomach for several hours. In the stomach, digestive juices break down the food more until it looks like a paste.

*In what part of the digestive system is digestion completed?*

From the stomach food passes into the small intestine. Digestion is completed in the **small intestine**. Digested food that the body will use passes through the walls of the small intestine into blood flowing through capillaries. The capillaries are in the lining of the small intestine. Food that is not digested is passed to the **large intestine**. This undigested food is moved out of the body as solid waste. The process of removing solid waste from the body is called a **bowel movement**.

FIGURE 8–6.

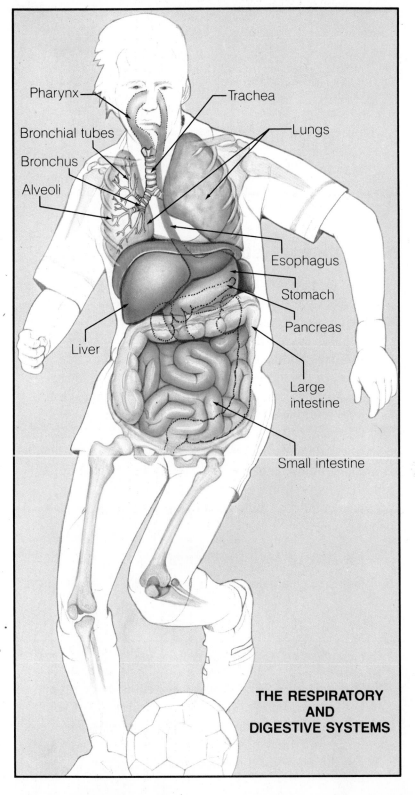

Pharynx

Bronchial tubes

Bronchus

Alveoli

Liver

Trachea

Lungs

Esophagus

Stomach

Pancreas

Large intestine

Small intestine

**THE RESPIRATORY
AND
DIGESTIVE SYSTEMS**

**FIGURE 8–7.**

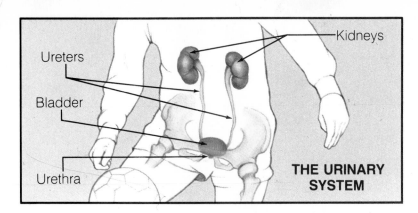

THE URINARY SYSTEM

Kidneys
Ureters
Bladder
Urethra

## The Urinary System

The **urinary** (YOOR uh ner ee) **system** removes liquid wastes from your body. The liquid wastes removed from the body make up **urine** (YOOR un).

*What is urine?*

Urine is made up of waste products and excess water. These waste products and excess water are removed from the blood in the **kidneys.** Each person has two kidneys. Each kidney lies below your bottom rib in your back.

As blood passes through your kidneys, excess water and wastes are filtered. These products are passed by tubes from the kidney to the urinary bladder. The **urinary bladder** is a muscular sac that stores urine. When the bladder is full, there is pressure on nerves in the bladder. The pressure creates an urge to get rid of the urine, or to urinate.

## Think About It

**8.** What might happen to your body if you had no kidneys?

## The Endocrine System

The **endocrine** (EN duh krun) **system** is made up of glands in your body. These glands control many of your body's activities. They do this by producing special chemicals called hormones (HOR mohnz). Hormones are released directly into the bloodstream.

*What are hormones?*

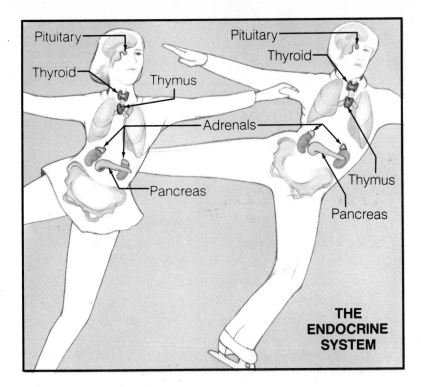

FIGURE 8-8.

THE
ENDOCRINE
SYSTEM

The main endocrine gland is called the pituitary gland.
The pituitary gland influences other glands in the body. See
Chapter 3.

The adrenal glands are another part of your endocrine
system. The **adrenal glands** release a hormone that helps
your body react suddenly. Suppose a dog is chasing you.
When you first see the dog, you might become scared. Your
heartbeat rate increases. Your muscles tighten. You run fast.
All these actions are due to hormones produced by your
adrenal glands. These hormones are helpful. They help your
body respond when necessary.

*What is one function of the
adrenal glands?*

 **Activity**

**Your Adrenals in Action**

Copy the following chart on a separate sheet of
paper. (1) In the left column, indicate five situations in
which you think your adrenal glands helped you to react.
(2) In the right column, list how you responded to
each situation. How did each reaction help to
protect your health?

**FIGURE 8-9.**

| Situation | How You Reacted |
|-----------|-----------------|
| 1. | |
| 2. | |
| 3. | |
| 4. | |
| 5. | |
| 6. | |
| 7. | |

The Endocrine System **111**

Another endocrine gland is the thyroid gland. The thyroid gland regulates the energy you get from food. If your thyroid gland makes too much of its hormone, you may become excited, nervous, and lose weight. If your thyroid gland makes too little hormone, you may become tired, sleepy, and gain weight.

## The Reproductive System

The parts of the body that are involved with producing offspring make up the **reproductive system.** Offspring are produced from sex cells. Sex cells unite to form a new cell. This new cell is the beginning of a new human being.

*What is the role of the pituitary gland in reproduction?*

The pituitary gland releases special hormones. These hormones influence glands in the reproductive system to release additional hormones. The release of reproductive hormones occurs around the ages of 11 to 13 in girls and 12 to 14 in boys. When this happens, changes begin to take place in the bodies of girls and boys. A girl begins to look more like a woman. A boy begins to look more like a man. The period in which these changes occur is known as puberty (PYEW burt ee).

You have seen how eight different body systems work. These systems work together and influence your health. You have gained some important knowledge about these systems. This knowledge will make you more informed about decisions that affect your body.

**FIGURE 8–10.** Healthy body systems work together to help you enjoy many types of activities.

Norman Tomalin/Bruce Coleman, Inc.

# Chapter 8
## Review

## Summary

1. The nervous system acts as a message center for the body. The spinal cord and brain are the main parts of the nervous system.  *8:1*
2. The skeletal system holds your body together and helps you move.  *8:2*
3. By relaxing and contracting, your muscles and bones work together to produce body movement.  *8:2*
4. The circulatory system is made up of blood, blood vessels, and the heart.  *8:3*
5. The respiratory system helps oxygen and carbon dioxide to be exchanged between the blood and the body cells.  *8:4*
6. The digestive system is the part of the body that enables you to use the food you eat.  *8:5*
7. The urinary system removes liquid wastes from the body.  *8:6*
8. Hormones released by the endocrine system control many of the activities in the body.  *8:7*
9. Hormones released by glands in the reproductive system cause changes in the body.  *8:8*

## Words for Health

*Below are vocabulary words and incomplete sentences. Complete each sentence with the correct vocabulary word. DO NOT WRITE IN THIS BOOK.*

| | | |
|---|---|---|
| adrenal glands | endocrine system | platelets |
| arteries | heart | reproductive system |
| blood | large intestine | skeletal system |
| brain | muscular system | small intestine |
| circulatory system | nervous system | urinary system |

1. The system involved in producing offspring is the _____.
2. Thinking, creating, and memory are controlled by the _____.
3. The system that removes liquid wastes from your body is the

   _____.
4. The _____ produce a hormone which helps your body react suddenly.
5. The system to which your bones belong is the _____.
6. The system to which your blood vessels belong is the _____.

7. Undigested food moves through the _____.
8. _____ are involved in the clotting of blood.
9. The _____ is a muscle which pumps blood through the body.
10. The _____ is made up of many glands.
11. _____ carries nutrients and oxygen to body cells.
12. The system of the body that acts as a message center is called the _____.
13. _____ carry blood away from the heart.
14. The skeletal system and the _____ help the body move.
15. In the _____, digestion is completed.

## Vocabulary

*Write a sentence which uses correctly each of these vocabulary words.*

| | |
|---|---|
| alveoli | red blood cells |
| bowel movement | respiratory system |
| blood vessels | skeleton |
| capillaries | spinal cord |
| digestive system | urinary bladder |
| kidneys | urine |
| lungs | veins |
| nerve cells | white blood cells |

## Look at Your Health

1. What are the main parts of the nervous system?
2. How do the brain and muscles work together?
3. What are two purposes of the skeletal system?
4. What is a function of bones?
5. What are two functions of blood?
6. What are some ways the alveoli can be harmed?
7. What is the path food takes in the body once it is swallowed?
8. What is the purpose of the urinary system?
9. How does the endocrine system control body activities?
10. Describe the period of a person's life that is known as puberty.

## Actions for Health

*Think about the following situations. Then respond to the questions that follow.*

*Situation:* You have just learned in school that eating a balanced diet is important for a healthy heart. Your younger brother, Pete, does not eat a balanced diet. When you ask Pete to eat a balanced diet, he says, "I'm too young to have my heart affected by what I eat."

1. Do you agree or disagree with Pete's statement? Why?
2. What would you tell Pete?

*Situation:* Your older sister breathes heavily when she walks up one flight of stairs. You think this might be due to the fact she smokes two packs of cigarettes per day.

1. How might cigarette smoking affect your sister's lungs?
2. How might you explain to your sister that she is damaging her health?

## Individual Research

1. Different diseases can affect body systems. List one disease that can affect each body system. Describe the symptoms of the disease. Write all answers on a separate sheet of paper.

2. Select one body system and write a report about how you can care for that system.

## LIFE MANAGEMENT SKILLS

- Keep your heart healthy by eating a balanced diet, exercising, and not smoking.
- Avoid smoking cigarettes to keep your lungs healthy.

# Having a Disability or a Handicap

World Wide Publications

*The artist is paralyzed. She cannot use her hands to hold the paint brush. She has learned to use her teeth and lips to hold the brush as she creates beautiful paintings. Despite her handicap, this artist works hard to accomplish her goals. Is there anything in your life that keeps you from doing your best?*

M ike has difficulty seeing the chalkboard at school. He wears eyeglasses so that he can do his school work. Alice has difficulty hearing others. She needs a hearing aid. Bob was born with only one leg. He has an artificial (art uh FIHSH ul) leg. Dana has both of her legs but she is unable to walk. She comes to school in a wheelchair.

Mike, Alice, Bob, and Dana may be different from you in some ways. They are also like you in many other ways. This chapter describes some ways that people are alike and some ways that people are different.

**GOAL:** *You will learn about disabilities, handicaps, and how the people who have them work to be at their best.*

## What Are Disabilities and Handicaps?

Mike, Alice, Bob, and Dana are in the same grade level at their school. They each have friends. They each like to do things that are fun after school.

However, Mike, Alice, Bob, and Dana may also differ from you. Each has a disability (dihs uh BIHL ut ee). A disability is a physical or a mental defect. A person can be born with a disability. A disability may also result from an accident, injury, or disease. Mike was born with poor vision. Alice lost some of her hearing in an automobile accident. Bob was born with a body part missing. Dana had a disease that left her unable to use her legs.

*What is a disability? What causes a disability?*

Wide World Photos, Inc.

**FIGURE 9–1.** Skiing continues to be an enjoyable form of exercise for Ted Kennedy, Jr.

*Define handicap.*

When you have a disability, you might be limited in what you can do. Such a limit is called a **handicap.** A handicap need not limit what you want to be, however. Some people who have a disability have a handicap. Others do not.

## Think About It

**1.** What is the difference between a handicap and a disability?

## Section

## 9:2

*Give examples of successful people who have had a disability.*

## Being at Your Best

You may have learned about many successful persons who had a disability. Franklin Roosevelt was the 32nd President of the United States. A disease called polio (POH lee oh) left him unable to use his legs. But he did not view his disability as a handicap. He worked hard to accomplish what he wanted to do in life.

Beethoven (BAY toh vun) was a musical genius. Did you know that he wrote some of his greatest works while he was deaf? Beethoven had a disability but it did not put limits on his musical work.

Stevie Wonder is a rock singer. Millions of people enjoy his records and performances. Stevie Wonder is blind. Yet he uses his talent to entertain people around the world.

Homer was a great poet in Ancient Greece. Homer was blind. His blindness was a disability. But blindness did not keep him from writing poetry.

Did you know that Helen Keller was blind and deaf? Yet she learned to do many things well in her lifetime. She was well known all over the world.

Many people are different on the outside. Some do not have legs. Some do not have fingers. Some cannot see. Some cannot hear. Some have difficulty in learning. When you look at people, what do you see? If they have a disability, it may be the first thing that you see. You may think of the limits caused by this disability.

Yet, the inside is the most important part of each person. Each person has something important to give to others. Franklin Roosevelt knew this. People saw him in his wheelchair but he used his inner strengths to become President. People knew Helen Keller could not see or hear but they admired her courage. They liked the inner character of Helen Keller.

All persons need to make use of what they have. Can you think of some reasons why people might not perform at their very best? Do you make use of all your talents? Do you put limits on what you can do or what you want to be?

Three things may keep you from being your best. They may handicap you and limit your success in life. These three things are the same for someone with or without a disability. They are fear, having poor feelings about yourself, and worrying about what others will think of you.

Jane has only one arm. She is supposed to give a report in front of her class. Jane is afraid. This fear handicaps or limits Jane. Jane should give the report. Then she will show others what she can do.

Tom cannot see. When classmates come to his house after school, he says that he is busy. Tom has poor feelings about himself. These feelings limit Tom. If Tom spent some time after school hours with his classmates, he might make friends. Then he would like himself better.

*How are all persons alike?*

*What are three things that keep people from being at their best?*

**FIGURE 9–2.**

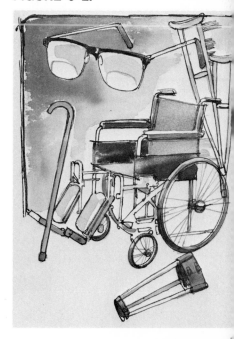

Nathan has brain damage. He does not think as easily or quickly as some others his age. The boys and girls in the neighborhood ask Nathan to join their basketball team. He says, "I'll never learn to play basketball. What will people think of me!" Nathan is worried about what others will think. His worries keep him from trying to be his best.

*How can you limit your success?*

When you are afraid, feel poorly about yourself, or worry about what others will think, you put limits on your success. Unfortunately, these may be more of a problem for someone with a disability. How can you help others overcome fear? How can you help others feel good about themselves? How can you show others that you think highly of them? How can you help others to do more than they think they can do? Knowledge about some disabilities may be helpful.

**FIGURE 9–3.** Many people are different on the outside. Some cannot hear, some cannot see, some do not have arms. But on the inside you are like others in many ways. You need to try to be at your best. Where would you put yourself on the scale?

## Think About It

2. How might a person's inner character differ from what you see on the outside?

3. How is fear a handicap?

4. Why do some persons with a handicap have poor feelings about themselves?

**DO YOU WANT TO BE AT YOUR BEST?**

0   10   20   30   40   50   60   70   80   90   100

I am sometimes at my best     I am usually at my best

I am never at my best     I am always at my best

**FIGURE 9–4.** Being blind has not kept Stevie Wonder from becoming a popular musical entertainer.

# Being Blind

Many people who can see think blindness is the worst possible disability. They have several beliefs that are not true. Perhaps you have some of the same beliefs. Do you think that being blind means being helpless? Do you think that a person who cannot see must always be helped by others? Do you think that all persons who are blind are unhappy? Knowing some facts about blindness may change some of your beliefs.

A person who is **legally blind** has 20/200 vision after correction in the better eye. What is meant by 20/200 vision? This person can see no more at 20 feet than a person with normal vision can see at 200 feet. Many persons who are legally blind have some usable vision. They can learn to make use of the vision they do have. They may need a guide dog or a cane to move about. They may need to read books printed in bold type. They may need to wear special eyeglasses.

*What does it mean to be legally blind?*

The **Braille system** is a method of touch reading and writing used by a person who is blind. In the Braille system, raised dots that represent letters of the alphabet are grouped together in different ways. A blind person touches these dot formations and can identify the letters.

*What is the Braille system?*

**FIGURE 9–5.** Small raised dots make up the Braille alphabet.

Did you know that many persons who cannot see can work and play? Many of these people work hard to overcome their disability. They do not want blindness to be a handicap. There is a person who is blind in almost every type of job and profession. Blind persons ride horses, bowl, swim, ski, and play golf and basketball. They marry and have children. They cook and clean their homes.

Being blind does not mean being helpless. Blindness need not be a handicap. Persons who are blind have the same needs as persons who are not blind. Do you have a healthy attitude about blindness? Are you doing as much with what you have as someone who must read Braille or play golf on crutches?

## Activity

### Blindfolded

You and another person in your class will be partners. Take turns blindfolding one another. While you are blindfolded, move about the room for five to ten minutes. Your partner will assist you. Copy and complete the sentences below on a sheet of paper.

**1.** When I was blindfolded, I felt _____.

**2.** The most difficult thing about not being able to see is _____.

**3.** The thing I liked best about not being able to see is _____.

**4.** I learned _____.

# Being Deaf

Close your eyes and pay attention to the sound in the room. How many different sounds do you hear? What can you learn from these sounds? What sounds frighten you? What sounds relax you? What sounds excite you?

In Chapter 7, you learned some important facts about sound. You learned that sound produces vibrations in the ear. You learned that nerve cells in your ear carry messages to your brain. The brain interprets these messages and you hear sound.

*What are two causes of hearing loss?*

One in ten persons has some loss of hearing. Some people have a hearing loss because the hearing path is blocked. The vibrations that produce sound cannot reach the middle part of the ear. Have you ever had excess wax in your ear? If you have, you know that you can hear again after a doctor removes the wax.

Other persons cannot hear because the nerve cells that carry messages to the brain are damaged or not developed. These persons often use a hearing aid.

*When is a person considered to be deaf?*

A person who cannot hear most sounds is considered to be **deaf.** Imagine that you are deaf. What would be your greatest problem? What might limit you? Most likely it would be communication. **Communication** is the exchange of information among people. A person who is deaf has to try hard to overcome two communication problems.

Riverside Methodist Hospital

**FIGURE 9–6.** Hearing tests can detect minor hearing problems.

Larry Hamill

**FIGURE 9–7.** Sign language is a very effective type of communication.

One problem a person who is deaf has is not being able to hear what is being said. You can communicate better with a deaf person by forming words clearly on your lips. Look at the person to whom you are speaking. This helps someone who cannot hear or who has a hearing loss.

A person unable to hear may also need to learn to speak. Some persons lose their hearing after they learn to talk. But others are deaf at birth or in childhood. When you learned to talk you made the sounds that you heard others make. What if you could not hear these sounds? Someone with training would have to teach you to talk.

*What does it mean to be mute?*

What if you could neither hear nor speak? You would be a deaf-mute (MYEWT). Persons who are mute use other ways to communicate. They might use sign language. To use **sign language,** you are taught to move your fingers and hands in different ways. Someone who is "listening" to you can learn the signs to know what they mean.

*What handicap might result from being deaf?*

Being deaf or having a hearing loss is a disability. The handicap is the limit on communication that results. You have some knowledge about hearing disabilities. Remember, you can help someone with a hearing disability to communicate at their best.

*How can you help a person who has a hearing disability?*

- When you speak, form your words clearly on your lips.
- Look at the person to whom you are speaking.
- If someone close to you is deaf, learn to read and use sign language.

## Activity
### *Sign Language*

Try to think of three ways that you could explain something without talking. Select a student in your class. Without talking, tell this person:

- There is a fire across the street.
- You have a new kitten.
- It is time for you to go home.
- You would like to ride bicycles together.
- Your feelings are hurt.

Did your classmate understand what you were trying to say?

---

# Having a Brain or Nerve Disorder

Your nervous system is made up of your brain, your spinal cord, and the nerves that travel throughout your body. Your brain controls your body by sending messages by way of your nerves. If your brain, spinal cord, and nerves are healthy, your body performs as it should. You are able to work, run, and do exercises. At school, you are able to think clearly and understand what you are learning.

But what happens if the cells in a person's brain, spinal cord or nerves become damaged? The messages between the brain and nerves will not be clear. The body will not respond as it should. This is called a **neurological** (noor uh LAHJ ih kul) **disorder.**

*How does your brain control your body?*

*What is a neurological disorder?*

**FIGURE 9–8.**

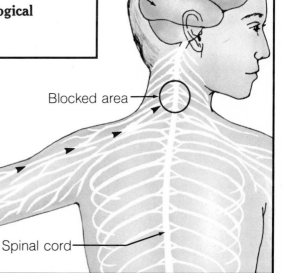

Brain

Blocked area

Nerve pathway

Nerves

Spinal cord

**FIGURE 9–9.** There are many ways that people who have a handicap can be at their best.

Jeffry Myers/Alpha

*What causes a neurological disorder?*

What causes a neurological disorder? When a baby is developing inside a pregnant woman, its nervous system is being formed. Suppose the mother-to-be takes harmful drugs. Or, she may have certain diseases. Then the baby's nervous system may be damaged. There are other causes of neurological disorders such as diseases, having too many X rays, malnutrition (mal noo TRIHSH un) (poor eating habits), and poisoning. Some neurological disorders are inherited. When you **inherit** a disorder, you get the disorder from the genes of one of your parents.

There are more than 200 neurological disorders. Each is a disability. Each one affects persons in different ways. A variety of handicaps result. Mike is a student your age with a neurological disorder. Mike may stumble or stagger when he walks. Donna has a hard time learning and understanding. Susan has difficulty breathing. Sometimes Mary has no feeling in her face or her right arm. Joshua walks with a cane.

Each of these students has a handicap or limit. These limits may produce fear, poor feelings about oneself, or worry about what others will think. Make a list of three things that you might do to help these persons to be at their best.

## Think About It

5. Why are there so many different neurological disorders?

## Other Types of Handicaps

Bernard Wolf wrote a book called *Don't Feel Sorry for Paul*. The book contains a true story about a boy named Paul. Paul was born with only two fingers on his left hand and no hand or fingers on his right arm. He had a steel hook at the end of his right arm. He used the hook as a hand. Some of his classmates were cruel and called him "Captain Hook." But Paul did his best to overcome his handicap. He explained that he was born this way. Then he showed his classmates how he used his hook. Paul learned to ride a horse, to ride a bicycle, and to play football.

Each year hundreds of children are born with handicaps. They may be born with a body part missing or a body part that does not work as it should. Other people have similar handicaps that are the result of accidents. They may be unable to move about the same as other people do.

Paul had no right arm or fingers. He had a handicap. The hook helped him overcome his handicap. He was able to pick things up with his hook. Other people overcome their handicaps in different ways. Perhaps they use a wheelchair or walk with a cane. They may wear special leg or arm braces.

People who are handicapped may appear different to you. Yet on the inside, they are like other people in most ways. Can you name three ways they are like others?

**FIGURE 9–10.** Some people overcome their handicaps by being active in sports.

## Think About It

6. How do you think Paul felt when his classmates called him "Captain Hook"?
7. Why do some people sometimes speak harshly and say cruel things about persons who have a handicap?
8. Why do people who have handicaps need to have friends who are not handicapped?
9. Why did Bernard Wolf title his book *Don't Feel Sorry for Paul*?

Thomas Zimmermann/fpg

# HEALTH HIGHLIGHTS

## "The Kids on the Block"

Ellen Jane stood in front of the class. She was ready to give her speech. Ellen Jane heard some giggles coming from the back of the classroom. She knew some of the children were making fun of her. She took a deep breath and said, "My name is Ellen Jane Peterson. I'm 17 years old. I'm happy to be in this class. I was born with Down Syndrome. It makes me have a disability. It makes me learn slow and takes long time to do things. I have job in animal hospital. Thank you."

Ellen Jane stood alone for a moment. The class started clapping. She smiled and said, "Do you have question for me? I like to talk with you."

What would you think if you saw a person like Ellen Jane? Would you stare? Would you have the courage to ask that person, "What is Down Syndrome?" Could you be a friend to a person like Ellen Jane?

Ellen Jane is a member of a puppet troupe called "The Kids on the Block." There are twenty one lifelike puppets in the troupe. "The Kids on the Block" speak, act, and dress like real children. Some of the puppets represent children with a handicap. Some do not.

Melody, 9 years old, is a nearsighted puppet that shares the stage with Mark. Mark, 11 years old, has cerebral palsy (SER uh brul•PAWL zee). He uses a wheelchair which he calls a "cruiser" to move about. He wears a helmet to protect his head. Melody plays the role of a child who is afraid of someone with a handicap. She expresses this fear by blurting out, "Gee, Mark. I don't know if I should play with you. What if I catch cerebral palsy?"

In 1975, a law was passed which permitted mainstreaming. Mainstreaming allows children with handicaps to attend public schools. It means that children with and without handicaps are in the same classes at school. "The Kids on the Block" is designed to show all children what it is like to have a handicap. They also teach children with and without handicaps how to become friends.

The Kids on the Block, Inc.

128

# Review

## Summary

1. Many persons have disabilities which may result in a variety of handicaps.  *9:1*
2. Three things that may handicap everyone are (1) fear, (2) having poor feelings about yourself, and (3) worrying about what others may think of you.  *9:2*
3. Being unable to see does not mean being helpless.  *9:3*
4. A person who is deaf or who has a hearing loss can learn to communicate in other ways.  *9:4*
5. Damage to the cells in a person's brain or spinal cord may result in a neurological disorder.  *9:5*
6. Many persons have a handicap because they are missing a body part.  *9:6*

## Words for Health

*Below are vocabulary words and incomplete sentences. Complete each sentence with the correct vocabulary word. DO NOT WRITE IN THIS BOOK.*

| | |
|---|---|
| Braille system | inherit |
| communication | legally blind |
| deaf | neurological disorder |
| disability | sign language |
| handicap | |

1. A person is _____ if the corrected vision in the better eye is 20/200.
2. Someone with a(n) _____ has a physical or a mental defect.
3. You are considered _____ if you cannot hear most sounds.
4. _____ is the use of hand and finger movements to communicate with others.
5. A(n) _____ may result from damage to the cells in the brain, spinal cord, or nerves.
6. The exchange of information among people is _____.
7. You _____ a neurological disorder when you get the disorder from one of your parents.

# Review

9. The _____ is a method of touch reading and writing used by a person who is blind.

10. A person is _____ if the corrected vision in the better eye is 20/200.

## Look at Your Health

1. What might cause a person to have a disability?
2. When does a disability result in a handicap?
3. Who are some people with disabilities who became successful?
4. What are three factors that may keep you from being at your best?
5. How might persons who have a loss of sight make use of the vision that they do have?
6. How many people have a hearing loss?
7. What is the most important handicap that a person who is deaf must overcome?
8. In what three ways can you help someone with a hearing disability communicate with you?
9. What are some causes of neurological disorders?
10. How are persons who are handicapped different and like others?

## Actions for Health

*Think about the following situations. Then respond to the questions that follow.*

*Situation:* There is a boy in your class who has a back that curves in a way that it should not. Some of your classmates make fun of him. They call him "hunchback." You have talked with this boy. You know that he was born with the curve in his back.

1. What are three things that you could do when your friends make fun of this boy?
2. What is the best thing to do? Give reasons for your answer.

*Situation:* You are on a baseball team with a classmate who is deaf. One of your friends on the same team cannot communicate with your deaf teammate. Your friend says, "I don't think that deaf people should play on our baseball team!"

1. Do you agree with your friend? Give reasons for your answer.
2. What suggestions would you make to help communication among the team members?

## Individual Research

1. Interview a person who works with children who are mentally retarded. Write a report that discusses:
   (a) What training do persons have who work with the mentally retarded?
   (b) What special problems do mentally retarded persons have?
   (c) How do people work with these problems to help the mentally retarded to be at their best?
   (d) Would this be a career that would interest you? Give at least two reasons for your answer.
2. Write a report on one of the more than 200 neurological disorders. Share your report with classmates.
3. Write a report that describes The March of Dimes or The National Society to Prevent Blindness. What is the purpose of this organization? How does this organization raise money? How is this money spent?
4. Learn two facts about the audiometer. Share these facts with your classmates.
5. Write a report about a physical therapist. What training does this person need? How does a physical therapist help others?

# LIFE MANAGEMENT SKILLS

- Develop positive feelings about yourself.
- Do not worry about what others think of you.
- Accept and appreciate persons with handicaps and disabilities.
- Learn to use sign language if a person close to you is deaf.
- Never joke or make fun of persons who have a disability.
- Be patient with classmates who learn more slowly than you.

# Consumer Health

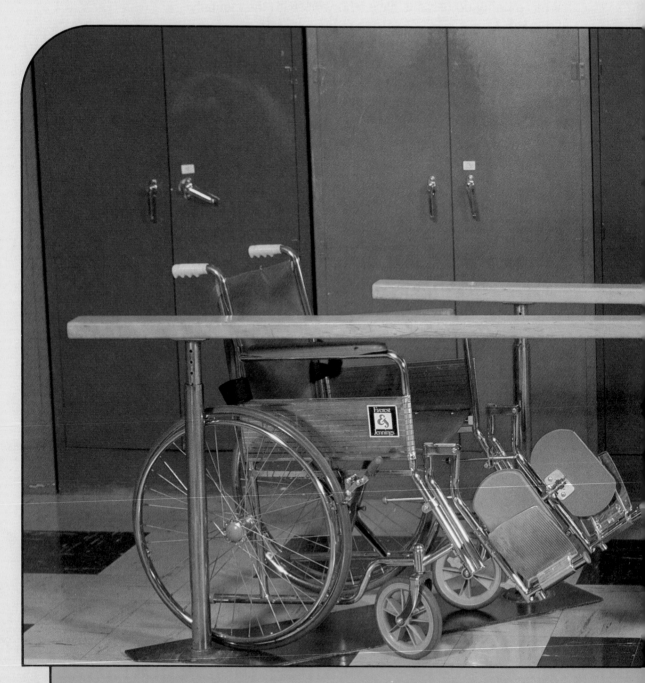

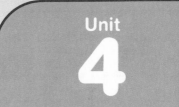

How can you be a wise health consumer?

Why is a physical examination important?

What kinds of care are available at hospitals?

Doug Martin/ Courtesy Children's Hospital, Columbus, OH.

# The Wise Consumer

Doug Martin

*Should he choose plastic frames? His friend has a pair of wire frames that look good on her. How will he choose? Eyeglasses can correct vision problems. But eyeglasses also influence a person's appearance. What other facts should he consider? It is wise to take enough time before making important decisions.*

**B**ill has a hard time seeing the chalkboard at school. His parents take him to an eye doctor to have his eyes checked. He needs to start wearing eyeglasses to see more clearly.

**GOAL:** *You will gain knowledge about how to make wise choices about health products and services for your physical, mental, and social health.*

## Who Is a Health Consumer?

Certain health products and health services help you to be at your best. When Bill went to the eye doctor, he bought a health service. A **health service** is a place or a person that helps others to be healthy. When Bill's parents bought eyeglasses, they bought a health product. A **health product** is something that you use to be at your best. It keeps you healthy.

Bill is a health consumer. A **health consumer** is a person who buys health products and health services. You are a consumer when you use health products or health services for your physical, mental, or social health. Look at the health triangle of physical, mental, and social health on page 136. In the center of the triangle is a picture of a happy, healthy person about your age. This person makes wise choices for health.

*What is a health service?*

*What is a health product?*

*Who is a health consumer?*

MENTAL

PHYSICAL

SOCIAL

THE HEALTH TRIANGLE

FIGURE 10–1.

## Section

## 10:2

*What do physical health products do?*

# Health Products for Physical Health

Health products for physical health keep your body healthy. Make a list of the products that you or your family use for physical health. Did you realize that there were so many health products to buy? Some students your age made a list of the health products their families bought recently. They were surprised to see how different their lists were.

Alice and her family were getting ready to go camping. She made a list of the things they would need. Many health products protect your physical health. Alice wanted to buy insect spray to keep bugs from biting her.

Mike remembered the list he had for shopping for his grandmother. Mike's 80-year-old grandmother lives with his family. Many health products help people with special physical needs to be at their best.

Jane has a very bad cough and a cold. Jane chose health products that will improve her health.

FIGURE 10–2.

| ALICE | MIKE | JANE |
|-------|------|------|
| toothpaste | ·batteries | ·cough syrup |
| dental floss | ·vaporizer | ·tissues |
| insect spray | ·false teeth | ·nasal spray |
| bandages | cleaner | ·thermometer |
| | ·hair brush | |

## Activity

### Products for My Physical Health

Make a list of ten products that you use for physical health. Which product is most important in keeping you healthy? Put the number 1 next to it. Then rank the remaining products in order of importance from 2 to 10. Are all ten products necessary for your health? Why or why not?

## Health Products for Mental Health

Health products for mental health influence the way you think or feel. The same students were asked to make a list of health products for mental health. No one could think of any. Can you think of any health products for mental health?

Then Mike said, "I read books. Are books a health product?" You may be surprised to learn that you are a consumer when you buy a book, play music, go to a movie, read a newspaper, watch TV, or exercise. In each case, you are doing something that affects your mental health.

Health products for mental health are often difficult to choose. When you buy eyeglasses, you know they are needed and good for your physical health. But what if you buy a book that does not make you use your mind? What if you go to a movie and do not learn anything? What if you watch a TV show that has crime and violence in it? Do you think you may have wasted your time and money?

*What do mental health products do?*

## Think About It

1. Why do people buy products for their physical health?
2. How can television programs affect your mental health?

Eric Hoffhines

**FIGURE 10–3.** When you buy sheet music you are choosing a health product for mental health.

# Health Products for Social Health

**FIGURE 10–4.**

*What do social health products do?*

Health products for social health influence the way you relate to others. At your age, you are interested in getting along with others. You want to have good social health. When you watch TV or read a magazine you see many products for social health. Do you know why? The people who make and advertise these products want you to buy their products. They want you to believe that you will relate better with other people if you use their products.

Look at the picture of the health products for social health in the margin. Some of these health products are needed for good social health. Others are needed for both physical and social health. You need to use soap to cleanse your body and shampoo to clean your hair. You may not need other health products. A girl does not need nail polish or lipstick. A boy does not need cologne (kuh LOHN). These are products that you choose to use for social health.

There are some important things to think about when you buy social health products. You should want to be clean and to look healthy. Health products can help you with this part of your social health. But you also need to act healthy to have good social health. Some people think that wearing nice clothes and smelling good is all that it takes to get along with others. Having good manners and saying "please," "excuse me," and "thank you" are part of social health.

## Think About It

3. How do health products help your social health?
4. How does having a clean body affect your social health?

# Health Services

*How is a health service provided?*

A health service can be provided by either a place or a person. To be a wise health consumer you need to know two other facts.

- Most health services located in a special place must meet certain standards. A **health standard** is a rule or way of doing things to protect your health. For example, if a restaurant does not meet health standards, it must close. The restaurant must be clean. The people who make and serve food must meet health standards. There are other health standards which concern other places. A drugstore has other standards to meet. There are people called **health inspectors** who have the job of checking to see if places like restaurants and stores meet health standards.

- People who provide health services must also meet standards. These standards assure you that these persons can do their job correctly. Usually they need to have a certain number of years of education. They may also need to have special training beyond that. A doctor and a nurse have special education, training, and experience. They must meet certain standards. There are people who have the job of making sure that people who provide health services meet certain standards.

## Think About It

**5.** Why do you think it is important to have standards for health services?

**FIGURE 10–5.** Hospitals offer a variety of health services.

*What is a health standard?*

*Why must a person who provides a health service meet certain standards?*

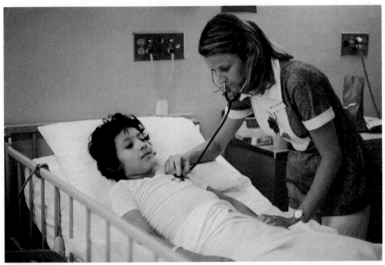

Windsor Publications/fpg

**FIGURE 10–6.** People who work in hospitals to provide health services must meet certain standards.

# Health Services for Physical Health

Students your age were also asked to make a list of health services for physical health. They thought of some places that were near where they live.

FIGURE 10–7. Valuable health reminders are offered by many organizations.

| PLACES THAT PROVIDE HEALTH SERVICES | |
|---|---|
| 1. rest home | 6. camp for people with handicaps |
| 2. speech clinic | 7. health office at school |
| 3. doctor's office | 8. school for people who are blind |
| 4. hospital | 9. emergency room |
| 5. Red Cross | 10. local heart association |

Then the students made a list of the people who provide health services. Mike wanted to put the pharmacist (FAR muh sust) first on the list. This is because Mike wants to be a pharmacist. Have you thought about getting the education and training to provide a health service? There are many interesting jobs in the health services.

Doug Martin

FIGURE 10–8. Pets often need medical attention.

## PEOPLE WHO PROVIDE HEALTH SERVICES

1. A **pharmacist** mixes drugs for medications.
2. A **speech pathologist** (puh THAHL uh just) studies and treats speech problems.
3. A **veterinarian** (veh trun ER ee un) prevents and treats diseases in animals.
4. A **medical technologist** (tek NAHL uh just) helps a doctor by doing certain tests in a laboratory.
5. A **dentist** examines and treats the teeth, mouth, and gums.
6. A **health educator** works to improve the knowledge, attitude, and behavior of people.
7. A **hospital attendant** helps hospital patients with daily activities.
8. A **medical doctor** examines patients to prevent, diagnose, and treat illness.
9. A **dietitian** (di uh TIHSH un) helps others plan balanced, healthy meals and special diets.
10. A **dental hygienist** (HI jeen ust) cleans and flosses your teeth and assists the dentist.
11. A **nurse** cares for the sick and injured.

## Activity

### *Health Services Concentration*

To play Health Services Concentration, you need 22 index cards. Write one of the names of the people who provide health services on each of 11 of the cards: (1) pharmacist, (2) speech pathologist, (3) veterinarian, (4) medical technologist, (5) dentist, (6) health educator, (7) hospital attendant, (8) medical doctor, (9) dietitian, (10) dental hygienist, (11) nurse. On the remaining 11 cards write one of the 11 job descriptions. Shuffle the cards. To play the game, place all 22 index cards facedown, side by side. Each player turns over two cards at a time. The object is to match the name of a person with the correct job description. If the two cards do not match, the player returns the two cards to their original position. Players take turns trying to match cards.

## Health Services for Mental Health

Eric Hoffhines

**FIGURE 10–9.** Guidance counselors are familiar with the needs of young people.

Some people have special education and training to help others to adjust to day-to-day problems. Religious leaders are trained to help others learn about the meaning of life. Many people who have problems go to these people to talk. In this way, mental health services are provided.

Your school may have a guidance counselor to help with problems. There may be social workers in your community. **Social workers** help people find resources to meet a variety of needs.

A **psychologist** (si KAHL uh just) assists people in problems of daily living by observing and testing behavior. A **psychiatrist** (suh KI uh trust) helps persons who have poor mental health. A psychiatrist is also a medical doctor.

There may be a mental health clinic near your home. Is there a psychologist at your school? Some industries have mental health services. Many psychologists and psychiatrists have their own offices while others work at hospitals.

## Health Services for Social Health

*How does a psychologist differ from a psychiatrist?*

*What is a social health service?*

Many places provide an opportunity for you to improve your social health. These places provide a social health service. The people who work or help with these activities are also providing a health service. Have you been a part of any of the activities listed below?

**FIGURE 10–10.**

### HAVE YOU BEEN A SOCIAL HEALTH SERVICE CONSUMER?

| | |
|---|---|
| YWCA/YMCA | swim team |
| YWHA/YMHA | band |
| church group | Bird Club |
| candy striper | Indian princess |
| Boy Scouts | Camping |
| Girl Scouts | Campfire Girls |
| choir | Little League baseball |

If you have, you were a consumer of social health services. Has one of your parents helped with one of these activities? If so, your parent provided a social health service.

## Making Wise Choices

It is important for you to look and feel your best. Others know this. They know that you use health products and services. They know that you have many choices to make. A **quack** (KWAK) is a person who tries to sell you useless products and services. Usually, these products and services do not make you more healthy. The method a quack uses to sell useless products or services is called **quackery.** A quack will say or do things to try to help you make up your mind. Some of these things are listed in the margin. Do not let statements made by quacks influence your choices.

*What is a quack? Quackery?*

As a consumer you spend your money and your time. How careful are you? How important is it for you to make wise choices?

*What are two things to consider when making wise choices?*

Bob goes to a skin doctor. The doctor advises Bob to eat different foods to help his problem. The doctor says it will take time for Bob's skin to become clear. Bob reads in a magazine about a skin cream with something new in it. Bob sends for the cream. It does not work.

Sally asks Alice to come over to her house to play backgammon. Alice does not know how to play that game. She says, "That will be too hard for me to learn." Alice stays home. She decides to watch TV. She gets frightened watching a program that has a lot of crime in it. That night she cannot sleep.

Bob spent money for a product that did not improve his physical health. The product did not help Bob to be at his best. Bob should have listened to his doctor. Alice spent time watching a television program that did not improve her mental health. Alice might have learned something new from Sally. Bob wasted his money. Alice wasted her time. Do you make wise choices when you spend time and money?

**FIGURE 10–11.** Do any of these statements sound familiar to you?

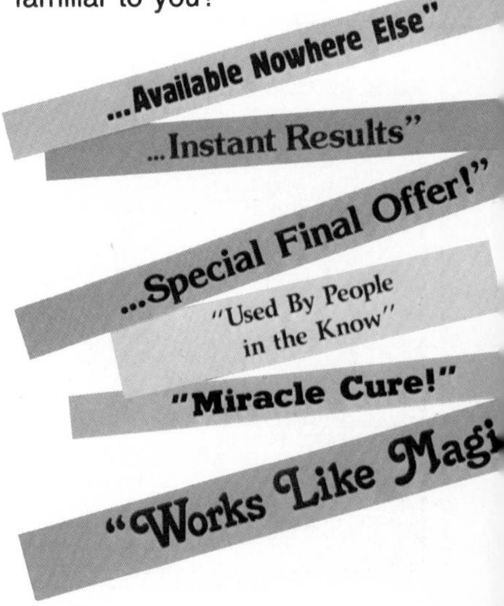

...Available Nowhere Else"

...Instant Results"

...Special Final Offer!"

"Used By People in the Know"

"Miracle Cure!"

"Works Like Magi

## UPC in the Supermarket

The letters UPC do not stand for a new chemical or a new football league. The letters UPC represent the words "Universal Product Code." If you have been through a checkout counter in a supermarket, then you have seen the UPC symbol. The symbol is on the packages of many different products.

Foods, paper towels, detergents, and many other products have the UPC symbol. The symbol consists of many closely spaced lines, bars, and numbers.

The lines and bars in the code symbol are unique to that product. The UPC symbol does not contain the price. It contains information about the name, manufacturer, and size of the product.

At the checkout stand the clerk slides the product, UPC side down, over a scanning device which uses a laser beam. As the product passes over the scanner, a message is sent to the store's computer. The computer does several things with the information in a matter of seconds.

First, the computer identifies the item, and then "rings" it up on the register at the checkout counter. It also prints a description of the item and the price on the customer's receipt.

The computer also helps the store manager. It gives the manager a lot of important information. The manager will know how much of a certain item is left on the shelf. It also reveals how fast an item is being sold, when and how much to reorder, and what products the shoppers like best.

The UPC system also is designed to serve the consumer. Two main reasons for using the system are checkout speed and reducing checkout errors. There are, however, some questions that some consumer groups have about the UPC system. Some see an advantage for increased checkout speed. But they say the supermarket may use the faster-moving lines as a reason to reduce the number of checkout stands. If this happens, the result would be faster-moving but longer lines.

Groups in favor of the system believe the computer will reduce checkout errors. Some consumer groups are concerned that the computer may be fed wrong information or the computer could break down.

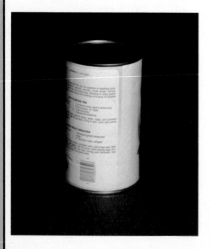

Gerard Photography

# Chapter 10

## Review

## Summary

1. A health consumer uses products and services for physical, mental, and social health. — *10:1*
2. Many health products protect your physical health. — *10:2*
3. Health products may influence the way you think or feel. — *10:3*
4. Some health products are needed to have good social health. — *10:4*
5. A health service may be a place or a person. — *10:5*
6. There are people and places that provide health services for physical health. — *10:6*
7. Many people have special training to provide health services for mental health. — *10:7*
8. Social health services provide places for people to enjoy being with each other. — *10:8*
9. A quack uses quackery to try to sell you useless products and services. You need to be wise about choosing health products and services. — *10:9*

## Words for Health

*Below are vocabulary words and incomplete sentences. Complete each sentence with the correct vocabulary word. DO NOT WRITE IN THIS BOOK.*

| | |
|---|---|
| dental hygienist | medical technologist |
| dentist | nurse |
| dietitian | pharmacist |
| health consumer | psychiatrist |
| health educator | psychologist |
| health inspector | quack |
| health product | quackery |
| health service | social worker |
| health standard | speech pathologist |
| hospital attendant | veterinarian |
| medical doctor | |

1. A _____ works to improve the health knowledge, attitudes, and behaviors of people.
2. A _____ prevents and treats diseases in animals.
3. A _____ is a person who tries to sell you useless health products and services.

# Review

4. A _____ cleans and flosses your teeth.
5. A place or a person that helps others to be healthy provides a _____.
6. A _____ checks to see if health standards are met.
7. A _____ provides a health service by observing behavior.
8. A _____ buys and uses health products and services.
9. A _____ examines and treats the teeth, mouth, and gums.
10. A _____ helps others plan balanced, healthy meals and special diets.
11. Someone who studies and treats speech problems is a _____.
12. When a quack sells you a useless product, it is called _____.
13. A person who works at a drugstore selling drugs is a _____.
14. A person who helps hospital patients with daily activities is a _____.
15. A _____ helps persons in your community to meet a variety of needs.
16. A _____ is a rule or way of doing things to protect your health.
17. A _____ is a medical doctor who helps persons with poor mental health.
18. A _____ helps the doctor by doing certain tests in the laboratory.
19. A _____ examines patients to prevent, diagnose, and treat illness.
20. A _____ is something that you use to be at your best.
21. A _____ cares for the sick and injured.

## Look at Your Health

1. In what way are a health product and a health service alike?
2. What are three products that can be used for physical health?
3. Why are health products for mental health difficult to choose?
4. What are two things that you need to have good social health?
5. Why must persons who provide health services meet certain standards?
6. List five places that provide health services for physical health.
7. List five jobs where people provide health services.
8. Name four people who provide mental health services.
9. What kind of service does a Boy Scout or Girl Scout leader provide?
10. What is the difference between a health product or service you get from your doctor and one you get from a quack?

## Actions for Health

*Think about the following situations. Then respond to the questions that follow.*

*Situation:* You would like to grow taller. Your health teacher tells you that people grow at different rates. You have not started to grow taller yet. In a magazine, you read about a product that will make you grow fast. You need to send $2 to get this product. You cannot get it anywhere else. Medical doctors do not recommend it.

1. What would you do?
2. What two things helped you make your decision?

*Situation:* You and one of your parents are reading this health book. Your parent says, "I would like to provide a social health service."

1. Name five social health services in which you might participate.
2. Which one would be the most fun for you and your parent?
3. Give reasons for your answer.

## Individual Research

1. Visit your local health department. Learn at least five health standards that must be met by schools.
2. Write a report about violent shows on television. Do you think persons your age should watch violent shows? Give reasons for your answers.
3. Movies are given different ratings. These ratings tell you who can and who cannot buy a ticket to see the movie. What are the different ratings? How do these ratings protect you as a consumer?
4. Write a report about a health service in your community.

# LIFE MANAGEMENT SKILLS

- Evaluate health products and services to avoid quackery.
- Report suspected cases of quackery to the appropriate agency.
- Read UPC register tapes to be aware of products and their prices.
- Select health products and services carefully.
- Identify people and places in your community that provide health services.

# The Physical Examination

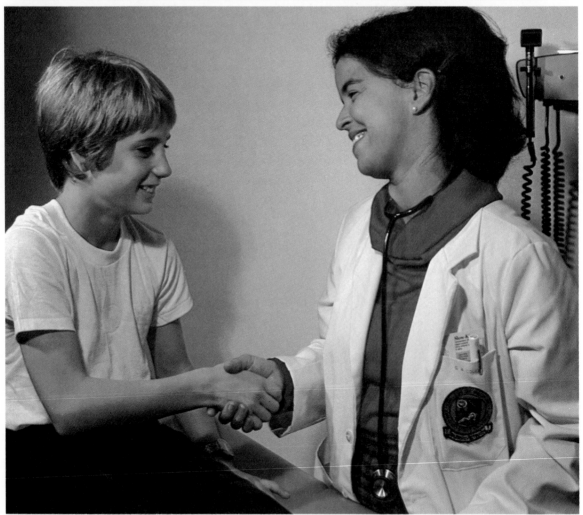

Doug Martin

*A doctor is a very important person in your life. When you are ill, you need someone who is trained and who cares about your health. When was the last time you were sick? How does a doctor discover what is causing you to be ill? How can a doctor help you to stay well? When did you have your last checkup?*

**Chapter**

**11**

An important factor will help you live a long and healthy life. This factor is having good medical care. Your medical care should include a physical examination at least every two years.

**GOAL:** *You will study about physical examinations and why they are important to good health.*

**Section**

## The Importance of a Physical Examination

**11:1**

Doctors can predict how long you may expect to live if you are accident-free. This is called your **life expectancy** (ihk SPEK tun see). Some things influence your life expectancy.

*What is life expectancy?*

- what you know about health
- what you do—your habits
- your heredity
- your environment
- the drugs that you take to make or keep you healthy

*What influences your life expectancy?*

Your doctor can help you make a plan to increase your life expectancy. The doctor assists you by gathering clues about you. These clues help you make a plan for your health. Sometimes the doctor will ask you questions. At other times, the doctor will check your body from head to toe. A **physical examination** includes checking your body and gathering information about you and your family.

*What does a physical examination include?*

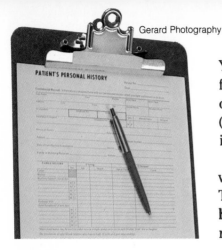

**FIGURE 11–1.** After you complete a health history form a doctor can plan for your future health.

*Define symptom and diagnosis.*
*What is a health record?*

Sometimes you go to the doctor because you are ill. You may have symptoms. A **symptom** is a change in bodily function from a normal pattern. A symptom is an indication of a possible problem. The doctor examines you to diagnose (DI ihg nohs) your illness. A **diagnosis** is the process of identifying a disease or disorder based on symptoms.

At other times, you go to your doctor for a checkup when you are healthy. You have no symptoms of an illness. The doctor keeps your information in a special file called a **health record.** As you grow and develop, the doctor will read your record and help you make a plan to stay healthy.

What does a doctor do when you have a physical examination? What might the doctor learn? In the rest of this chapter, you will learn some of the ways a doctor gathers information about you.

## Think About It

1. Why is it important to go to a doctor when you are healthy?
2. How is a health record used?

## Section

## 11:2

*What is a health history?*

**FIGURE 11–2.** Computers can recall patient health information in seconds.

## Health History

The doctor will ask you many questions to gather facts for your health history. The **health history** includes facts about your past health and your habits. Your doctor may also ask your parents questions about you. How much did you weigh when you were born? What illnesses have you had? Do you eat breakfast? How many hours of sleep do you get each day? What drugs have you taken when you were sick? Your health history gives the doctor clues about your present health. Your health history may be helpful in diagnosing and treating a future illness.

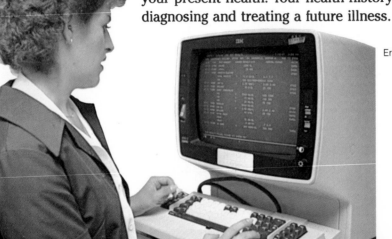

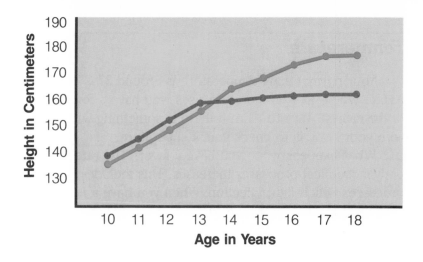

**FIGURE 11–3.** The graph indicates the average differences in heights between boys and girls as they grow from age 2 to 18.

Girls

Boys

---

# Weight and Height

There is always a scale in a doctor's office. The doctor wants to know how much you weigh. If you lose or gain much weight, it may be a symptom of an illness. If you are underweight for your age and size, you may not be digesting your food properly. Perhaps some other body part is not functioning normally.

*Why are some people underweight?*

If you are overweight, you may eat too much or may not exercise enough. As a result, fat is stored under your skin. The doctor will suggest that you lose some weight. For every extra pound of fat, your body needs one more mile of blood vessels. Your heart has to work harder to pump blood through these extra blood vessels.

*Why does the heart of an overweight person have to work more?*

The doctor will measure you to see how tall you are. The doctor may use a height-weight grid. This grid shows the height and weight that someone with your body build should have. The grid gives a range rather than a definite height and weight. The doctor reads the grid for your height. Then the doctor can check to see if you are in the correct weight range for your height. What do you think the doctor would ask you to do if you weighed too little or too much?

## Think About It

3. Why does the heart of any overweight person beat more often than the heart of an underweight person?

# 11:4

*What is normal body temperature?*

*What happens to your body when you have a fever?*

## Temperature

Your normal body temperature is around 37°C or 98.6°F. When your temperature rises, you have a **fever.** One of the easiest ways to learn if there is something wrong with your body is to check your temperature.

What happens when you have a fever? The rate of your body's chemical processes increases. This includes the processes which fight infection. When you have a fever, it is an indication that your body is resisting an infection. But when things in your body speed up, your body uses energy. You become weak and tired. Your doctor will tell you to rest. You may need medicine to reduce your fever.

## Activity

### *Thermometer Readings*

The thermometer that you have in your home is most likely marked in Fahrenheit (FER un hite) degrees. Your normal body temperature is 98.6°F. A hospital thermometer is usually marked in Celsius (SEL see us) degrees. Your normal body temperature is 37°C. You can change Fahrenheit temperature to Celsius.

**1.** Subtract 32 from the Fahrenheit temperature.

**2.** Multiply the remainder by ⅝ and the result will be in Celsius degrees.

Complete the following chart on a sheet of paper.

| Temperature in Degrees Fahrenheit | Subtract 32 | Multiply by ⅝ to get Temperature in Degrees Celsius |
|---|---|---|
| 99.5°F | 99.5 − 32 = ____ | ____ × ⅝ = ____ |
| 100.0°F | 100.0 − 32 = ____ | ____ × ⅝ = ____ |
| 101.0°F | 101.0 − 32 = ____ | ____ × ⅝ = ____ |
| 101.5°F | 101.5 − 32 = ____ | ____ × ⅝ = ____ |

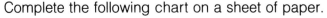

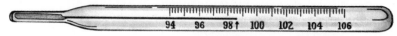

Normal    Fever

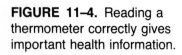

**FIGURE 11–4.** Reading a thermometer correctly gives important health information.

# Eyes and Ears

Bill's eyes sparkle. Maria's eyes shine. Gina's eyes are clear. People often describe the eyes of others in such terms. Eyes give the doctor many clues about your health. The doctor uses an instrument called an **ophthalmoscope** (ahf THAL muh skohp) to shine light into your eye. This allows the doctor to see the internal parts of your eye. The doctor can also see if your blood vessels are healthy.

*Why does a doctor shine a light into your eyes?*

A doctor may learn symptoms of illness in other parts of your body from looking at your eyes. If your eyes seem deep, dark, or sunken, you may have lost weight rapidly. There is a fat layer under each eye. When you lose weight, some of this fat is lost.

You may not be growing as fast as you should and you may feel tired. The doctor notices that your eyes bulge. The thyroid gland controls growth. Bulging eyes are a symptom that this gland is not functioning normally.

The doctor uses an **otoscope** (OHT uh skohp) to look inside your ears to examine the ear canal and the eardrum. If there is a buildup of wax, the doctor will remove it. If you have an infection, the inside of the ear may be swollen. There may be pus in your ear. Pus is a yellowish-white matter produced by an infection.

*What is an otoscope?*

You may be asked to repeat words that the doctor whispers. This is a simple test to learn if you can hear normal sounds. If you cannot hear the whispered words the doctor will suggest that you have an ear specialist check your ears.

**FIGURE 11–5.**

Doug Martin

Doug Martin

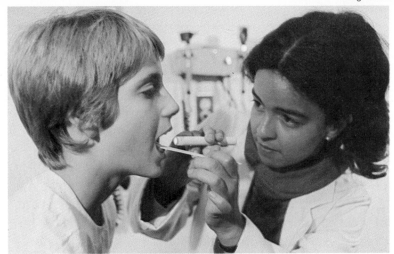

**FIGURE 11–6.** Tissues in the mouth and throat are healthy when they are pink.

## 11:6

### Nose

*Why does the doctor use a nasal speculum?*

The doctor uses a **nasal speculum** (SPEK yuh lum) to spread apart your nostrils. A nasal speculum is used to check if there is anything that blocks your breathing. If the wall between the two parts of your nose is cracked or separated the doctor will record this in your health record.

*What happens when your mucous membranes become irritated?*

Your nose has a protective lining called **mucous** (MYEW kus) **membranes.** When your mucous membranes become irritated, they are red. They produce more mucus which is a slimy secretion. You have a runny nose. If you have had a cold, you have had these symptoms.

Section

## 11:7

### Mouth and Throat

A **tongue depressor** (dih PRES ur) is a wooden stick that is used to hold down the tongue. The doctor will ask you to say "ah" so that your tongue will be flat. Then the doctor will use a flashlight to see the inside of your mouth and throat. The doctor will look for any postnasal

*What is postnasal drip?*

(pohst NAY zul) drip. **Postnasal drip** is a heavy discharge that drains from the nose to the throat. It is a symptom of infection.

The doctor looks at your teeth and gums and smells anything unusual about your breath. An unusual smell may indicate that you have something wrong inside your body. If your tongue is pale, you may not have enough red cells in your blood. A dry and shriveled tongue means that your body needs more water. People who breathe through their mouths or who smoke may have a coated tongue.

A person usually has tonsils on both sides of the throat at the base of the tongue. The doctor checks to see if the tonsils are large or infected.

## Reflex Tests

Your nerves control your body movements. These nerves can be destroyed by a disease or by an accident. A reflex test checks to see if your nerves will cause you to have certain movements or reflex actions. A reflex action occurs when a body part moves without being directed to by the brain. Here are some reflex tests the doctor may perform.

*What is a reflex test? Reflex action?*

- You put your arm out in front of you with one finger up and you look at your finger. The doctor shines a light in your eye. Your pupil gets very small.

*Give examples of reflex tests.*

Peter Gridley/Alpha

**FIGURE 11–7.** Quick reflexes are a sign that a person's nervous system is healthy.

- The doctor sticks your arm gently with a sharp pin. You twitch or move.
- You sit on a chair or on the examination table with your legs crossed. The doctor strikes your leg just below the kneecap with a small rubber-tipped hammer. Your leg jerks forward.

## Section 11:9

### Palpation or Feeling

*What is palpation?*

A doctor has some ways to tell what is going on inside you. One way is to touch or feel your body to learn how it is functioning. This is called **palpation** (pal PAY shun). During palpation, the doctor checks the location and size of various organs. A check is made for firmness, softness, swelling, and pain. The doctor may feel your neck. If there is swelling or if your neck feels tender, you may have an infection.

*What is percussion?*

## Section 11:10

### Percussion or Tapping

**FIGURE 11–8.** Some lumps or infected tissues in the body can be easily felt by palpation.

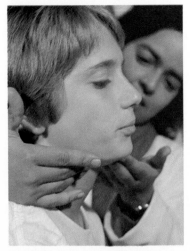

Doug Martin

The doctor may tap on your chest, abdomen, or back with his/her fingers. This tapping is called **percussion** (pur KUSH un). The sounds that are made also tell your doctor what is going on inside your body.

Usually the lungs are soft and full of air. When the doctor taps on your chest or back, the sound indicates the condition of your lungs. The doctor is trained to recognize the sounds. The doctor listens to determine if you have an infection in your lungs.

### Think About It

4. How does the knee jerk reflex differ from kicking a football?
5. Why are quick reflex actions a sign of good health?
6. What can a doctor learn about your lungs by listening to sounds?

Doug Martin

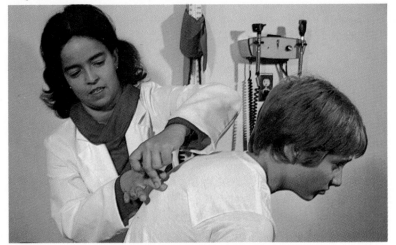

**FIGURE 11–9.** A body produces sounds that a doctor recognizes.

## Activity
### Sounds

To learn about tapping and sounds, do an experiment using three jars of water.

• one empty jar  • one full jar  • one half-full jar

Tap each of the three jars with your finger. How does each sound? Now close your eyes and tap each jar. Do you know which jar you are tapping?

## Auscultation or Listening

The doctor listens to sounds in your body. This is called **auscultation** (aw skul TAY shun). A **stethoscope** (STETH uh skohp) is an instrument that your doctor uses to hear body sounds.

The doctor listens to your heartbeat with a stethoscope. The valves in your heart normally make sounds as they open and close. The doctor will listen in three to four different places to hear the valves opening and closing.

Next, your doctor listens to your lungs. You will be asked to breathe with your mouth open. The doctor listens for a wheezing or whistling sound. Unusual sounds may be symptoms of an illness.

*What is auscultation? What instrument is used?*

# Blood Pressure and Pulse

Have you ever turned on a hose and had water come out very fast? Do you know how to make it come out more slowly? The rate at which water comes out of the hose depends upon pressure. Your blood moves in blood vessels through your body because of the force of the heartbeat. The force of blood against the walls of the blood vessels is measured as **blood pressure.** When your heart muscle pushes blood out of your heart, your blood pressure rises. The doctor measures this pressure when the heart is pumping. This is one measure. A second measure is taken when the heart is resting between beats. Blood pressure is read by stating the two measures like a fraction. The first measure is stated first. A **sphygmomanometer** (sfihg moh muh NAHM ut ur), or blood pressure cuff, is used to measure the two blood pressure readings.

There is a normal blood pressure for your age, sex, and body build. When you rest or sleep, your blood pressure is low. When you exercise, your blood pressure is higher. If someone should scare you, your blood pressure increases. Soon, your blood pressure goes back to normal.

*How is blood pressure measured?*

**FIGURE 11–10.** Blood pressure is measured in two readings.

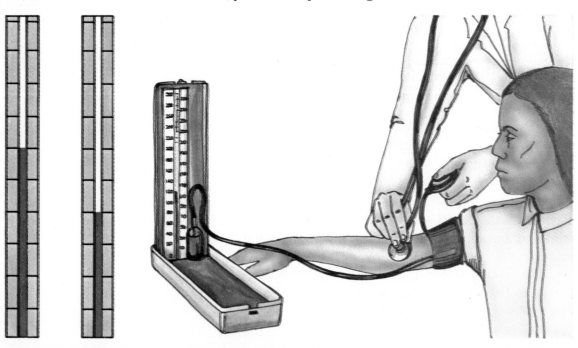

Some people have high blood pressure. Their blood pressure remains higher than normal. They may need medicine, surgery, a salt-free diet, or a change in lifestyle. People who are overweight may have high blood pressure. Their doctor will suggest that they lose weight. People who smoke usually have higher blood pressure than those who do not smoke. What do you think their doctor will ask them to do?

About half of the people who have high blood pressure do not know it. A blood pressure test is one of the best ways to see how healthy you are. There are some ways to help keep your blood pressure in a normal range.

- Keep your weight in a normal range for your age and height.
- Do not smoke.
- Exercise at least three times a week.
- Get enough sleep.
- Do not eat too much salt.

A doctor can use another test to learn about your health. The doctor will hold your wrist to feel your pulse and count the number of times your heart beats. When your heart muscle is strong, your heart may not beat as often. There is more time for your heart to rest between beats.

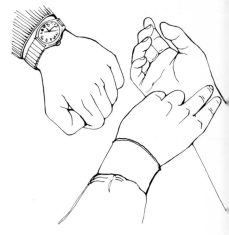

**FIGURE 11–11.** Heartbeat rate can be detected by the pulse at the wrist.

*What can you do to keep your blood pressure in a normal range?*

## Think About It

7. Why do you think most doctors believe that blood pressure information tells the most about your health?
8. How can you try to keep your blood pressure normal?

## Blood Sample

A doctor may learn many things from taking a sample of your blood. A blood sample is usually drawn from one of your veins. The blood sample is sent to a local laboratory where several checks are made. Do you have enough red blood cells? Red blood cells are needed to carry oxygen to all parts of your body. Do you have an increase in the normal number of white blood cells? If you do, you may have an infection in your body.

*How does a doctor get a blood sample?*

## Disease Prevention

One reason to visit a physician is for a regular physical examination. You might also visit a physician because you have disease. A *communicable disease* is an illness caused by a pathogen that enters the body. A *noncommunicable disease* is an illness that is not caused by a pathogen.

The most common communicable disease is the cold. You can take steps to avoid catching a cold. The most important step is to avoid contact with a person who has a cold. The first 24 hours a person has a cold is the most communicable.

It is important to realize that there is no medical cure for the common cold. However, if you follow good health habits, you can make your body stronger and fight pathogens more easily.

Two of the major noncommunicable diseases that affect many people are heart disease and cancer. Heart disease can often be traced to poor health practices that began at a young age. You can reduce your risks of getting heart disease by choosing not to smoke, exercising daily, avoiding fatty foods, maintaining a desirable weight, and learning ways to deal with stress.

Certain factors you cannot control to avoid heart disease. One factor is your family history. Risks of heart disease increase if members of your family have had heart disease. However, practicing healthful habits can still reduce your risks.

Cancer is the other major noncommunicable disease. Cancer is a disease in which abnormal cells grow throughout the body and destroy healthy cells.

There are many kinds of cancer. Medical researches believe that by following healthful behaviors you can decrease the risks of getting these cancers. You can avoid skin cancer by avoiding the sun's rays when they are strongest.

This occurs between 10:00 A.M. and 3:00 P.M. During these hours, wear a sunscreen or keep exposed body parts covered when you are in the direct sun.

Health authorities agree that almost all cases of lung cancer could be avoided if people did not smoke. Most cases of cancer of the mouth would not occur if people did not use smokeless tobacco. There is also evidence to indicate that eating healthful foods will help reduce the chances of cancer of the digestive system.

Learn the facts about heart disease and cancer. Then follow healthful practices to reduce your risks of having these diseases.

Tom McGuire

160

# Chapter 11

# Review

## Summary

1. Your doctor will ask you questions and do a physical examination to gather information about your health.     *11:1*

2. Your health history includes facts which may help a doctor diagnose and treat a future illness.     *11:2*

3. A height-weight chart tells the doctor a range for good health measurements.     *11:3*

4. Checking your body temperature is one of the easiest ways to learn if you have an illness.     *11:4*

5. A careful check of your eyes and ears is a standard part of a physical checkup.     *11:5*

6. During a physical examination, your doctor will use a nasal speculum to check for anything that blocks your breathing.     *11:6*

7. Your doctor uses a tongue depressor and a flashlight to see the inside of your mouth, throat, teeth, gums, and tonsils.     *11:7*

8. Your doctor will do several reflex tests to examine your nerves and their reflex actions.     *11:8*

9. During palpation, a doctor touches or feels your body to learn how it is functioning.     *11:9*

10. The doctor may tap on your chest, abdomen, or back to listen for sounds which indicate good or poor health.     *11:10*

11. The doctor uses a stethoscope to listen to the sounds made by your heart and lungs.     *11:11*

12. The doctor uses a sphygmomanometer to measure your blood pressure.     *11:12*

13. A doctor may learn many things from tests on a sample of your blood.     *11:13*

## Words for Health

*Below are vocabulary words and incomplete sentences. Complete each sentence with the correct vocabulary word. DO NOT WRITE IN THIS BOOK.*

| | | |
|---|---|---|
| auscultation | health record | physical examination |
| blood pressure | life expectancy | postnasal drip |
| diagnosis | mucous membranes | symptom |
| fever | palpation | |
| health history | percussion | |

# Review

1. _____ is touching or feeling the body to learn how it is functioning.
2. The doctor listens to sounds in your body by a process of tapping called _____.
3. _____ moves your blood through your blood vessels.
4. Your _____ is how long you can expect to live.
5. A(n) _____ is a change in bodily function that indicates a possible problem.
6. Tapping or _____ makes sounds that tell your doctor what is going on inside you.
7. A(n) _____ is the process of identifying a disease or disorder from symptoms.
8. _____ is a heavy discharge that drains from the nose to the throat.
9. A(n) _____ is an increase in your body temperature that is not normal.
10. A doctor does a(n) _____ to check your body and gather information about you and your family.
11. Your nose has a protective lining called _____.
12. A(n) _____ is a special file that contains information about your health.
13. A(n) _____ includes facts about your past and present health habits.

# Vocabulary

*Below are the names of health instruments used by your doctor. There are also incomplete sentences. Complete each sentence by writing in the name of the correct instrument. DO NOT WRITE IN THIS BOOK.*

nasal speculum      sphygmomanometer
ophthalmoscope     stethoscope
otoscope               tongue depressor

1. Your doctor uses a(n) _____ to examine your eyes.
2. Your doctor uses a(n) _____ and a flashlight to see inside your mouth and throat.
3. Your doctor uses a(n) _____ to examine the ear canal and the eardrum.
4. Your doctor uses a(n) _____ to spread apart your nostrils.
5. Your doctor uses a(n) _____ to measure your blood pressure.
6. Your doctor uses a(n) _____ to listen to your heart and lungs.

## Look at Your Health

1. What are some things that influence your life expectancy?
2. How does your doctor gather information about your health?
3. How does a doctor use your health history?
4. What happens inside your body if you are overweight?
5. What happens when you have a fever?
6. What can a doctor learn by looking at your eyes?
7. What is a simple test to learn if you can hear normal sounds?
8. What does a doctor learn from palpation?
9. What does your doctor learn from tapping on your back and chest?
10. What is the difference between the first measure and the second measure of blood pressure?
11. What can you do to keep your blood pressure normal?
12. What can the doctor learn from a blood sample?

## Actions for Health

*Think about the following situation. Then respond to the questions that follow.*

*Situation:* You go to your doctor for a physical examination. Your doctor asks questions about your health. Do you get a good night's sleep? What concerns do you have about your health?

1. What will you tell your doctor?
2. How important is it for your doctor to have this information?

## Individual Research

1. Write a report on hypertension (high blood pressure).
2. Write a report about an EEG or an EKG.

## LIFE MANAGEMENT SKILLS

- Have physical examinations at regular intervals.
- Keep a well documented health history.
- Be able to take body temperature and read a thermometer.
- Have blood pressure checked regularly and know your reading.

# Doctors and Hospitals

St Jude Children's Research Hospital

*Hospitals are special places. St. Jude is very special because it is a hospital for children. It is also a research hospital. Possible cures for illnesses which affect children are constantly being studied there. Have you thought about the career you would like? Perhaps working in a hospital like St. Jude would interest you. How could you learn about the kinds of jobs available at hospitals like St. Jude?*

What do each of these people have in common? Mrs. Jones is ready to give birth to a baby. Sarah has been in a serious automobile accident. Mr. Green has had a sudden heart attack. Bradley needs to have his tonsils removed. Doctors do not know what is the matter with Tyler.

**GOAL:** *You will learn about hospitals, patients, and people who work in hospitals to give health care.*

**Section**

## What Is a Hospital?

**12:1**

Each of these persons needs to go to a hospital. A **hospital** is a special place where people receive medical care, diagnosis, and treatment. People who are in the hospital for medical care or treatment are called **patients.**

There are at least five main reasons that people become patients in hospitals.

- Mrs. Jones is at the hospital to give birth to a baby. The hospital has special equipment that will make the birth easier and safer. Most women go to a hospital to give birth to their babies.
- Sarah has been in a serious automobile accident. The accident was not expected to happen. An accident is one kind of an emergency. An **emergency** is an unexpected illness or injury that requires immediate medical attention. People usually go to a hospital for such care.

*What is a hospital? A patient?*

*List five reasons people become patients.*

**FIGURE 12–1.** General information about a patient is given in the admitting office.

- Mr. Green had a sudden heart attack. There are special machines at the hospital that might help keep him alive. People go to a hospital when special machines are needed for medical care or treatment.
- Bradley needs an operation to have his tonsils removed. An **operation** is a procedure where the body is made healthier by surgery. People go to a hospital when they need to have surgery.
- Doctors have not been able to diagnose Tyler's illness from his symptoms. At the hospital, they will examine Tyler carefully. They will conduct tests to give them information. From this information they will be able to make a diagnosis. People go to the hospital to have tests to learn why they are not healthy.

What are five reasons that people become patients in hospitals? What hours of the day do these patients need care?

A hospital never closes. It is open 24 hours a day to give patients the treatment needed. A hospital does not even close on a holiday. Day and night, weekdays and holidays, people are ill or injured and babies are born.

*Why are hospitals always open?*

## Think About It

1. Why is it important for a hospital to stay open on a holiday or weekend?

# Types of Doctors at the Hospital

If you are a patient in a hospital you may meet many kinds of doctors. You may meet an intern. An **intern** is a doctor who has finished medical school and is completing a year of further study at a hospital. This extra year of study is called an **internship.**

*Who is an intern? What is an internship?*

You may meet a resident. A **resident** is a doctor who is getting advanced training in special areas of medical care or surgery. This advanced training is called a **residency.** The doctor who is caring for Mr. Green is doing a residence in heart care. She is doing advanced study under the direction of other doctors. She wants to become a specialist. A **specialist** is a doctor who works in one special area of medicine.

*Who is a resident? What is a residency?*

At some hospitals, there are interns and residents who are learning more about medical care. There are also doctors who have finished their formal training. These doctors teach the doctors who are still in training. They plan the medical care and treatment for their patients. Then they check to see that the interns and residents carry out these plans. They all work together to provide good medical care.

## Think About It

**2.** How is an intern different from a resident?

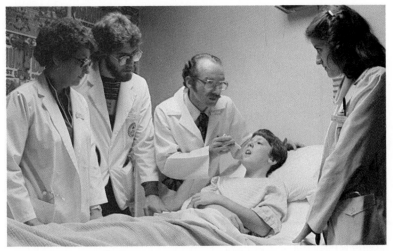

Hickson-Bender Photography/Community Medcenter Hospital, Marion, Ohio

**FIGURE 12–2.** Doctors work together to help a patient.

# People Who Work at the Hospital

Many other people work at a hospital. There are people working day and night. These people care about the patients in the hospital. Because they care, they work closely as a team. The patient needs the help of each team member. The hospital would not run smoothly without each team member. Table 12-1 contains a description of the people who work at a hospital.

## Activity
### Hospital Careers

Look at the chart "People Who Work at a Hospital." Select one of these people. Write a report on this hospital career. Describe the training needed by this person. Describe what responsibilities this person has at the hospital.

*Table 12-1*

| People Who Work at a Hospital | |
|---|---|
| * **Administrator** | The person who runs the hospital and plans the budget. |
| **Clerical Helper** | A person who does typing and helps with the medical records. |
| * **Dietitian** | A person who plans meals for patients. |
| * **Doctor** | A person who is trained to study disease and diagnose and treat sickness. |
| * **Licensed Practical Nurse** (LPN) | A person who assists the registered nurse. |
| * **Medical Technologist** | A person who does blood, urine, and other tests. |
| **Nursing Assistant** | A person who helps the nurse care for patients. |
| * **Occupational Therapist** (THER uh pust) | A person who retrains patients in skills of daily living. |
| * **Physical Therapist** | A person who helps patients move. May work with exercises, heat, light, crutches, braces. |
| * **Registered Nurse** (RN) | A person who cares for patients under the orders and instructions of the doctor. |

* Must be licensed after completion of training and passing state examinations.

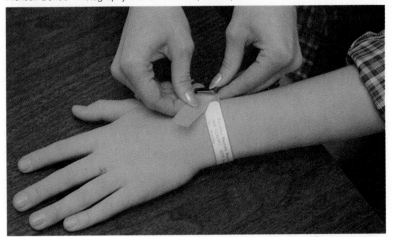

**FIGURE 12–3.** An identification bracelet can help reduce confusion in an emergency situation.

# A Day at the Hospital

Do you remember Bradley? Bradley needed to go to the hospital to have his tonsils removed. Let us follow Bradley's stay in the hospital as a patient.

First, Bradley arrives at the hospital with his parents. They stop first at the registration desk. A record will be made of Bradley's entering the hospital for care. The person at the desk asks many questions. What is Bradley's full name and address? Who is his doctor? How will Bradley's father arrange to pay for the hospital stay?

Then Bradley's name is placed on a small card. He is given a hospital number which is typed on the card too. The card is put in a plastic bracelet. Bradley wears the plastic bracelet on his wrist. Hospitals use these plastic bracelets for identification. If Bradley is in surgery or asleep, someone can check his bracelet for his name.

*Why do hospital patients wear an identification bracelet?*

Next some tests are done. A nurse will record Bradley's height and weight. Bradley's temperature is taken. A nurse takes blood from Bradley's arm with a needle and draws blood into a glass tube. The glass tube has Bradley's hospital number on it. Then Bradley is asked to go to the bathroom. He collects urine in a cup. A medical technologist then examines the blood and urine samples. The results of all the tests will be added to Bradley's medical record.

Bradley must also have a chest X ray as do all hospital patients. An X ray is a picture of his lungs. A specially-trained person knows how to read the X ray. It may show signs of certain diseases. In Bradley's case the X ray showed his chest to be healthy.

Now Bradley is taken to his room. He puts on a hospital gown and gets into bed. The bed has rails on the side to keep patients from falling out of bed. Bradley is in a very large room called a ward with several other patients.

He looks around the ward. It is very clean. Hospitals are kept clean to be free of germs. Next to each bed is a cord or a button that can be used to notify the nurse that a patient needs help.

One of the patients in Bradley's ward has a wheelchair. This patient cannot walk. Soon a new patient arrives on a stretcher. A **stretcher** is a table upon which a person is moved. Sometimes a stretcher is on wheels.

Many things are happening in the ward. Bradley hears someone call a doctor's name over the loudspeaker. Then the nurse tells him it is time for dinner. Bradley has a table next to him that fits right over his legs when he is in bed. He can move the table himself.

After dinner, Bradley hears that visiting hours have begun. All hospitals have special hours when families and friends come to see patients. The visiting time is limited so

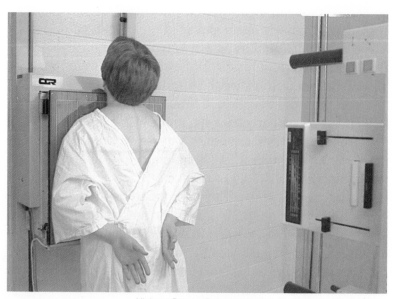

**FIGURE 12–4.** Chest X-ray photos reveal important information to the doctor.

Hickson-Bender Photography/F.C. Smith Clinic, Marion, Ohio

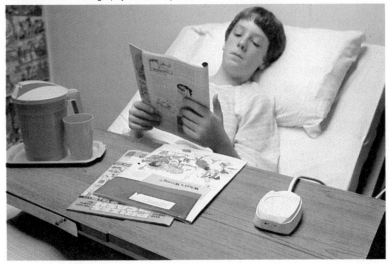

**FIGURE 12–5.** Hospital patients require rest.

patients do not get too tired. Patients need time to rest and take many tests. Bradley's mother comes during visiting hours to see him.

After visiting hours, a nurse wheels a cart around the ward. There are cups filled with medicines on the cart. One cup has Bradley's name and hospital number on it. This is to be certain that he gets the right medicine. Bradley needs to sleep. Tomorrow he will have his operation.

## Activity

### *Hospital Pamphlet*

Write a pamphlet about hospitals. Remember to include the following information.

1. What is a hospital?
2. Reasons people become patients in hospitals.
3. Types of doctors at hospitals.
4. People who work at the hospital.
5. What a patient can expect to happen when checking into a hospital.

## Think About It

3. Why does the identification bracelet have a number on it?
4. Why is it important to have all medicine cups labeled with a name and number?

# The Operating Room

The **operating room** is a separate place in a hospital where surgery is done. The people who work at a hospital call it O.R. The people who work in O.R. wear special clothes. They cannot wear their regular clothes because there may be germs on them. The clothes are usually blue or green. This is to cut down on glare from the bright lights in the O.R.

Each person in surgery wears a mask to cover the lower half of the face. A cap covers the hair. Outside O.R. there is a scrub room. The **scrub room** is a room in which everyone scrubs hands, wrists, and arms thoroughly.

After Bradley is wheeled into the operating room on a stretcher, he is moved to the operating room table. The operating room table is really not a table. It is more like a machine. It tilts and moves forward or back, up or down, or to the side. This makes it easier for the doctor and the assistants to work. Bradley is covered with clean blankets and made very comfortable. He has been given drugs to make him sleep through the operation. He will not feel any pain while the doctor operates to make him well.

After the operation, Bradley stays in the recovery room until he is awake. The **recovery room** is a special room where nurses check Bradley's heartbeat and breathing. They want to be certain that Bradley is recovering. **Recovering** means returning to normal health after surgery or an illness. Then Bradley is taken back to his hospital room. When Bradley is ready to go home, his doctor will tell him how to care for himself.

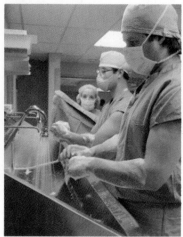

Hickson-Bender Photography/Community Medcenter Hospital, Marion, Ohio

**FIGURE 12–6.** Doctors and nurses scrub their hands and arms thoroughly with a special soap before an operation.

*What is the purpose of an operating room?*

*Describe an operating room table.*

*Why are patients taken to a recovery room after surgery?*

# The Emergency Room

The **emergency room** is the special place in the hospital that handles unexpected illnesses or injuries. A person might have been injured in an automobile accident or fire. Or perhaps someone swallowed poison or fell from a high place.

*Why do people go to the emergency room?*

Dan McCoy/Rainbow

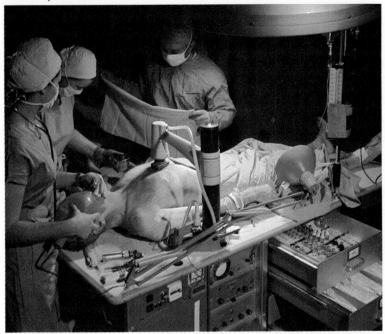

**FIGURE 12–7.** People who work in an emergency room are trained to handle unexpected situations.

Most people are brought to the hospital by someone they know. Others may need to be rushed to the hospital. When someone needs emergency care, you can call the police or fire department. You can also call the emergency medical service for ambulance service.

*How do most people get to the hospital when there has been an emergency?*

As soon as a patient arrives at the emergency room a medical record is started. If the patient cannot answer questions someone who is with the patient answers.

If you take someone to the emergency room, here are some things you should do.

- Be calm.
- Remember others may need to be helped first.
- Stay with the patient until the nurse or doctor comes.
- Try to remember the facts about an accident.
- Write down instructions for when you go home.

## Think About It

5. Why are some people upset while they are waiting in an emergency room?

6. Why are there usually more people in an emergency room on a weekend or holiday?

## Summary

1. Patients in hospitals receive medical care, diagnosis, and treatment for illnesses or injuries.
2. At a hospital, there may be many types of doctors—interns, residents, and specialists.
3. Many people work in teams to give good hospital care to patients.
4. When a person becomes a patient in the hospital, a record of admittance and several medical tests are made.
5. The operating room is a separate room in the hospital where patients have surgery.
6. The emergency room is a special place in the hospital that handles unexpected illnesses or injuries.

## Words for Health

*Below are vocabulary words and incomplete sentences. Complete each sentence with the correct vocabulary word. DO NOT WRITE IN THIS BOOK.*

| | | |
|---|---|---|
| emergency | internship | residency |
| emergency room | operation | resident |
| hospital | recovery room | specialist |
| intern | | |

1. A(n) _____ is a special place where people receive medical care, diagnosis, and treatment.
2. The _____ is a special place in the hospital that handles unexpected illnesses or injuries.
3. A(n) _____ is completing advanced training in medical care or surgery.
4. A (n) _____ is a procedure where the body is made healthier by surgery.
5. Advanced training completed by a resident is called a (n) _____.
6. After an operation, a patient is taken to the _____.
7. An unexpected illness or injury that requires immediate medical care is a (n) _____.
8. A (n) _____ is a doctor who has finished medical school and is completing a year of further study at a hospital.
9. A (n) _____ is the year of study that an intern completes at a hospital.
10. A doctor who works in one special area of medicine is called a (n) _____.

## Look at Your Health

1. What are four reasons that people become patients in hospitals?
2. What are three types of doctors that might be found at a hospital?
3. Name some people who work at the hospital.
4. Why do patients wear plastic name bracelets at the hospital?
5. What is a chest X ray?
6. What is a ward?
7. Why are visiting hours at a hospital limited?
8. Why do people who work in the operating room wear special clothes?
9. What are two reasons for going to an emergency room?
10. What is a fast way to get to the emergency room?

## Actions for Health

*Think about the following situation. Then respond to the questions that follow.*

*Situation:* You and your best friend are playing in your backyard. Your friend falls and cannot move. You suspect that your friend needs help.

1. What three things might you do?
2. Which one is the best to do? Why?

## Individual Research

1. Write a report about the Intensive Coronary Care Unit that may be found in many hospitals.
2. Make a list of the different kinds of specialty hospitals. What type of service is provided at each?

## LIFE MANAGEMENT SKILLS

- Identify hospitals in your community and know about services they provide.
- Be aware of the different types of specialists you might need for medical care.
- Consider various hospital health careers.

# Drugs, Alcohol, and Tobacco

How are drugs classified?

How do alcohol and tobacco affect the body?

How can you make responsible decisions about drugs?

Larry Hamill

# Some Facts About Drugs

Eli Lilly and Co.

*The machinery will direct the capsules along the line until they are finally packaged. What do the capsules contain? What will the label say? Who will buy them? When is it safe to use drugs?*

**E**very day you make choices about many different things. You may need to make a choice about spending time with your friends or going someplace with your parents. You might have to decide on a gift for a friend's birthday. No matter what kind of a choice you make, there are certain things to consider.

Among your considerations are the following:

- Is the action I will follow safe?
- Is the action I will follow healthful?
- Is the action I will follow legal?
- Will the action follow my parents' guidelines?

**GOAL:** *You will learn how different types of drugs can harm the body.*

## What Is a Drug?

What is meant by the word "drug"? Several young people your age were asked to define this term. Here are a few of their answers.

- A drug is something that helps a sick person get better.
- A drug is something that can be dangerous.
- A drug is a pill you swallow.
- A drug is a type of medicine.

Each answer is correct. Yet each answer only partly defines the term drug. A **drug** is any chemical that you put in your body that changes the way you think or feel. The kind of change a drug causes in your body depends on the type of drug you use.

*What is a drug?*

## Think About It

1. How do you think a drug differs from food?

**FIGURE 13–1.**

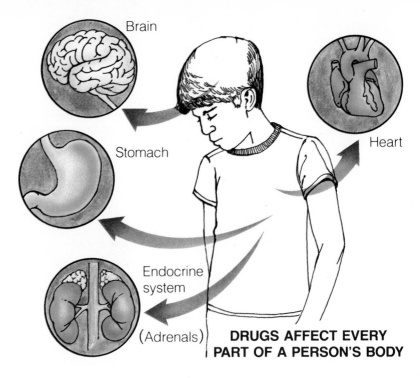

Brain

Stomach

Heart

Endocrine
system

(Adrenals)  **DRUGS AFFECT EVERY
PART OF A PERSON'S BODY**

## Section

## 13:2

*What is a depressant?*

*Describe one way depressants are helpful.*

# Depressants

A **depressant** is a drug that slows down the rate of the body's activities. As a result, body parts do not work as they should. Depressants belong to a large group of drugs. They can be abused, if they are not used safely.

Depressants have many medical uses. Doctors may give their patients depressants called barbiturates (bar BIHCH uh ruts) if these patients cannot sleep well. Sometimes doctors will give patients pills called tranquilizers. Tranquilizers are depressants. Tranquilizers may be prescribed by a doctor for nervous conditions or extreme cases of illnesses.

You may sometimes have trouble falling asleep. You may be nervous at times. For example, you may worry about a test at school. Most people your age experience feelings like that. They are normal. But these feelings of restlessness and worry do not need to be treated with depressants. These feelings will go away.

Some depressants are called narcotics. Narcotics are dangerous drugs. Morphine is a narcotic. It is not legal to use morphine except with a doctor's permission. Heroin is another narcotic. It is not legal to buy, sell, or use heroin.

Taking barbiturates and tranquilizers with a doctor's permission is legal. However, some people do not use these drugs the right way even when they are prescribed by a doctor. Some people may take more of these drugs than they should. Perhaps they should take one pill every four hours. Instead, they may take two pills at one time. This is a form of drug abuse. The drug is not being used as the doctor intended it to be used.

People who abuse drugs like this can harm themselves. If these people give a depressant to another person, that person can also be harmed. It is not legal for a person to give another person a depressant drug.

Depressants can be abused in another way. If a person takes two depressant drugs at the same time, that person can become very ill. Two drugs of any kind should be taken together only with a doctor's knowledge and permission.

There is risk involved in using depressants. Using some drugs can become a habit. A **habit** is something that is repeated again and again until it becomes an automatic behavior.

Using a depressant can also lead to tolerance (TAHL uh runts). **Tolerance** means that the body needs larger and larger amounts of a drug to get the same effect.

Use of depressants can lead to physical dependence. **Physical dependence** is a bodily need for a drug. Physical dependence is also called addiction (uh DIHK shun). If people become addicted to a drug, they will go through withdrawal when that drug is taken away.

**Withdrawal** is an illness. It occurs when a drug which causes physical dependence is no longer taken by a person. Withdrawal symptoms, such as vomiting and headaches, are similar to other illnesses. In most cases, a person who takes drugs under a doctor's care will not become physically dependent, and therefore will not experience withdrawal.

Psychological (si kuh LAHJ ih kul) dependence is another term you should know. **Psychological dependence** is

*What is a habit?*

*What is physical dependence?*

**FIGURE 13–2.** These depressant drugs are legal to use only with a doctor's written permission.

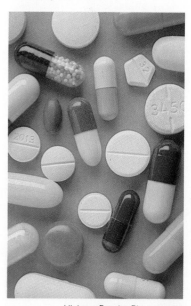

Hickson-Bender Photography

Depressants **181**

an emotional need for a drug. This need does not cause the same serious signs of withdrawal as those caused by physical dependence on a drug.

Remember, using and abusing depressants is dangerous. Depressants can cause physical dependence, tolerance, and withdrawal. Depressants can also be habit-forming and can cause psychological dependence. Because they can be dangerous, depressants should be taken only under a doctor's orders.

*Why can misuse of depressants be dangerous?*

## Think About It

**2.** Why do some people who cannot fall asleep use depressants?

**3.** How is withdrawal similar to other illnesses?

**4.** Why might physical dependence on a drug be more dangerous than psychological dependence?

---

## Section

## 13:3

## Stimulants

*What is a stimulant?*

There are several drugs that belong to a group of drugs called stimulants. **Stimulants** are drugs that speed up the rate of the body's activities. As a result, body parts do not work as they should.

**FIGURE 13–3.** Chocolate products contain caffeine. The seeds inside the cocoa pod are a source of caffeine.

One kind of stimulant is caffeine. **Caffeine** is a stimulant found in cola soft drinks, coffee, cocoa, and tea. The caffeine in these drinks is a minor stimulant. Yet many people know that the caffeine in these drinks is strong enough to affect them. For example, a person may choose not to drink a cola soft drink in the evening before going to sleep. The caffeine in the cola may make it difficult to fall asleep. Instead, this person may choose a more healthful drink such as fruit juice or milk.

Because many people do not want to drink caffeine, many companies make caffeine-free products. Some of these are caffeine-free soft drinks, tea, and coffee. Some drinks are available with reduced caffeine content.

Ian Berry/Magnum Photos

Tim Courlas

**FIGURE 13–4.** There is a variety of low-caffeine or caffeine-free products.

Some stimulants produce effects that are stronger than those of caffeine. They are major stimulants. Amphetamines (am FET uh meenz) are a group of major stimulants. It is not legal to buy or use these stimulants without a doctor's written permission. Amphetamines cause the heartbeat rate to increase. This causes the heart to work harder than it should. Amphetamines also cause the blood pressure and breathing rate to increase. They have a direct effect on a center in the brain that influences appetite. Because of these effects, the medical use of amphetamines is limited.

Using amphetamines is dangerous. Amphetamines may cause a person's moods to change rapidly. The use of amphetamines can lead to tolerance and psychological dependence and can also cause death.

*How do stimulants affect the heart?*

## Think About It

**5.** How can amphetamines affect a person's sleep?

# Hallucinogens

A **hallucinogen** (huh LEWS un uh jun) is an illegal drug that affects a person's senses. A person who uses hallucinogens may not hear or see things as they really are.

There are several kinds of hallucinogens. Some examples are PCP, LSD, and mescaline (MES kuh leen). There are many different harmful effects from each of these drugs. The effects can be different each time the drug is used. The effects of taking these drugs can be very dangerous. People can become scared. They may have a false sense of power. This might cause them to do something which can injure or even kill themselves and other people.

## Think About It

**6.** Why are hallucinogens very dangerous?

# Marijuana

**FIGURE 13–5.** Marijuana

**Marijuana** (mer uh WAHN uh) is a drug that contains many harmful ingredients including THC. Marijuana is the leaves, stems, and flowering tops of the cannabis plant. This drug is illegal to use, sell, or buy.

Many of the effects of marijuana are caused by THC. When a person smokes marijuana, THC can cause many changes in that person's body. Great stress is put on the circulatory system. The heartbeat rate and blood pressure increase. This can harm the heart and blood vessels.

Marijuana changes the way a person's nervous system works. Messages from the brain to the muscles are not sent properly. This causes poor muscle coordination and increases the chances of having accidents. A person's moods also change. Marijuana causes confusion and changes in a person's senses.

Research shows that long-term use of marijuana may cause lung diseases including lung cancer. Long-term use causes tolerance and dependence in some people.

# Prescription Drugs

A **prescription** (prih SKRIHP shun) is a doctor's written order that allows a person to get a special medicine. This special medicine is called a **prescription drug.**

*Define prescription.*

Maria is not feeling well. This morning she awoke with a sore throat and a fever. She went to her doctor who ordered a medicine to help her feel better. The doctor wrote the name of this medicine on a special form. Some other information was also written on the paper. Maria took this paper to a store that sells prescription drugs. At the store she paid for her medicine and took it home.

Maria's doctor wrote a prescription. You can get prescription drugs only from a pharmacist. A **pharmacist** is a person who reads the doctor's prescription and fills the order. Only a doctor can order a prescription drug.

The same prescription drug can affect people differently. Every person's body is different. A doctor knows how a person's body works. The doctor knows the kind of prescription drug your illness requires. Prescription drugs will often help you get better when you are ill.

*Why should prescription drugs be prescribed only by a doctor?*

Prescription drugs can cause side effects. A **side effect** is an unwanted result after taking a drug. Dizziness is an example of a side effect. If you get a side effect from a drug, stop taking it and contact your doctor.

---

## HOW YOU CAN SAFELY USE PRESCRIPTION DRUGS

**FIGURE 13–6.**

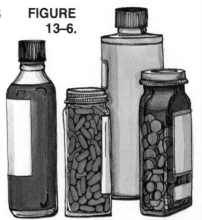

- Know the name of the drug.
- Know when and how often the drug should be taken.
- Know if the drug can be taken with other medicines.
- Know what the possible side effects are.
- Know if you should finish the entire prescription even if you feel better.
- Read the label of the drug container each time to make sure you are taking the right drug.
- Do not take a drug prescribed for someone else.
- Call your doctor if you get a side effect from a prescription drug.

---

## Think About It

**7.** Why is it dangerous to take another person's prescription drug?

**8.** Why should you call a doctor if you have a side effect after taking a drug?

## Section

### 13:7

## Over-the-Counter Drugs

Tim had an important meeting at the office. After the meeting, he got a headache. On his way home from the office, Tim stopped at a store that sells drugs. He saw a medicine on the shelf that helps relieve headaches and he bought it. After taking one pill, his headache went away.

*Define OTC.*

Tim bought an over-the-counter drug. An **over-the-counter drug,** or **OTC,** is a drug that can be bought without a doctor's prescription. OTC drugs are sold at drugstores, supermarkets, and other places. OTCs are not as strong as prescription drugs. This is why OTCs can be purchased without a doctor's prescription. They are used to treat problems such as occasional headaches and minor aches and pains. Aspirin is a common OTC drug.

*What problems do OTC drugs treat?*

**FIGURE 13–7.** Different kinds of drugs can be purchased in a drugstore.

Gerard Photography

## WHAT YOU SHOULD KNOW ABOUT OVER-THE-COUNTER DRUGS

Always read OTC labels for the following information.

- The symptoms treated by the drug.
- How often the medicine should be taken.
- The amount of medicine that should be taken.
- The number of days the medicine should be taken.

Read warning labels.

- If the OTC drug does not relieve symptoms, see a doctor. You might allow a serious illness to go untreated.
- Read the label for possible side effects.
- Read the label for possible cautions.
- If side effects occur, stop taking the drug.
- Inform a doctor if you intend to take OTCs with a prescription drug. Taking both types of drugs at the same time could cause serious problems.

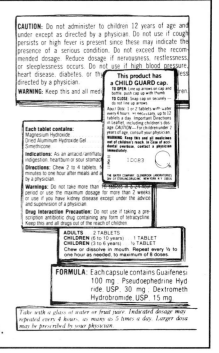

**FIGURE 13–8.**

## Activity

### OTCs Can Be Dangerous

Many people think that OTC drugs are safe at all times. This is not true. Almost every label or container of an OTC drug has a caution or warning written on it. (1) Look for five OTC drugs in your home. (2) Write the name of each drug in the left column. (3) Write the warnings or cautions in the right column. Write all answers on a separate sheet of paper. (4) What information surprised you?

| Name of Drug | Cautions or Warnings |
|---|---|
|  |  |
|  |  |
|  |  |

## Think About It

**9.** What are some examples of OTC drugs?

**10.** Why should you read the labels on OTC drugs?

## Tamper-Resistant Drug Packaging

Think about the last time you were in a store in which prescription and over-the-counter drugs were sold. Have you ever thought about how many over-the-counter drugs there are? These drugs have different forms—pills, capsules, liquids. Regardless of the type of OTC drug you may have seen, all drugs must meet certain government standards before they can be sold. This requirement helps make the drug safer to use.

Companies that make drugs must test all new drugs. Some tests may take as long as seven years before a drug is considered safe. This is one way people who buy and use these drugs are protected.

There is another way that OTC drugs are made safer for use. Drugs are sold in tamper-resistant packages. A tamper-resistant package is a sealed container. It is easy to determine whether or not the container has been opened before it is purchased. If there is evidence that the package has been opened, it should not be purchased. The drug may not be safe to use.

There are different kinds of tamper-resistant seals or closures.

- **Inner membrane seals.** These are paperlike seals under screw-top jar caps. They cover the opening at the top of the drug container.

- **Lid bands.** These are bands that must be broken the first time a lid is opened.

- **Shrink bands.** These are bands that are heated and sealed around a lid. They have to be peeled from a lid.

- **Unit-dose packaging.** These are capsules that are sealed at the capsule joint. Capsules usually contain a single dose of the medicine.

There is another regulation concerning tamper-resistant packaging. Drug companies must place a message on the outside of drug packages. This message states that the product must not be bought or used if the seal is broken. According to health officials, the best defense for protection is an educated buyer. All consumers must be educated about tamper-resistant packages.

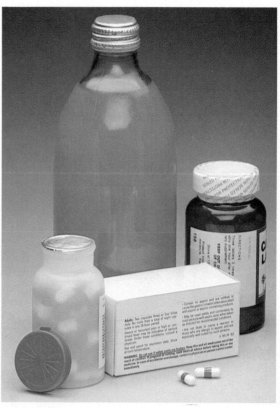

Hickson-Bender Photography

## Summary

1. A drug is something put in the body that changes the way a person thinks or feels.　　*13:1*
2. Depressants can be habit-forming and cause physical and psychological dependence.　　*13:2*
3. Stimulants are harmful drugs with limited medical use.　　*13:3*
4. Hallucinogens are harmful drugs that affect a person's senses.　　*13:4*
5. Marijuana is a harmful drug that is illegal to use, sell, or buy.　　*13:5*
6. Prescription drugs can be very helpful when they are taken properly.　　*13:6*
7. Before taking an OTC drug, you should read the label on the container.　　*13:7*

## Words for Health

*Below are vocabulary words and incomplete sentences. Complete each sentence with the correct vocabulary word. DO NOT WRITE IN THIS BOOK.*

| | |
|---|---|
| caffeine | physical dependence |
| depressant | prescription |
| drug | prescription drug |
| habit | psychological dependence |
| hallucinogen | side effect |
| marijuana | stimulant |
| OTC | tolerance |
| pharmacist | withdrawal |

1. _____ is a drug made from parts of the cannabis plant.
2. Something that is repeated again and again is a(n) _____.
3. A drug which slows the rate of the body's activities is a(n) _____.
4. _____ is a stimulant drug found in coffee.
5. A drug that can be bought without a doctor's prescription is called a(n) _____.
6. A type of drug which speeds up the body's activities is called a(n) _____.
7. A bodily need for a drug is called a(n) _____.

# Review

8. A drug that affects the body's senses is a(n) _____.
9. The general name for a chemical that causes changes in the body is a(n) _____.
10. When a person's body needs larger and larger amounts of a drug to get an effect, this person is said to have a(n) _____ for the drug.
11. An order written by a doctor that allows a person to get a special medicine is called a(n) _____.
12. An unwanted result after taking a drug is called a(n) _____.
13. People who are addicted to a drug and are then not able to take that drug may go through _____.
14. A medicine that a person can get only by a doctor's permission is called a(n) _____.
15. An emotional need for a drug is known as _____.
16. The person who reads a doctor's prescription and fills the order is called a(n) _____.

## Look at Your Health

1. What is a drug?
2. How do depressants affect your body?
3. What are some benefits of depressants?
4. Why is it dangerous to build up a tolerance to a drug?
5. How might physical dependence be more dangerous than psychological dependence?
6. Why is coffee considered a stimulant?
7. How can stimulants be dangerous?
8. Name three kinds of hallucinogens.
9. What is an example of a side effect?
10. Where are OTC drugs sold?

## Actions for Health

*Think about the following situations. Then respond to the questions that follow.*

*Situation:* Your aunt is a very nervous person. She says she cannot fall asleep unless she takes special sleeping pills her doctor has prescribed.

One night your aunt says, "I'm really having a lot of trouble falling asleep. I think I will take three pills instead of one. That should help me for sure."

1. Do you think your aunt should take three pills instead of one pill? Why or why not?
2. What could you tell your aunt?
3. What could you do if your aunt did not want to listen to your advice?

*Situation:* Your friend Sharon has had a headache every day for the past week. Sharon tells you that she has been taking aspirins each time her headache appears. She is now taking 10 aspirins each day. Each time Sharon takes aspirins, she says her headache is relieved.

1. Why might you suggest that Sharon see a doctor?
2. What would you tell Sharon?
3. What could you do if Sharon does not listen to you?

## Individual Research

1. Articles about drugs appear often in the newspapers. Cut out newspaper articles about drugs for one week.
2. Write a report about a new drug that has been developed to treat or cure a disease.
3. Check for medicines in your home. Which medicines can still be used? Which medicines do you feel should be thrown out? Why? This activity should be conducted with an adult member of your family.
4. Make a list of the different drug commercials on radio and television you hear or see during one week. Which types of drugs are advertised most often? Why do you think they are advertised most often? Which of these drugs do you have in your home?

# LIFE MANAGEMENT SKILLS

- Try to use products that are caffeine-free.
- Follow safety rules for using prescription drugs.
- Know how to read an OTC drug label.
- Avoid the use of any illegal drug.

# Alcohol and Tobacco

Ruth Dixon

*Different kinds of tobacco are used in different products. Some tobacco plants need full sunshine; others grow better in shade. All tobacco plants contain drugs. How do these drugs affect your health? How can you protect yourself from the harmful effects of the drugs in tobacco?*

There are many facts you need to know about alcohol and tobacco. These facts will make you aware that alcohol and tobacco contain drugs that can harm a person's body. When you learn the facts about these drugs, you can make responsible choices.

**GOAL:** *You will learn that alcohol and tobacco contain drugs which influence the function of your body.*

---

## What Is Alcohol?

**Alcohol** is a depressant drug found in beer, wine, whiskey, and some other drinks. It forms when yeast cells act upon certain grains, vegetables, or fruit sugars. The action of the yeast cells upon grains, vegetables, or fruit sugars is called **fermentation** (fur mun TAY shun).

The alcohol made from this type of fermentation is called **ethyl** (ETH ul) **alcohol,** or grain alcohol. Alcohol also can be made from wood products and petroleum by another process. This type of alcohol is called **methyl** (METH ul) **alcohol,** or wood alcohol. Methyl alcohol is poisonous. A person who drinks methyl alcohol can become blind or die. Ethyl alcohol is the kind of alcohol found in alcoholic beverages. It, too, is dangerous. This is why it is not legal for young people like you to buy or drink alcohol in public places.

Alcohol is a colorless and clear liquid. When a person drinks alcohol, a burning sensation is felt. This feeling can occur in the mouth, throat, or chest area. The greater the amount of alcohol in a drink, the greater the burning feeling. A sip of whiskey produces a greater burning feeling than the same amount of beer. This is because whiskey has more alcohol in it than beer does.

*What is alcohol?*

*What kind of alcohol is found in alcoholic beverages?*

There are three main kinds of alcoholic drinks. One kind is beer. Beer has less alcohol than the other kinds of alcoholic drinks. American beer usually contains about 3 to 6 percent alcohol. Wine is another general kind of alcoholic drink. Most wines contain about 12 percent alcohol. Some wines have more alcohol. These wines may contain up to 22 percent alcohol. The third kind of alcoholic drinks, hard liquors, contain the largest amount of alcohol. Hard liquors include brandy, gin, vodka, rum, and whiskey. Hard liquors contain as much as 50 percent alcohol.

## Think About It

1. Why is methyl alcohol dangerous?
2. Why might a person feel more of a burning sensation when drinking brandy than when drinking beer?

Ward's Natural Science Establishment, Inc.

**FIGURE 14–1.** Wines are made from the sweet juices of grapes.

## What Alcohol Does in the Body

*Name three kinds of alcoholic drinks.*

When you eat food, it enters your digestive system. Once in your digestive system the food is chemically changed. It takes about eight hours for food to be digested. The bloodstream carries the digested materials throughout the body. Cells are nourished by these materials.

Alcohol does not need to be digested. Alcohol begins to enter the bloodstream soon after a person drinks it. In the bloodstream, alcohol is circulated to all parts of the body, including the brain. The effects of alcohol can be felt several minutes after drinking it. A person might feel light-headed and act silly. The rate at which alcohol can affect a person depends on several things.

## How alcohol enters the bloodstream

*Name three conditions that determine how quickly alcohol will affect the body.*

Alcohol enters the bloodstream mostly from the stomach and the small intestine. If a person's stomach is empty, some of the alcohol will pass quickly into the small intestine. If there is food in the stomach, alcohol will not pass as quickly to the small intestine. Alcohol will enter the bloodstream more slowly from the stomach than from the small intestine. Therefore, food in the stomach will reduce the effects alcohol will have on a person.

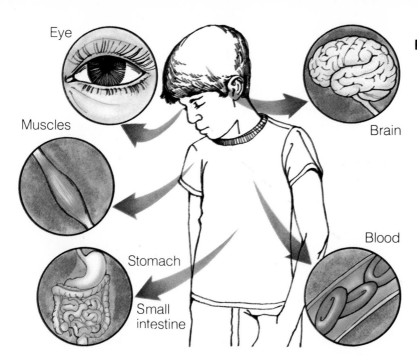

Eye

Muscles

Stomach

Small intestine

Brain

Blood

## The amount of alcohol in a drink

Different types of alcoholic drinks contain different amounts of alcohol. For example, whiskey contains more alcohol than wine. A person who drinks whiskey may begin to feel the effects of the alcohol sooner than a person who drinks wine.

## Blood alcohol level

With each drink, the amount of alcohol in a person's blood increases. The level of alcohol in a person's blood is called the **blood alcohol level**. Larger persons have more blood and other fluids in their bodies than smaller persons. Therefore, a larger person who drinks the same amount of alcohol as a smaller person will have a lower blood alcohol level. The greater a person's weight, the greater the amount of alcohol required to produce an effect.

## Think About It

3. How can food in a person's stomach determine the effects of alcohol on the body?

4. Why might alcoholic drinks affect smaller people sooner than larger people?

# How Others' Drinking Can Affect You

**MADD**FACTS
Mothers Against Drunk Drivers / 916 966-MADD

**ALCOHOL RELATED CRASHES...**
Are the leading cause of death between the ages of 15 and 24.
Cost over 5 billion dollars annually.
Took over 25,000 lives last year
   **731 died in Ohio alone (36% of all crashes)**

2/3 of all alcohol related fatal crashes are caused by identifiable problem drinkers.

Any given Friday or Saturday night, 1 out of 10 drivers is driving while legally intoxicated.

Less than 40% of all those arrested for driving while under the influence are convicted.

65% of drivers who kill themselves in single-car wrecks are drunk.

Of every 2,000 drunken drivers, only one is arrested.

**AND THE PROBLEM GOES ON.**

**FIGURE 14–3.** Some parent groups want to protect the lives of young people.

*Why is knowledge about alcohol important?*

Since most people your age do not drink, you may question why you need to know about alcohol. The story that follows may change your thinking. Someone else's drinking can affect you.

It is time for you to leave the wedding party. Uncle John, who is 5'10" tall and weighs 130 pounds, says he will drive you home. He drank an ounce of whiskey. Uncle Fred is the same height and weight as Uncle John. Uncle Fred drank an ounce of wine. Both uncles are good drivers. With which uncle would you feel safer?

You would be safer riding with Uncle Fred. The wine he drank would not have the same effect as an ounce of whiskey. Knowledge about alcohol can help you make a decision which can help protect your safety.

It is a well-known fact that alcohol in a person can cause that person to have an accident. A driver who drinks is much more dangerous than a driver who does not drink. Each year, thousands of young people suffer injuries and death because of people who drink and then drive.

Alcohol also causes other problems. Young people may be affected by a close family member who drinks. This person may be difficult and unpleasant. Normal activities like studying at home may suffer.

## Think About It

5. What is the relationship between drinking alcohol and a person's ability to concentrate?

6. Why can alcohol-related problems cause family relationships to suffer?

## Protecting Yourself

There are some ways for you to help yourself and others avoid the effects of alcohol.

J. Kevin Fitzsimons

**FIGURE 14–4.** Seeking help for an alcohol-related problem is a wise decision. A young person does not have to drink alcohol to have alcohol-related problems.

## Stand by your decisions

If another person's drinking can affect you, try to protect yourself. You can say "No, thank you" when asked to ride with a person who has had too much to drink.

*Name two ways you can protect yourself and others from the effects of alcohol.*

## Seek help

You can help people with alcohol-related problems. Ask your parents, teacher, or guidance counselor to give you information about local community groups that help people affected by alcohol. Groups that help people with alcohol-related problems are listed in the telephone directory.

### Activity
**Seeking Help**
There are many sources of help for people with alcohol-related problems. Look through your telephone book and list five organizations or programs you think can help persons in your community with alcohol-related problems. Along with your classmates, make one large list of all the places available for help.

**Section**

## Cigarette Smoking: Your Concern

**14:5**

People your age know that cigarette smoking is harmful to health. Studies show that beginning to smoke at an early age is harmful to health. Some people your age think that smoking cannot affect them.

*What is the relationship between smoking and age?*

Ted Rice

**FIGURE 14–5.** Bad habits can lessen your enjoyment for work and life just as bad habits can affect your tennis game.

They make statements such as:

- I'm too young to get heart disease.
- Lung cancer only strikes older people.
- If I don't die from cigarette smoking, I could die getting hit by a car. So why stop something I enjoy?

People who make statements like these are not aware of the facts about smoking. These people may not know that the effects of their health habits can remain for a lifetime. What they do now will affect them when they are older. Look at the development of an athlete. To be an athlete, you must develop skills. Suppose you have the skills to become a great tennis player. When you play against people your age, you usually win. However, you have a bad habit. You shift your feet the wrong way when getting ready to hit the ball. The longer this habit is continued, the more difficult it is to break. While you may be winning now, it probably will not last. The bad habit will affect your play.

Developing healthy habits which do not include smoking is also important. However, smoking is a more difficult habit to break than a wrong foot shift in tennis. The following section will explain why.

## Think About It

7. Why is it important for people your age to learn the facts about cigarette smoking?
8. Why is cigarette smoking a habit?

## Tobacco and Your Health

Did you know that cigarette smoke contains over 1000 different substances? Many of these substances are drugs. As with other drugs, you can develop a psychological dependence to the drugs in tobacco. **Nicotine** is one example of a stimulant drug in tobacco. When a smoker inhales or breathes in nicotine, changes occur in the body. One such change is heartbeat rate. Each cigarette smoked causes an increase in a person's heartbeat rate. This causes a smoker's heart to work harder than it should.

*Name one stimulant drug found in tobacco.*

Another dangerous substance in cigarettes is tar. **Tar** is a brown, sticky substance in cigarette smoke. Tar can cause cancer in smokers. A smoker will have tar along the air passages leading to the lungs. The air passages include the mouth, throat, and windpipe. Tar also forms a lining in the lungs of smokers. This interferes with the exchange of oxygen from the lungs to the bloodstream. The heart must work harder to pump oxygen to body parts. The buildup of tar in the lungs can affect people even your age. Look at the chart about Lorraine and Gail.

| Lorraine, Smoker | Gail, Nonsmoker |
|---|---|
| • Breathes fast after walking up one flight of stairs<br>• Cannot run ¼ mile<br>• Tires easily during physical activity | • Breathes at resting rate after walking up one flight of stairs<br>• Can run a mile<br>• Can play during physical activity without tiring too easily |

Lorraine and Gail might be similar in many ways. However, Gail does not smoke. Gail seems to be in better physical condition than Lorraine. Do you think smoking affected Lorraine?

Clark is on the school track team. As part of his training, Clark runs five times around the block in his neighborhood every evening. One of his neighbors was watching Clark as he ran. The neighbor was smoking a cigarette. When Clark finished, the neighbor said, "I couldn't even run once around the block." But the neighbor continued smoking.

Perhaps you have heard smokers make similar remarks at one time. If a smoker made that comment to you, what would you say?

**FIGURE 14–6.**

*What is tar?*

## Think About It

9. Why should people who have heart disease not smoke?

10. Why should athletes not smoke?

## Sidestream Smoke

**FIGURE 14–7.** Sidestream smoke can be either visible or invisible. It can cause your breath and clothes to smell.

You may feel that smokers have a right to smoke. You may believe that smoke from another person's cigarette cannot affect you. However, studies now show that sidestream smoke can be dangerous to your health. **Sidestream smoke** is smoke you inhale from other people's cigarettes even if you are not smoking. Studies show that nonsmokers who work in a smoky area can be harmed. They can suffer the same effects as if they smoked one to ten cigarettes a day.

Most states now have laws that protect the nonsmoker from cigarette smoke. There are separate areas in restaurants, theaters, and other public places for nonsmokers and smokers. What are some other nonsmoking areas? Most smokers and nonsmokers support this idea. To protect your lungs, it is wise to stay away from people while they are smoking.

## Smokeless Tobacco

Most people are aware of the hazards of cigarette smoking. Because of this, some of these people have decided to use smokeless tobacco. Smokeless tobacco comes in two forms—chewing tobacco and snuff. Chewing tobacco is made from chopped tobacco leaves that are pressed together. The tobacco is placed between the cheek and gums. Snuff is powdered tobacco that is placed between the cheek and gums.

Both chewing tobacco and snuff are dangerous to health. People who use these forms of tobacco increase their chances of getting cancer of the mouth and throat. Smokeless tobacco also damages gum tissue. This may lead to tooth disease as well as cause teeth to fall out.

Like smokers, users of smokeless tobacco find it difficult to stop using tobacco. The nicotine in smokeless tobacco has the same habit-forming effects as the nicotine in cigarette tobacco.

# Review

## Summary

1. Alcohol is a depressant drug that can be harmful to a person's body. *14:1*
2. The effects alcohol can have on a person's body depends upon how much food is in the person's stomach, the amount of alcohol in a drink, and the blood alcohol level of the person. *14:2*
3. Your health and safety can be affected by another person's drinking. *14:3*
4. You can help yourself and others from the effects of alcohol. *14:4*
5. Starting to smoke at an early age is extremely harmful to health. *14:5*
6. Tobacco contains many substances that are harmful to the body. *14:6*
7. Nonsmokers are harmed by the smoke from a smoker's cigarette. *14:7*
8. Smokeless tobacco causes many health problems and is habit-forming. *14:8*

## Words for Health

*Below are vocabulary words and incomplete sentences. Complete each sentence with the correct vocabulary word. DO NOT WRITE IN THIS BOOK.*

| | |
|---|---|
| alcohol | methyl alcohol |
| blood alcohol level | nicotine |
| ethyl alcohol | sidestream smoke |
| fermentation | tar |

1. The amount of alcohol in a person's blood is called the _____.
2. The smoke a person inhales from a smoker's cigarette is called _____.
3. Another name for grain alcohol is _____.
4. A stimulant drug found in tobacco is _____.
5. When yeast cells act upon grains, vegetables, or fruit sugars, a process called _____ takes place.
6. The depressant drug found in wine is _____.
7. Another name for wood alcohol is _____.
8. The brown, sticky substance found in cigarette smoke is called _____.

## Look at Your Health

1. What are three examples of drinks made with alcohol?
2. What is the difference between ethyl and methyl alcohol?
3. Which type of liquor contains the largest amount of alcohol?
4. What are three factors that determine how fast alcohol can affect a person?
5. Why can alcohol affect a smaller person sooner than it can affect a larger person?
6. How can you be affected by another person's drinking?
7. What are two things you can do to protect yourself or others from the effects of alcohol?
8. Why is a habit like cigarette smoking dangerous to a person's future health?
9. What are two dangerous substances found in cigarette smoke?
10. Why can sidestream smoke be a problem for the nonsmoker?

## Actions for Health

*Think about the following situations. Then respond to the questions that follow.*

*Situation:* You and a friend are riding bikes in the street. You see a person getting ready to get in a car and drive. This person appears to act silly. This person cannot walk straight, and has trouble trying to open the car door with a key.

1. Why might this person be acting this way?
2. Why might it be dangerous for you and your friend to continue riding bikes in the street?
3. What should you and your friend do?

*Situation:* Your friend Dan seems to be sad during the past several days. When you ask Dan if anything is wrong, he says everything is fine. Your friend Wanda lives next door to Dan. Wanda tells you that she feels sorry for Dan. She said Dan's father has been coming home drunk each night and getting into arguments with everyone in the family.

1. What assumption about Dan might you make?
2. Name three things you can do to help Dan.
3. Of the three things you can do to help Dan, which do you think might be the best? Why?

## Individual Research

1. Cut out three alcohol advertisements from newspapers or magazines. How do these advertisements encourage people to buy these products? What is it about the advertisements that helps to sell alcohol?
2. Write an advertisement that tells people not to drink. What points would you try to get across? What should people know about responsible drinking?
3. A psychiatrist may help people who have alcohol-related problems. Describe how a person becomes a psychiatrist.
4. Copy the following chart with different body parts listed. In the column to the right, describe how each body part can be affected by cigarette smoke.

| Body Part | How It Is Affected by Cigarette Smoke |
|-----------|----------------------------------------|
| mouth | |
| heart | |
| lungs | |
| brain | |
| throat | |

# LIFE MANAGEMENT SKILLS

- Avoid any drinks that contain alcohol.
- Be aware of how another person's drinking can affect you.
- Stick with your decisions not to drink.
- Be aware of the harmful effects of tobacco on your health.

# Making Responsible Choices

Ellen Lappa

*Decisions, decisions. Which trail would you choose for skiing? Which code applies to you? Are you a beginner? If you are, that fact would help you to decide on the beginner's hill. Some decisions are more difficult to make. How do you make decisions? What are some things that influence your choices?*

# Chapter 15

n this chapter, you will learn that there are important guidelines to consider in making decisions. These guidelines focus on what is safe, healthy, and legal, and on what actions follow parents' rules.

**GOAL:** *You will gain an understanding about how choices are made and how important it is to make responsible decisions.*

**Section**

## Decision Making

**15:1**

In this story, Sheryl has two choices. If you were Sheryl, what would you do?

Sheryl delivers newspapers in her neighborhood. The money she earns is put in a savings account in the bank. Sheryl is saving money to pay for her college education. On her paper route one day Sheryl saw a bicycle for sale. It was just the kind she had always wanted. Sheryl knew that if she bought it she would have to use some of the money in her savings account. Sheryl must make a decision. Should she buy the bicycle with the money she is saving for college? Should she not buy the bicycle?

**Decision making** is deciding which of two or more choices to make. Sheryl can use some of her money she is saving for college to buy a bicycle. If Sheryl were not interested in buying a bicycle, she would not need to make a decision. All of her money would be used for college only.

*Define decision making.*

**FIGURE 15–1.** Decision making involves making a choice to help you be at your best.

Decisions about drugs are some of the most important decisions you will have to make. When making a decision about drugs, here are four important questions you will need to answer.

- Is this drug safe to use?
- Will this drug be helpful to my health?
- Is it legal to buy or use this drug?
- Would my parents approve of my using this drug?

All decisions about drugs should consider the above questions. An answer of "no" to any of these questions will indicate that the best decision would be not to use a drug.

## Think About It

1. Why are two or more choices needed to make a decision?

**Section**

**15:2**

## Factors That Influence Decisions

Have you ever thought about some of the ways that your decisions are influenced? You may or may not be aware of some of these things.

## Facts

When you make decisions, you must be aware of the facts. At some time in your life, you will make decisions about drugs. Some of these decisions may be
- whether or not to smoke a cigarette.
- whether or not to take a certain medicine.
- whether or not to drink alcohol.

Chapters 13 and 14 in this unit presented some facts about drugs. When you know the facts about drugs, you are better prepared to make an informed decision about drug use. An **informed decision** is a choice that is made after considering the facts.

*What is the relationship between knowing facts and making a decision?*

## Peer pressure

Peer pressure plays an important role in your decisions. **Peer pressure** is the influence people of your age group have upon you. Think about some of the things you do each day. Have you ever thought about why you do these things?

*Define peer pressure.*

> You and your friend are shopping for something to wear to your class graduation party. Your friend says, "Buy this shirt. The colors are great. Besides, that's the same kind I'm going to buy. I know some of the other people at the party are going to wear the same kind."

*What kinds of effects can peer pressure produce?*

Perhaps you decide to go along with your friend's suggestion. Although you may not know it, you were feeling peer pressure. Your friend might have pressured you into buying that shirt. Peer pressure can have a positive, healthy effect on your decision. It can also produce a negative, unhealthy effect.

Let us see how peer pressure can have a positive or negative effect on your decisions. Perhaps you wanted to buy the shirt described above. You may have said to yourself, "I really like this shirt, but I do not know if it will look good on me." Your friend says, "I think that shirt will look great on you." You decide to buy the shirt. Your friend helped you to make a decision. Later, you feel glad that you bought the shirt. In this case, peer pressure had a positive effect. Your friend went along with your feeling. In many cases, peer pressure can help you make a positive choice.

**FIGURE 15–2.** Will you be affected by the influence of your peers when you shop for clothes?

Larry Hamill

Peer pressure can also have a negative effect. Suppose you tried on the shirt. While looking in the mirror, you say, "This shirt looks terrible on me." Your friend says, "You should buy the shirt. It doesn't look that bad." Suppose you buy the shirt. After buying the shirt, you decide not to wear it. You are not happy about your choice. You realize you bought the shirt because your friend said you should. In this case, peer pressure was negative.

Peer pressure will play a role in many choices you will make as you grow up. Some of these choices may involve drug use. Whether or not you will use drugs may depend upon how your friends influence you.

## Your family

Your family members play an important role in your decisions. Many of your decisions are based upon what your family members believe and do. Studies show that persons your age are less likely to misuse drugs if they feel loved by their families. Studies also show that persons your age often follow the behavior of their parents. For example, you are less likely to smoke if your parents do not smoke. Many people believe that the family is the best prevention for drug misuse.

## Your parents' knowledge

Your parents have more experience and are older than you. They may know many things that you do not know. They can use this knowledge to help you make responsible decisions.

## Your family's understanding of your needs

Family members can help each other. Since you most likely are with your family more than other people, your family is aware of your needs. Many people who misuse drugs may have a certain need. For example, some persons may misuse drugs because they have a need to be liked by their friends. They feel their friends may not like them unless they use drugs. If you tell your family members about your concerns, they can help you. Perhaps you can do things together when you are having problems with your friends. How else do you think your family can help you?

**FIGURE 15–3.** Many young people respect the influence their families have on their decisions.

Doug Martin

Roger Burnard

**FIGURE 15–4.** Your family can understand your needs by sharing important activities together.

## Your family as listeners

All people need someone with whom they can talk. Think about the last time you had a problem. Did you talk with someone? Did you feel better after your talk? Everyone has problems. When you have a problem, there are several things you can do. Many people share their problems with someone who will listen. Family members can be good listeners. People who have someone with whom they can discuss a problem are less likely to take drugs. They may then solve their problem.

*Why is it important to discuss problems with family members?*

## Activity

### Who Influences Your Decisions?

Many people may play a role in the decisions you make. On a sheet of paper, describe a decision you made recently. Then answer the following questions. (1) Who was involved in influencing your decision? (2) Who played the most important role in influencing your decision? (3) Why did you make the decision? (4) How valuable was the influence of others in your decision? (5) Why were you pleased or not pleased with your decision?

## Think About It

2. Why should you know the facts about drugs?

3. How is peer pressure a strong influence on decisions?

4. Why are members of your family important to you?

## How You Make a Decision

When you make a decision, there are many things you must consider. In this story, many steps take place before a decision is made.

Some of your friends have come to your house after school. After awhile, your friend Glenn suggests that everyone go outside and play basketball. Your other friend, Sol, has another idea. Sol says, "I have some cigarettes. Why don't we try smoking them?" You have a concern. You do not want to smoke. You know that your parents do not allow anyone to smoke in your home. You want to follow their rules. You tell Sol, "No one is going to smoke here." Sol says, "You're chicken. You're afraid to smoke."

Here are the steps to take before making a decision. Consider each one carefully.

*What are the five steps involved in making a decision?*

### Identify the problem

The first step in making a decision is to identify the problem. One problem in the story was whether or not to smoke. For every decision, you must identify the problem.

### Identify ways to deal with the problem

There are several ways to deal with Sol. You can suggest that he can smoke if he wants to. You can agree with him and you can smoke. You can also ask him to leave your house. You can tell Sol you want him to stay but that

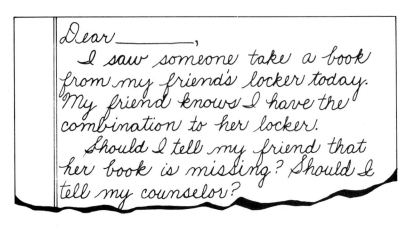

**FIGURE 15–5.** When you have to make a decision about a problem, it sometimes helps to write down your thoughts.

Dear _____,
I saw someone take a book from my friend's locker today. My friend knows I have the combination to her locker.
Should I tell my friend that her book is missing? Should I tell my counselor?

he cannot smoke in your home. Besides identifying a problem, you should look at different ways to solve the problem.

## Think about the possible results

You should think about the pros and cons of all possible decisions. For example, what would be the pros and cons of smoking when Sol asked you? What would be the pros and cons of asking Sol to leave your home? What would be the pros and cons of allowing Sol to smoke? What are the pros and cons of telling Sol you want him to stay but he cannot smoke in your home? Looking at pros and cons helps you make an informed decision.

## Make a decision

After you examine the advantages and disadvantages, you should make a decision.

## Evaluate the decision

To evaluate means to judge or rate. When you take a test, your teacher may place a number or a score on your test paper. This helps the teacher determine what you know and do not know. This is one way your teacher can evaluate your knowledge.

When you make a decision, you should evaluate the results. Suppose you told Sol he cannot smoke in your house. You listened to Glenn, and you and your friends went outside to play basketball. If you evaluate this decision, you may find the following.

- You felt good because you exercised instead of smoking.
- You felt good because you did not have to worry about getting caught by your parents.
- You felt good because you stood by your feelings.

After evaluating this decision, you probably would say you made the best choice. People who use drugs often fail to go through all the steps in making a decision. They may not identify the problem. They may not think about the different choices they can make. Remember, a responsible decision should consider what is safe, what is healthy, what is legal, and how it follows parents' guidelines.

*What does evaluate mean?*

**FIGURE 15–6.** The results of making a healthy decision will make you feel good about yourself.

Larry Hamill

**FIGURE 15–7.** Healthy decisions are often made by working with other people.

 **Activity**

*How You Make A Decision*

Read the following case study. After this case study are the five steps needed to make a decision. For each step, describe what would take place.

> You are at a party at your friend's house. One of your friends suggests that everyone taste some wine that was brought to the party. Everyone else has a taste of the wine. The bottle is now handed to you.

1. Identify the problem.
2. Identify ways you can deal with the problem.
3. Think about the possible results of your decision.
4. Make a decision.
5. Evaluate your decision.

## Think About It

5. In making a decision, why is it important to identify the problem?
6. How can you tell when you have made a good decision?

---

## Section

## 15:4

# How to Be Drug-Free

*What is meant by being drug-free?*

Almost everyone at times uses prescription or OTC drugs. What does it mean to be drug-free? To be **drug-free** means to do things without the misuse of drugs.

## Choose friends who are drug-free

You saw how peer pressure can be positive and negative. Studies show that people who use drugs have at least one close friend who also uses drugs. How do you think friends who use drugs can affect you? Choose friends who help you to always be at your best.

## Attend only drug-free activities

You can avoid drugs if you do not go where they may be. For example, you may decide to stay home if you know that some people will be drinking at a party.

## Identify goals for yourself

A **goal** is something you work toward. When you identify goals, you have something to work toward. When you reach your goal, you feel good. If you feel good, you enjoy life. Many people take drugs because they have no goals.

## Follow healthy habits

People who follow healthy habits feel good. When you exercise, eat the proper foods, and take good care of your body, you feel healthy. People who feel healthy often avoid drugs.

## Think About It

7. Why do you think friends can be an important influence on your decision about drugs?

8. What is the relationship between having nothing to do and drug use?

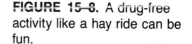

*Name four ways to be drug-free.*

**FIGURE 15–8.** A drug-free activity like a hay ride can be fun.

213

## Crack and Designer Drugs

Cocaine use has become a major drug problem for people of all ages. Cocaine is an illegal stimulant drug that is obtained from the leaves of the coca plant. It is usually used by sniffing.

Cocaine is an extremely harmful drug. It can cause blood pressure to rise and can damage the heart. Cocaine can also kill. It causes the electrical waves in the heart to work abnormally. This can lead to heart failure. In the summer of 1986, a famous college basketball player who was going to play professionally lost his life because of cocaine use.

Now there is a new drug that has become a major health problem. This drug is called crack. Crack is an illegal and harmful drug that is made from cocaine.

Users of crack are harmed in many ways. Crack harms the electrical functioning of the brain. This can result in unclear thinking as well as seizures. Crack is also linked to heart attacks and lung damage. Because it produces physical dependence very easily, users of crack often resort to violent crimes to get money for this drug.

Another group of drugs has caused serious health problems. They are called designer drugs. Designer drugs are drugs that are made in homemade labs. They imitate the effects of other kinds of drugs. Unfortunately, the problems resulting from the use of designer drugs often are more dangerous than those caused by the original drugs.

Unlike some other drugs, designer drugs are made by a company that tests them. As a result, these drugs can be made with just about anything. Users of designer drugs have been known to acquire lifelong disorders from these drugs. The users of designer drugs also place their lives in jeopardy. Many users have died because they experimented with designer drugs.

The evidence is clear about crack and designer drugs. They are extremely dangerous. Any use of these drugs could be fatal.

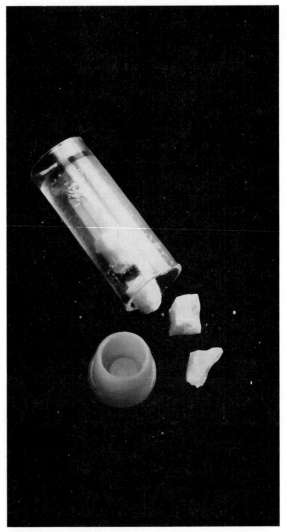

Ed Gallucci

# Review

## Summary

1. A responsible decision is one that is healthy, safe, legal, and one that respects parents' guidelines.    *15:1*

2. Facts, peer pressure, and your family are some of the things that influence your decisions.    *15:2*

3. Making a decision requires that you consider the following steps: identify the problem, identify ways to deal with the problem, think about the possible results of your decision, make a decision, evaluate the decision.    *15:3*

4. Some of the ways to be drug-free are to: choose friends who are drug-free, attend only drug-free activities, identify goals for yourself, follow healthy habits.    *15:4*

## Words for Health

*Below are vocabulary words and incomplete sentences. Complete each sentence with the correct vocabulary word. DO NOT WRITE IN THIS BOOK.*

> decision making
> drug-free
> goal
> informed decision
> peer pressure

1. A choice you make after looking at the facts is called a(n) _____.
2. Something you work toward is called a(n) _____.
3. The process of selecting between two or more choices is called _____.
4. People in your age group who try to influence your decisions are said to use _____.
5. People who are _____ do not misuse drugs.

## Look at Your Health

1. What are two things about which people your age often make decisions?
2. Why are facts important in making a decision?
3. What are some decisions people might have to make about drugs when they get older?

# Review

4. How can peer pressure play a role in making decisions?
5. How can your family play a role in your decisions?
6. In what ways can a family help prevent drug misuse?
7. What is the relationship between having someone to talk to and taking drugs?
8. What are the five steps involved in making a decision?
9. Why is it important to evaluate decisions?
10. List two things people can do to be drug-free.

## Actions for Health

*Think about the following situations. Then respond to the questions that follow.*

*Situation:* You have been invited to a party at your best friend's house. One of your friends tells you that some of the people at the party are going to smoke cigarettes. You do not want to smoke nor do you want to be at a party where others will smoke. However, you promised your best friend you would go to the party.
Respond to the following steps in making a decision.

1. Identify the problem.
2. Identify ways you can deal with the problem.
3. What are some possible results of your decision?
4. What is your decision?
5. Evaluate your decision.

*Situation:* Your older sister is having a party at home. You are at home during the party but your parents are not. You and your sister know that your parents do not allow alcohol to be used in your home. At the party, some of your sister's friends bring a bottle of wine. You observe your sister and her friends drinking. Your sister does not know you have seen her drink.
Respond to the following steps in making a decision.

1. Identify the problem.
2. Identify ways you can deal with the problem.
3. What are some possible results of your decision?
4. What is your decision?
5. Evaluate your decision.

## Individual Research

1. There are many people who sometimes have trouble making a decision. As a result, they turn to others for help. Copy the following chart and list five kinds of persons who can help others who have problems. Describe the special skills or training that enables each of these people to help others.

| Persons Who Can Help Others | Special Skills or Training |
|---|---|
| 1. | |
| 2. | |
| 3. | |
| 4. | |
| 5. | |

2. Interview five friends in your age group. Ask your friends to answer the following question: "What do you think are the three most important things about which people your age need to make decisions?" Ask the same question to people who are about 10 years older than you. Then compare the answers given by members in both age groups. How were the answers similar? How were they different? What kinds of decisions do you think you might have to make ten years from now?

3. There are many books in your library which try to help people make decisions. List the titles and authors of three books that have been written as a guide for helping people make decisions.

# LIFE MANAGEMENT SKILLS

- Apply the criteria for making responsible decisions.
- Choose friends who support healthful behaviors.
- Understand the difference between positive and negative peer pressure.
- Consider your parents' rules when making a decision.
- Choose to be drug-free.

# First Aid and Safety

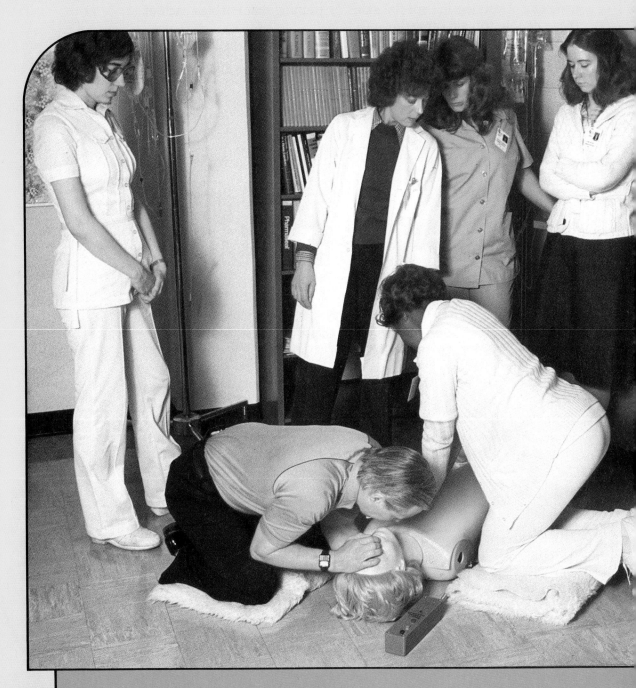

What are first aid procedures for common medical emergencies?

How are heat and cold problems treated?

How are sports and play injuries treated?

Doug Martin/Courtesy Grant Hospital, Columbus, OH.

# Medical Emergencies

Larry Hamill

*Can you hear the siren? Other drivers will pull their cars over to the side of the street to let the ambulance pass. Why is the ambulance in such a hurry? What kind of help will be needed? What training do the people in the ambulance have?*

At some time, you may be near a person who is injured or becomes ill. When this happens, your help will be needed. What you are able to do may save that person's life. This chapter will describe some important things you should know about helping an injured or ill person.

**GOAL:** *You will study first aid procedures for some common medical emergencies.*

## What Is a Medical Emergency?

Paul fell off his bicycle. His elbows and knees were scraped.

Mr. Brown had strong pains on the left side of his chest. He told his son he thought he was having a heart attack. Then he fainted.

Suppose you saw Paul and Mr. Brown in the above situations at about the same time. Whom would you help first? You should help Mr. Brown before Paul. Mr. Brown has strong pains in his chest. Chest pains and fainting are signs of a medical emergency. A **medical emergency** is an illness or injury that requires quick treatment. In a medical emergency, a person's life may be in danger. If Mr. Brown received no help, he might die. Since Paul has only scraped his elbows and knees, he will not bleed much. His life is not in danger.

*Define medical emergency.*

In a medical emergency, you might help someone by giving first aid. **First aid** is the quick care given to an injured or ill person. This care is given until a doctor arrives or an ambulance transports the person to a hospital.

*What is first aid?*

**FIGURE 16–1.** Bicycle injuries are one of the most common recreational emergency situations.

Every day, many people need first aid. The first aid for some medical emergencies will be described. This information might help you save a life.

## Think About It

**1.** Why might chest pains be considered a medical emergency?

 **Activity**

***Medical Emergency***

List or describe three medical emergencies you have heard about or seen. For each emergency describe the first aid that was given.

---

**Section**

**16:2**

## General Rules for Emergency Care

Suppose you are with a group of friends at a park. One of your friends has a radio. As you and your friends listen to the radio, your name is mentioned. The announcer says that if you call a certain number within three minutes, you will win a bicycle.

How would you react if this really happened? Would you be nervous? Would you remember the telephone number given on the radio? How would you go about finding the nearest telephone?

Many people do not know what to do first when placed in an unusual situation. They are not able to think clearly. People who cannot think clearly may make mistakes.

If you experience a medical emergency, you might become nervous. This is normal. Knowing what to do will make it easier to stay calm. Unlike other times when you must act suddenly, you cannot make a mistake in a medical emergency. Making a mistake can mean the difference between life and death for someone else or yourself.

Here are some guidelines to follow in any medical emergency.

1. Keep calm.
2. Plan what you want to do.
3. Send for a doctor or emergency squad.
4. Keep the injured or ill person still and comfortable.
5. Encourage the injured or ill person by saying, "help is on the way" and "things will improve."

Following these guidelines is helpful even if you do not know what else to do.

## Think About It

2. Why might it be easy to make mistakes in unusual situations?
3. Why should you always send for a doctor or emergency squad in a medical emergency?

**FIGURE 16–2.** Training classes are sponsored by many organizations such as the Red Cross.

*What can happen if a person cannot think clearly?*

*What are five guidelines to follow in a medical emergency?*

**Section**

**16:3**

## First Aid for Heart Attacks

Heart attacks are a leading cause of death in the United States. A **heart attack** is damage that occurs to a part of the heart. This damage is caused by a blocked blood vessel. When the blood vessel is blocked, blood cannot pass through all parts of the heart. The parts of the heart that do not receive blood can be damaged. Too much damage can cause death.

A heart attack is one of the most common serious medical emergencies. Perhaps you have seen a person suffer a heart attack. If you are near when a person has a heart attack, you can help save a life.

*What is a heart attack?*

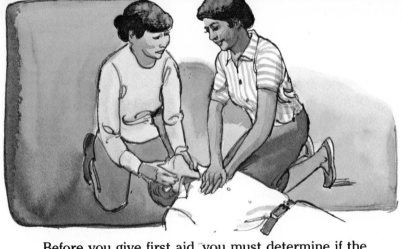

**FIGURE 16–3.** There are health organizations in your community where CPR training is given. The basics of the CPR procedure are shown.

Before you give first aid, you must determine if the person may be having a heart attack. Here are the warning signs of a heart attack.

*What are the warning signs of a heart attack?*

- A prolonged pain in the center of the chest. This pain may feel as if the chest is being squeezed or that a heavy object is on it.
- A pain that travels to the shoulder, arm, neck, or jaw. Usually the pain will be on the left side of these body parts.
- Sweating, nausea, vomiting, and shortness of breath.

All of these warning signs may go away and then return after a short while. If these signs last two minutes or more, a person might be having a heart attack.

If you think a person is having a heart attack, you can do the following.

- Place the person in a comfortable position. The person can be seated. Do not lie the person flat.
- If lying down, the person's back and head should be raised.
- Call for an ambulance or emergency squad.
- Keep the person calm. Say that help is on the way.

If the person stops breathing, someone trained in cardiopulmonary (KARD ee oh PUL muh ner ee) resuscitation, CPR, can help. **CPR** is a first aid procedure to help circulation and breathing start again if they have stopped.

*Define CPR.*

## Think About It

4. Why is it important to know the warning signs of a heart attack?
5. Why should you have CPR training?

# First Aid for Strokes

Strokes are another leading cause of death. A **stroke** is caused by a clogged or burst blood vessel in the brain. When this happens, blood cannot get to all parts of the brain. This will cause damage to some parts of the brain. A person can become paralyzed (PER uh lized). To be **paralyzed** means to lose the use of a part of the body.

*What is a stroke?*

A stroke usually occurs suddenly. A person's arms and legs might feel weak. There might also be a tingling or numb feeling in the arms and legs. Vision may also be blurred. The arms, legs, or face may become paralyzed. A stroke victim can become unconscious and die.

*What are the signs of a stroke?*

A stroke victim may be helped by doing the following.
- Make sure that the victim can breathe.
- Make the person feel comfortable. The person can be seated or lying down. If lying down, be sure the top half of the body is raised.
- Loosen clothing around the neck and waist.
- Keep the person warm.
- If breathing stops, CPR may be applied by someone who has been trained in the procedure.

## Think About It

6. Why could a broken blood vessel in the brain cause paralysis?

**FIGURE 16–4.**

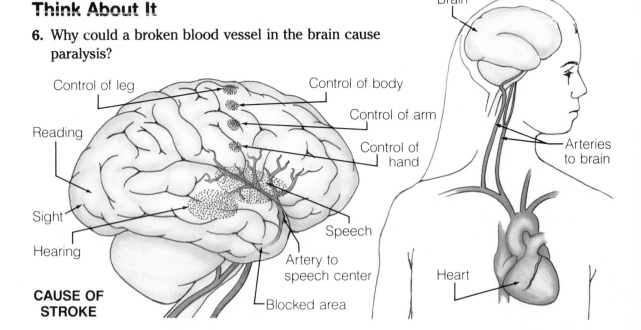

CAUSE OF STROKE

**FIGURE 16–5.** Asthma inhalers should be used according to a doctor's directions.

*What is an allergy?*

*What is a wheeze?*

## First Aid for Asthma

Many people have allergies (AL ur jeez). An **allergy** is an unusual reaction from something breathed in, eaten, or worn. Insect stings and bites may also cause allergies. A person who has allergies to materials breathed in may have a disease called asthma (AZ muh). **Asthma** is a disease that affects the parts of the body used in breathing.

When persons with asthma come in contact with something to which they have an allergy, they may have an asthma attack. During an asthma attack, a person has difficulty breathing. The person will usually wheeze (WEEZ). A **wheeze** is a whistling sound made when a person breathes. The person may also cough often.

There are ways you can help a person keep calm during an asthma attack. This alone can help reduce the effects of the attack. Most asthma sufferers have special medicines. These medicines should be taken during asthma attacks. Sometimes asthma attacks can be serious and medicine does not help. In these cases, medical help should be obtained immediately.

You might be frightened if you see a person having an asthma attack. The large blood vessels in the neck might stand out. The person's face might turn blue. These signs often occur in young children. With the right treatment, these signs shortly disappear. Rarely does an asthma attack cause death.

## Think About It

7. Why is it important to keep an asthma victim calm?

*Where is the appendix located?*

## Appendicitis

Appendicitis (uh pen duh SITE us) is a common emergency among people your age. **Appendicitis** is an inflammation of the appendix. The appendix is a small organ located slightly lower than waist level on the right side of your body. The appendix is attached to the intestine and has no known function.

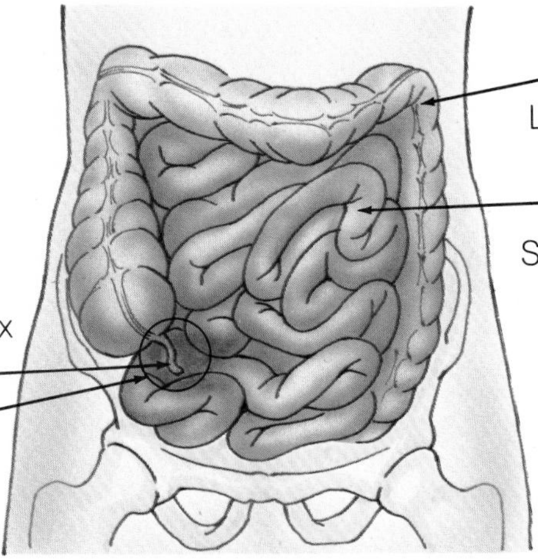

**FIGURE 16–6.** An appendix may become inflamed.

One usual sign of appendicitis is a pain in the stomach area. It might feel like a stomach ache. The pain slowly moves to the right side of the body midway between the navel and the hipbone. If this area is pressed, pain will occur as the pressure is removed.

*Name some signs of appendicitis.*

Other signs of appendicitis are tiredness, loss of appetite, nausea, and vomiting. A person's body temperature may rise. These signs can last for several hours, and then the pain can disappear. If the pain disappears, it may mean that the appendix has burst. If the appendix bursts, a person is seriously ill and may die.

It is not easy to know when a person has appendicitis. Sometimes the usual signs may not appear. The pain may not always be located on the lower right side. Only a doctor can diagnose appendicitis.

A person who has appendicitis needs medical attention immediately. Until medical help is available, prop up the person's head and shoulders. An ice bag or something else that will stay cold can be placed on the lower right side of the waist. Never give the person anything to eat or drink except little sips of water. Medicine should not be given.

The treatment for appendicitis is surgery. In surgery, the appendix is removed.

*What is the treatment for appendicitis?*

## Think About It

8. Why might it be difficult for you to diagnose an appendicitis attack?

**FIGURE 16–7.** Insulin bottles are filled in a sterile environment.

## Section

## 16:7

## Diabetic Coma

*What is the purpose of insulin?*

Certain chemicals in your body change food to energy. One such chemical is insulin (IHN suh lin). **Insulin** controls the use of sugar in your bloodstream. Some people do not produce enough insulin. A person whose body cannot produce enough insulin has a condition called **diabetes** (di uh BEET us). Diabetes usually affects people in your age group or people after age 40. When it affects people your age, it is because the body produces no insulin. People over age 40 who get diabetes usually have some, but not enough, insulin produced in their bodies.

*What causes a diabetic coma?*

One serious problem of diabetes is the danger of a diabetic (di uh BET ihk) coma. A **diabetic coma** occurs when a person's body does not have enough insulin. Several signs include a flushed face, cherry color lips, and dry skin. Often, the person's breath may smell like nail polish remover. The person may breathe heavily. These signs may occur over a period of several hours. There may be other signs, such as thirst, that occur over a period of several weeks. The person must also urinate frequently.

When a person is going into a diabetic coma, medical attention is needed. The person should be given large amounts of fluids to drink. If the person is a known diabetic, medication is usually nearby. Diabetics your age usually take an injection of insulin. An older diabetic usually takes insulin tablets. If a person goes into a diabetic coma and does not receive insulin, death can result. A person who goes into a diabetic coma needs a doctor immediately.

## Think About It

**9.** Why might a diabetic go into a diabetic coma?

## Insulin Shock

**Insulin shock** is a condition in which the body has too much insulin. This may be caused by too little food or too much insulin injected into the body.

A person in insulin shock may look pale. The skin will be cold and moist. The person may feel weak and faint. Medical attention is necessary immediately.

A person who goes into insulin shock can be given something sweet. Orange juice or 2 to 3 teaspoons of sugar in a glass of water can be given.

*What is insulin shock?*

## Activity

### Emergency Ranking

Copy the chart which lists the medical emergencies described in this chapter. Rank each medical emergency, beginning with the one you consider the most serious or needing the most attention and ending with the least serious. The one that is the most serious should have a rank of 1. Give a reason for each ranking. Do not write in this book.

**FIGURE 16–8.**

| Type of Medical Emergency | Ranking | Reason |
|---|---|---|
| Heart Attack | | |
| Stroke | | |
| Asthma | | |
| Appendicitis | | |
| Diabetic Coma | | |
| Insulin Shock | | |

## Think About It

**10.** How does insulin shock differ from a diabetic coma?

# HEALTH HIGHLIGHTS

## Sports Specialists

What is a sports injury? Perhaps you have heard the terms hip pointer, tennis elbow, torn ligaments, and shin splints. All of these are injuries that commonly occur during different sports activities. Certain sports have injuries that are common to them. For example, tennis elbow is common among tennis players. It is caused by straining the muscles and joints in the arm. Can you think of another sporting activity that may cause tennis elbow?

Sports medicine is the specialized study of all things that happen to a person's body during exercise. The purpose of sports medicine is to help all athletes reach and maintain physical fitness. Many types of sports injuries can easily be prevented. This is being done through sports medicine.

There are now more than 5000 doctors who are specialists in the field of sports medicine. In the United States there are over one hundred schools that teach sports medicine. After medical school, doctors can continue their medical training to become specialists. A sports medicine doctor is trained to diagnose and treat athletic injuries and problems. For example, he/she learns different surgical skills for operating on joints. He/she also learns how to determine the best sport for a person. For instance, if a person has a health problem, the sports medicine doctor will advise a sport that will prevent injuries or problems.

A person does not have to be a doctor to be involved in sports medicine. Many colleges offer programs which train people for a sports medicine career. Two popular careers are athletic trainer and physical therapist.

Athletic trainers are employed by high schools, colleges, and professional teams. Their job includes giving first aid, helping to prevent injuries, caring for and fitting equipment, checking playing fields and courts, and helping athletes in their physical fitness program.

Physical therapists involved in sports medicine work with injured athletes. The physical therapist uses treatments such as whirlpools, heat, ice, and special exercises to help the injured athlete. Physical therapists usually work under the direction of a doctor.

There is a physical fitness boom in the United States. Because of this, sports medicine has become an exciting and popular area in which to work. Does sports medicine sound interesting to you?

Doug Martin

230

# Review

## Summary

1. Knowing what to do can help save lives in a medical emergency.   *16:1*
2. There are general guidelines you can follow in giving care to a victim of a medical emergency.   *16:2*
3. Quick and proper care that is given to a heart attack victim can save a life.   *16:3*
4. A stroke victim should be given immediate medical attention. If breathing has stopped, CPR should be given.   *16:4*
5. Asthma is a disease which affects the parts of the body involved in breathing.   *16:5*
6. A first aider needs to seek immediate medical help for a person who is having an appendicitis attack.   *16:6*
7. Diabetic coma and insulin shock are two effects of diabetes which require first aid.   *16:7, 16:8*

## Words for Health

*Below are vocabulary words and incomplete sentences. Complete each sentence with the correct vocabulary word. DO NOT WRITE IN THIS BOOK.*

| | |
|---|---|
| allergy | heart attack |
| appendicitis | insulin |
| asthma | insulin shock |
| CPR | medical emergency |
| diabetes | paralyzed |
| diabetic coma | stroke |
| first aid | wheeze |

1. Cold, moist, and pale skin is a sign of _____.
2. Damage due to a blocked blood vessel in the heart causes a condition known as a(n) _____.
3. A whistling sound made by a person's breathing is known as a(n) _____.
4. A first aid procedure that helps to restart a person's breathing and circulation is known as _____.

# Review

5. A flushed face, cherry color lips, and dry skin are signs of a(n) _____.

6. An illness or injury that requires quick treatment is called a(n) _____.

7. A swelling and inflammation of the appendix is known as _____.

8. When a person's body cannot produce enough insulin, that person has a disease called _____.

9. When a person loses the use of a part of the body, that part is said to be _____.

10. A disease that affects the parts of the body used in breathing is called _____.

11. The use of sugar in your bloodstream is controlled by _____.

12. A clogged or burst blood vessel in the brain is called a(n) _____.

13. The quick care given to an injured or ill person is called _____.

14. An unusual reaction from something that is breathed in, eaten, or worn is called a(n) _____.


## Look at Your Health

1. Why is it important to provide quick treatment to a person during a medical emergency?
2. Why is it important to know how to give first aid?
3. Why is it important to remain calm during a medical emergency?
4. What are three guidelines to follow in any medical emergency?
5. What happens to a person's heart during a heart attack?
6. What are two signs of a stroke?
7. Why might it be frightening to see a person having an asthma attack?
8. What are four signs of appendicitis?
9. What are the first aid steps for a person in a diabetic coma?
10. How might you know if a person is in insulin shock?

## Actions for Health

*Think about the following situations. Then respond to the questions that follow.*

*Situation:* You are in your friend's house playing. Your friend's father says he does not feel well. He says, "I'm going to lie down. I have a sharp pain in my chest and I feel as if I'm going to faint. You two play quietly and don't disturb me. I need the rest."

1. What concern might you have for your friend's father?
2. What are two things you can do in this situation?
3. What do you think is the most important thing you can do?

*Situation:* On your way home from school, your friend Jim says he feels weak. You notice that he looks pale. You also know that Jim has diabetes.

1. What concerns might you have about Jim?
2. What could you do to help Jim?
3. What would you do if you were not sure what was causing Jim's condition?

## Individual Research

1. Many communities have emergency telephone numbers a person can call to get help for an injured or ill person. Look for these numbers in your telephone book. If there are no such numbers, make a list of important telephone numbers you should know. Keep this list near your telephone.
2. Find out what agencies in your community offer CPR courses. Share this information with your class.
3. Visit the emergency rescue squad headquarters in your community. Make a list of the most common types of medical emergencies to which they respond.
4. Make a list of the first aid supplies in your home. What supplies do you think you need?
5. There are many workers in hospitals who help patients adjust to their stay in the hospital. Find out what some of these educators for patients do in their jobs.

## LIFE MANAGEMENT SKILLS

- Follow the general rules when performing first aid.
- Know the signs and symptoms of a heart attack and follow the appropriate first-aid rules.
- Apply appropriate first-aid procedures for a stroke victim.
- Know the signs and symptoms of an appendicitis attack.
- Provide sweets to a person going into insulin shock.

# Dealing with Heat and Cold

H. Gritscher/Peter Arnold, Inc.

*The cross-country skier is doing his favorite kind of exercising. He is enjoying the stillness of the woods and the beauty of the snow. What happens if he is not dressed warmly? How long can he stay outdoors in such cold weather? If you live in this kind of climate, how do you stay warm? Have you ever been out in cold weather for a long time?*

F ew people enjoy being in temperatures that are very hot or very cold. Indoor temperatures often can be controlled. However, many people today enjoy being outdoors during all seasons. Outdoor temperatures cannot be controlled. Because of this, many people suffer needlessly from the effects of extreme heat and cold. Although the weather cannot be controlled, the effects of weather can. This chapter will describe how you can prevent illnesses and injuries due to the effects of heat and cold.

**GOAL:** *You will study the importance of knowing how to give first aid for problems caused by heat and cold.*

**Section**

## Heat Cramps

**17:1**

**Heat cramps** are muscle pains that result from extended physical activity. Heat cramps usually occur during warm or hot temperatures. Affected muscles feel tight and can be painful.

*What are heat cramps?*

Pat went to see her sister, Joan, run in a race for the state high school championship. It was a very hot and humid day. The race began. Joan was leading with a lap to go. Suddenly, she began to feel a pain in the calf of her leg. She could hardly run. She finished in second place. When Pat asked what happened, Joan said, "My calf muscle got tight and it hurt."

Joan suffered from heat cramps. Many cases of heat cramps occur in the calf muscle. The calf muscle is in the back of each leg, halfway between the knee and ankle.

**FIGURE 17–1.** A muscle cramp in the calf can be treated quickly by stretching and squeezing the muscle.

Pain will start suddenly. If you feel the muscle, it will be hard because it is tight. Heat cramps may also occur in the stomach or other parts of the body.

Heat cramps may also happen when the body loses too much salt. Salt is lost through perspiration. Pat's muscle cramps were not unusual. She took part in extended physical activity by running a long distance. She also ran in hot weather. This caused her to perspire a great deal and to lose salt from her body.

*What are two ways to treat heat cramps?*

Heat cramps can be treated easily. Rest and inactivity are important. Although heat cramps may disappear after several minutes, they will reappear if activity is begun too soon. If heat cramps are caused by a loss of salt from the body, the salt must be replaced. One teaspoon of salt dissolved in a quart of water should be given to drink.

Gentle stretching of the calf muscles is also needed. The person can sit on the ground. The legs should be together and extended to the front. By pointing or pulling the toes toward the body, the calf muscle will relax.

## Think About It

1. Why is salt important in your diet in hot weather?
2. What is the relationship between heat cramps and perspiration?

# Heat Exhaustion

**Heat exhaustion** (ihg ZAWS chun) is a physical reaction to being in a warm temperature for too long a time. It is usually due to extreme physical activity and sweating while in a warm temperature. It is not unusual to see runners during a long race get heat exhaustion in warm weather. Heat exhaustion occurs most often to people who are not used to warm weather and who sweat heavily.

The signs of heat exhaustion are pale, cool, and damp skin. Heavy sweating also will occur. Even though the skin may feel cool, the body temperature will be either normal or only slightly above normal. In many cases, a person will become dizzy and faint.

If you experience any of these signs of heat exhaustion, you should seek treatment. Treatment consists of

- getting to a cool place, lying down, and loosening clothing,
- drinking cool liquids, and
- sponging down with cold water.

Normally these actions will treat heat exhaustion. If a person does not respond well to these actions, medical help is needed. This person should be taken to a hospital. Each year, people die needlessly from heat exhaustion. To avoid heat exhaustion, physical activity should be reduced in hot weather. Drinking liquids and wearing the proper clothing also will reduce the risk of heat exhaustion.

## Think About It

3. Why do runners often suffer from heat exhaustion?
4. Why is drinking cool liquids important in treating heat exhaustion?

Tom McGuire

**FIGURE 17–2.** Playing in cool water during hot weather will help prevent heat exhaustion.

*Define heat exhaustion.*

*What are the signs of heat exhaustion?*

*What is the treatment for heat exhaustion?*

# Heatstroke

**Heatstroke** occurs when the body temperature is very high because of being in the sun or heat. Heatstroke is sometimes called sunstroke. In heatstroke, a person stops

*What causes heatstroke?*

sweating. The increase in body temperature occurs when sweating stops. Sweating is a healthy sign because sweat that is on the body evaporates in the warm air. This causes the body to feel cool. When sweating stops, the body cannot be cooled fast enough and the body temperature increases. When this happens, a person would experience headaches, nausea, and weakness. The skin may be hot, red, and dry. The person may act confused and appear to be clumsy. It is not unusual for the body temperature to rise to 40°C (105°F) or even to 44°C (110°F). A high body temperature destroys body tissues. The higher the temperature, the greater the tissue damage.

Several years ago, people in the southwest region of the United States suffered from an extended period of hot weather. The temperature stayed above 38°C for many days in a row. This resulted in death for many people who had heatstroke.

Heatstroke is a medical emergency. The person should be taken to the nearest hospital immediately.

Some people think heatstroke and heat exhaustion are the same thing. They are not. Heatstroke is more dangerous. Make sure you know the different signs of each.

Heatstroke can be easily prevented by remaining in cool places during hot, sunny weather. Reducing the amount of physical activity will also help.

*How can heatstroke be prevented?*

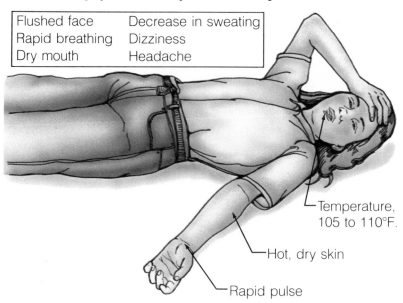

| Flushed face | Decrease in sweating |
| Rapid breathing | Dizziness |
| Dry mouth | Headache |

Temperature, 105 to 110°F.

Hot, dry skin

Rapid pulse

**FIGURE 17–3.** Heat stroke is a medical emergency that requires a doctor's attention.

## Activity

### *Heatstroke and Heat Exhaustion*

Many people confuse heatstroke with heat exhaustion. Copy the following chart on a separate sheet of paper. Complete the information.

| Condition | Cause | Signs | Treatment |
|---|---|---|---|
| heatstroke | | | |
| heat exhaustion | | | |

**FIGURE 17–4.**

## Think About It

**5.** Why is heatstroke more dangerous than heat exhaustion?

---

# Prickly Heat

**Prickly heat** is a skin rash that occurs in hot weather. It is caused by sweat glands that do not work well. Prickly heat looks like little raised dots. It causes a person to itch.

Prickly heat occurs often during physical activity. When it does occur, it should be treated. Sweat irritates prickly heat. Heat should be avoided since it may cause sweating. Bathing in cool water three or four times a day and drying thoroughly is helpful. Dusting the body lightly with medicated powder is also helpful. Avoid putting creams or lotions on prickly heat. This can block the pores or openings in the skin.

*What is prickly heat?*

*How can prickly heat be treated?*

## Think About It

**6.** Why does prickly heat occur during hot weather?

---

# Sunburn

Many people are affected by the sun each year. Some think that developing a tan is healthy. This is not true. Other than helping to relieve some conditions such as asthma or acne, lying in the sun is not healthy. In fact, too much sunburn causes the skin to begin to age sooner than it normally would. Too much of the sun's rays can cause skin cancer.

The American Cancer Society reports that 300 000 people each year develop skin cancer in the United States. Here are the warning signs of skin cancer.

- a sore that does not heal
- a change in the size or color of a wart or mole
- the development of any unusual color in a small area of the body

Most of these signs are caused by the sun. If one of these signs occur, have a medical checkup immediately.

The most common sun-related problem is sunburn. Some people are at a greater risk from sunburn than others. People with dark skin are less likely to get sunburned than are people with light skin.

There are many things you should know about sunburn protection.

- Between the hours of 10 AM and 3 PM the sun's rays are the strongest. Initially, do not lie in the sun for more than 15 minutes during these hours. After the first day, the length of stay in the sun can increase by five minutes each day.
- Clouds will not protect you from the sun. About 70 to 80 percent of the rays of the sun that cause sunburn pass through clouds.
- When you are moving around, you are less likely to become sunburned than when you are staying in one place.

Steve Lissau

**FIGURE 17–5.** Sunburn can be prevented. A sunburn can keep you from having a good time.

- You can become sunburned in the snow. Eighty-five percent of the sun's rays can be reflected from the snow.
- Use a sun lotion that contains PABA. **PABA** is a chemical that screens out the sun's ultraviolet rays which cause burning.
- Some lotions or creams can block all the sun's rays from your skin. One such cream is **zinc oxide.** If you notice a lifeguard with white cream on the nose or lips, it most likely is zinc oxide.

*Define PABA.*

If you do become sunburned, you can apply ice or towels soaked in cold water to the affected area. Cold baths and some lotions are helpful. A pharmacist can help you select the best product to treat your sunburn. Severe sunburn can cause fever and blisters. Medical help may be required.

## Think About It

**7.** Why do some people think sunburns are healthy?

**Section**

**17:6**

## Frostbite

Extreme cold may also affect your body. **Frostbite** is an injury to a part of the body due to freezing temperatures. The parts of the body most commonly affected by frostbite are the ears, nose, hands, and feet.

When cold air is combined with wind, the air temperature may feel cooler. Chances of frostbite increase. Look at Figure 17-7. You can see the relationship between wind and temperature. If you are going to remain outdoors in cold weather, you should know the wind speed and temperature. This will give you a better idea about how cold it really feels.

The signs of frostbite are usually easy to notice. At first, the affected area will be painful. There will also be a tingling feeling. If this person is not moved into a warm area, the body part will become numb and look waxy. A white cold spot will appear at the affected site.

*What is frostbite?*

**FIGURE 17–6.** The effects of frostbite can cause some serious problems. Often, toes must be removed to prevent infection throughout the body.

Lawrence Bruder/Tom Stack & Associates

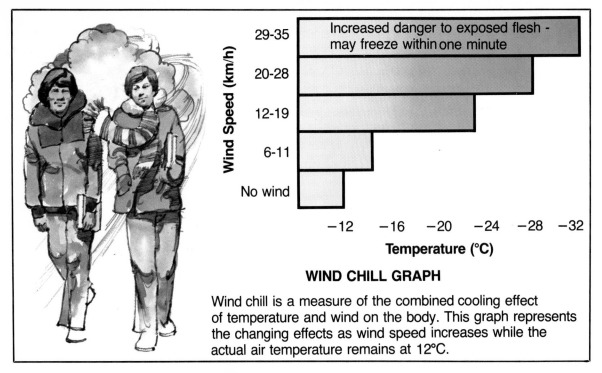

WIND CHILL GRAPH

Wind chill is a measure of the combined cooling effect of temperature and wind on the body. This graph represents the changing effects as wind speed increases while the actual air temperature remains at 12°C.

**FIGURE 17–7.**

## Activity

### *Protection from Frostbite*

Pretend you are going to be outdoors for two hours. The temperature is below freezing. Describe how you would protect each of the following body parts from becoming frostbitten—nose, ears, toes, fingers, cheeks, and legs.

*What is the first aid for frostbite?*

Medical help is needed for frostbite. If medical help is not available, first aid can be started. The frostbitten part of the body should be placed in warm water which is at body temperature. Keep the frostbitten part in the water for 20 to 40 minutes. As the body part rewarms, it will redden. Pain might also be felt. This means the frostbite is being treated properly. After 40 minutes, remove the frostbitten area from the water. Dry the area gently with a warm towel. Then keep the area warm. The person should be checked by a doctor.

## Think About It

**8.** Why are the ears, nose, hands, and feet most commonly affected by frostbite?

# Hypothermia

Hypothermia (hi poh THUR mee uh) is a condition in which the body temperature is lowered. This is due to cold, dampness, and wind. This condition can occur at temperatures above freezing. If the day is windy, chances of hypothermia increase. Think back to times when you have been swimming. On a warm windless day you did not feel cold when you got out of the water. On a cool windy day you felt cold when you got out of the water. These conditions are some that cause hypothermia.

*What is hypothermia?*

If you are outdoors on a cool day and you perspire because you are dressed too warmly, you may begin to chill. Perhaps you have been out in the rain. Your clothes got wet and you remained outdoors. If the temperature was cool, you would get chilled. Chills are a sign that the body temperature is dropping and that hypothermia might occur. Other signs of hypothermia are tiredness and poor muscle coordination. Untreated hypothermia will result in continued lowering of body temperature. If the body temperature drops too low, death can result.

*What are the signs of hypothermia?*

First aid for hypothermia includes warming the body. The person should be moved indoors and given dry clothing. Hot fluids to drink will be helpful. The person should also be wrapped in a blanket. If the person is not warm after several minutes, get medical help quickly.

## Think About It

9. What is the relationship between hypothermia and cold, damp weather?
10. Why is a person with hypothermia given dry clothing?

**FIGURE 17–8.** Providing a blanket for warmth is an important step in treating a person with hypothermia.

## Deep-Freeze Surgery

Hypothermia can be a serious medical emergency. However, the effects associated with hypothermia can be used by doctors to save lives.

During hypothermia, body activities slow down gradually. Breathing, heart rate, and blood flow decrease as the body temperature drops. Body tissues also require less oxygen to stay alive. This condition, however, can only last for a few hours. With this knowledge doctors are able to cause artificial hypothermia to help people.

Most surgical operations are performed at normal body temperature. However, doing some types of surgery at that temperature can create some problems. For example, at normal temperature many organs would be damaged if they did not get enough oxygen. By using artificial hypothermia, the blood flow can be safely stopped for an hour or longer.

At the University of Washington doctors are able to duplicate the effects of hypothermia in infants. Babies born with heart defects receive corrective surgery this way. Before surgery, an infant is given a drug to make it sleep during the operation. Then, the infant is placed in a cooling tub and surrounded with bags of crushed ice. The infant's temperature is lowered slowly to about 30° to 28°C. At this point, the doctor stops the heartbeat. This allows the doctor to operate on the tiny heart without any problems.

After surgery the infant is placed in warm water. The doctors start the heart again by gently rubbing it.

Tumors deep in the brain can also be removed with the aid of artificial hypothermia. In one such operation, doctors used artificial hypothermia to stop an adult patient's heart. This stopped the flow of blood to the brain temporarily so the doctors could perform the delicate operation more easily.

During the operation, the patient was connected to a heart-lung machine. The machine provided two functions. First, the patient's blood was passed through the machine to be cooled. The cooled blood returned to the patient's body and duplicated the effects of hypothermia. The surgery lasted 30 minutes and the tumor was safely removed.

Then, after the operation, the patient's blood was warmed, instead of cooled, as it passed through the heart-lung machine. The patient's body temperature was returned to normal after 34 minutes.

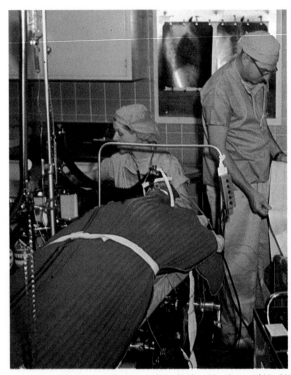

Courtesy of the National Institutes of Health

# Review

## Summary

| | |
|---|---|
| 1. In warm or hot temperatures, extended physical exercise can lead to heat cramps. | *17:1* |
| 2. Heat exhaustion can be dangerous if first aid is not given immediately. | *17:2* |
| 3. Heatstroke occurs when a person's body temperature increases too much due to being in the sun or heat. | *17:3* |
| 4. Prickly heat is a minor problem that occurs to the skin during hot weather and physical activity. | *17:4* |
| 5. Sunburn is the most common sun-related problem. Sunburn protection can be provided in several ways. | *17:5* |
| 6. A person who becomes frostbitten should be given first aid. | *17:6* |
| 7. Under certain conditions, being outdoors on a cool day can cause hypothermia. | *17:7* |

## Words for Health

*Below are vocabulary words and incomplete sentences. Complete each sentence with the correct vocabulary word. DO NOT WRITE IN THIS BOOK.*

frostbite          hypothermia
heat cramps        PABA
heat exhaustion    prickly heat
heatstroke         zinc oxide

1. A skin rash that occurs in hot weather is known as _____.
2. A cream that a person can put on the skin to block the sun's rays is called _____.
3. A person can get _____ if the body temperature rises due to being in the sun or heat.
4. An injury to a part of the body that is due to freezing temperatures is called _____.
5. A chemical in suntan lotions that helps prevent sunburn is called _____.
6. Pale, cool damp skin, and heavy sweating are signs of _____.
7. A cooling of the body temperature due to cold, dampness, and wind may result in a condition called _____.
8. Muscle pains that result from extended physical activity are known as _____.

## Look at Your Health

1. Name one cause of heat cramps.
2. How can heat cramps be treated?
3. What are three signs of heat exhaustion?
4. What are two ways to prevent heat exhaustion?
5. What is the relationship between high body temperatures and body tissues?
6. How can heatstroke be prevented?
7. Why should a person avoid putting creams or lotions on prickly heat?
8. What are three warning signs of skin cancer?
9. What parts of the body are most affected by frostbite?
10. What weather conditions cause hypothermia?

## Actions for Health

*Think about the following situations. Then respond to the questions that follow.*

*Situation:* You and your friends are playing a game of tag. After running for a while, one of your friends drops to the ground. Your friend says, "My leg really hurts. The calf muscle feels real tight. I can't stand."

1. What might be wrong with your friend's calf?
2. What may have caused your friend's condition?
3. What could you do to help your friend?

*Situation:* You are watching a long foot race. A runner crosses the finish line and collapses. The runner's skin looks pale, cool, and damp. Someone in the crowd says, "Leave the runner alone. The weather is warm enough. If we all gather around, the runner will not be able to get fresh air. Some fresh air will do the trick."

1. What might you think is wrong with the runner?
2. What could you do to help the runner?
3. What could happen to the runner if you did nothing?

*Situation:* You and your friend are going to watch your local high school football team play. The temperature is 3°C, and it is raining and windy. You probably will remain in the rain and wind for close to three hours.

1. How could this weather possibly be dangerous?
2. What kind of clothing could you wear to watch the football game?

## Individual Research

1. Collect newspaper or magazine articles that describe instances in which some of the conditions discussed in this chapter have occurred.

2. Visit a drugstore or other places where drugs are sold. Make a list of five products that help protect people from the effects of the sun. What is different about each product? What do each of the products share in common?

3. Copy the following list of different conditions that can affect you. For each condition, describe the clothing you would wear that can help prevent that condition.

| Condition | Clothing You Can Wear |
|---|---|
| Heat exhaustion | |
| Heatstroke | |
| Frostbite | |
| Hypothermia | |

4. Select a sport that you like. For this sport, describe one condition of heat or cold that is common to this sport. For example, heat cramps might be common to long distance runners. Then describe what can be done to prevent the condition common to that sport.

5. Write a report on how to become a trainer for athletes.

# LIFE MANAGEMENT SKILLS

- Stretch gently to relieve heat cramps.
- Place a person suffering from heat exhaustion in a cool place and provide something cool to drink.
- Avoid overexposure to the sun between 10 AM and 3 PM.
- Place a frostbitten body part in warm water.
- Know the first signs of hypothermia to avoid any related problems.

# Sports and Play Injuries

Walter Iooss Jr./Sports Illustrated

*The injury is painful, but he will soon get to a hospital. Meanwhile, he has received excellent first aid treatment. He is warm and safely tied to the sled. Have you ever been rescued after an injury? Why would it be a good plan to be trained to treat injuries?*

A basketball court, a playground, a jogging trail, and a schoolyard are similar. Each is an area where you can play or be active. In each of these areas, many people also become injured every day. You probably have had an injury at one time while playing. Most of the injuries received in these places are not serious. This chapter will describe the common injuries received during sports and play. Even if you do not participate in sports, you should know the information in this chapter. All of the injuries described can also occur during other activities.

**GOAL:** *You will learn how to treat and prevent injuries that are common in sports and play.*

## Scrapes

What is similar about each of the following?
- A person slides into a base during a softball game.
- A person trips and falls on the sidewalk while running.
- A person falls off a bicycle.

In each situation, the same type of injury can occur. A **scrape** is a wearing away of the outer layers of skin against a hard surface. A scrape usually results from a fall. The parts of the body usually scraped are the hands, elbows, and knees. These areas usually hit the ground first when you fall.

*What is a scrape?*

When a part of your skin is scraped, nerve cells are irritated. This is why scrapes are painful.

*Why are scrapes painful?*

Most scrapes are not serious. Usually very little bleeding will occur. Some baseball players call scrapes "strawberries" because of their appearance.

Tom McGuire

**FIGURE 18–1.** Cuts and scrapes can be prevented by wearing protective equipment.

*What can happen if germs are not removed from scrapes?*

Treatment for scrapes is simple. Wash the injured area with soap and warm water. This will clean and remove germs from the area. A bandage should be placed over a scrape that continues to bleed. This is done after the scrape is cleaned. A scab will form shortly after a scrape occurs. A scab is nature's way of covering a scrape. It is made up of red blood cells that harden. The **scab** is dried blood that forms over a cut or injury. Platelets in your blood cause the blood to clot and dry.

If germs are not removed, an infection can result. With an **infection** there is swelling and redness to the injured area. Pus will also be seen in an infection. **Pus** is a whitish material that forms around scrapes or cuts. It is made up of dead white blood cells and germs. Infections should be treated by a doctor.

Possible scrapes to some parts of the body can be prevented. Many people who play football or who roller skate wear knee and elbow pads. Wearing long sleeved shirts and pants can also help protect the knees and elbows. What other things can be done to help protect you from scrapes?

## Think About It

1. Why is there usually little bleeding from scrape wounds?
2. Why should infection be treated by a doctor?
3. Why should a scrape be cleaned before a bandage is placed over it?

## Section 18:2

### Cuts

Many people get cuts when they are playing. They may fall against a fence or step on a sharp object. There are many other ways cuts occur.

Most likely you have had a cut. Perhaps your cut healed without being treated. Usually, cuts heal without causing any permanent scar. Yet, all cuts should be treated.

*How should shallow cuts be treated?*

Like scrapes, cuts should be cleaned. A shallow cut can be washed with soap and water. If dirt remains in the cut, infection can result. Dirt is more likely to remain in cuts than in scrapes.

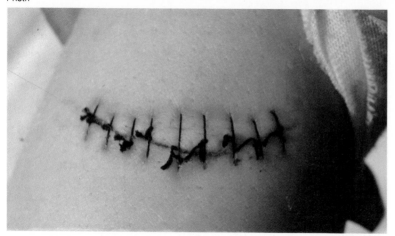

**FIGURE 18–2.** A deep cut may require stitches so the wound can heal quickly and properly.

Most cuts bleed. To stop bleeding from minor cuts, apply pressure with a bandage. This usually is enough to stop bleeding. If a cut appears deep and bleeds heavily, try to stop the bleeding by placing pressure on the cut. Get medical treatment. A doctor can close the cut area with stitches and provide any other treatment needed.

Most cuts can be prevented. Whenever playing, you should make sure the play area is free from hazards such as broken glass. Schoolyards, playgrounds, and parks should be safe. Sometimes they are not. Hazards you discover should be reported to the proper persons.

## Think About It

4. Why is dirt more likely to remain in cuts than in scrapes?
5. Why is medical treatment needed for deep cuts?

**Section 18:3**

## Sore Muscles

Sue likes to jog. She runs 1500 meters each day after school. One day, Sue's friend Jane said, "Exercise is great. I think I'll run with you today." This is the first time Jane has run very far. Although she had a difficult time keeping up with Sue, Jane completed the distance. The next morning, Jane's muscles were sore. Why do you think her muscles were sore?

Many people make the same mistake as Jane made. Jane tried to do too much too soon. She overused her muscles by running too far. Muscles that are forced to do things they are not ready to do can become injured. In Jane's case, her muscles became sore. Although sore muscles are not a serious injury, they are painful. Through proper training, muscles can be made ready to work hard and not be sore.

*How can sore muscles be prevented?*

Sore muscles can be relieved by applying warm, moist towels to the painful area. Taking a hot shower or bath will also ease the pain. These treatments should be repeated as needed.

There is a way Jane could have run 1500 meters without getting sore muscles. Whenever you start an activity that requires the use of certain muscles you should do so gradually. Jane should have run a shorter distance on her first try and increased the distance each time she ran. She would soon be able to run 1500 meters easily.

**FIGURE 18–3.**

| SPORT OR ACTIVITY | MUSCLES |
|---|---|
| 1. running | calves and upper legs |
| 2. | |
| 3. | |

## Activity
### *Muscle Soreness*
Many different activities can make your muscles sore. Copy the chart on a separate sheet of paper. In the left column, list four sports or activities you play. In the right column, identify the parts of the body in which muscles used for this sport can become sore. An example is completed.

You can get sore muscles from any activity. Perhaps you may decide to play catch with a friend and you have not thrown a baseball all winter. It is spring and the muscles you use to throw a baseball have not been used for a while. If you throw a ball too many times, the muscles in your shoulder may become sore. What could you do to prevent muscle soreness?

## Think About It
6. Why is it important to take time to train for special activities?

7. Why are sore muscles easy to prevent?

**FIGURE 18–4.** Fingers often become dislocated if a ball is not caught correctly.

# Dislocations

Your fingers, elbows, and knees are body parts that bend. They bend at a joint. A **joint** is a place where two bones meet. If you had no joints, no part of your body would be able to move. Sometimes a joint can become injured. One type of injury to a joint is a dislocation (dihs loh KAY shun). A **dislocation** occurs when a bone is forced away from a joint.

*What is a joint?*

*Define dislocation.*

Dislocations are common in many sports. Dislocations of fingers are common in basketball. When a person jumps to get a basketball that is coming down, the fingers are extended. If the basketball lands on top of an extended finger, a dislocation can result. The joint in the middle of the finger usually becomes dislocated.

If a joint is dislocated, pain and swelling will result. The pain increases if there is movement at the joint. The joint will usually be misshaped.

A dislocated finger can sometimes be treated by pulling the finger beyond the joint. Cold packs should be applied afterwards to the area. A dislocated thumb should never be pulled. A broken bone may be present. All thumb dislocations should be treated by a doctor.

*How should a dislocated finger be treated?*

## Think About It

8. Why might shoulder dislocations occur more often in football than in basketball?
9. Why should cold packs be applied to a dislocation?

# Safety in Running

Over 30 million Americans of all ages jog or run. Many of these people suffer needless injuries. There are many things you can do to prevent running injuries.

## Clothing

*What types of clothing should be worn in summer?*

Always dress for the weather. If you are running in cold weather, wear several thin layers of clothes. Do not wear a single heavy layer of clothing. Several thin layers help keep your body warmer. This can help prevent hypothermia. In warm weather, wear clothing made of lightweight fabrics. Clothes made of cotton will keep you cooler than clothes made of nylon because air goes through cotton easier.

Most running injuries occur to the feet and knees. Wear a good pair of running shoes. Good running shoes are well cushioned for foot support. Basketball and tennis shoes are not made the same way as running shoes. Your feet and knees can become injured easier if you run in these shoes.

## Running Surface

Select a running surface you like. Many people like to run on roads. For some, running on roads can injure the knees. The force of each step on the hard surface places stress on the knees. Wearing well-cushioned shoes and running on soft surfaces like grass can solve this problem.

Eric Hoffhines

**FIGURE 18–5.** Choose correct equipment for running.

Larry Hamill

**FIGURE 18–6.** Proper training includes stretching leg muscles before running.

## Training

Prepare, or train, the right way. Do not run too fast or too long at first. This can cause injury. Do you remember the story about Jane? She ran too far too soon and got sore muscles. There are other injuries worse than sore muscles. Knee and ankle injuries can result from improper training. Often surgery is needed to heal injuries to these areas. Always build up to the distances you want to run. Do not increase the distance you run by more than 10 percent each week.

*What is a good rule to follow in building up your running distance?*

## Activity

### Sport Safety

Copy the chart below on a separate sheet of paper. (1) Write the name of a sport in the left column. (2) In the middle column, describe the proper clothing or equipment needed for this sport. (3) In the right column, describe the ways you can train properly for this sport.

| Sport | Proper Clothing or Equipment | Proper Training |
|-------|------------------------------|-----------------|
|       |                              |                 |
|       |                              |                 |

## Safety in Team Sports

Most people play in team sports at some time in their lives. In team sports, you play with other members of a team. Baseball, football, and soccer are examples of team sports. Most people also play individual sports. Individual sports are played without other members playing at the same time. Some individual sports are golf, archery, and skiing.

In a team sport, many people play at the same time. When many people play at the same time, the chances of injury increase. There are things you can do to reduce the chances of becoming injured in a team sport.

### Wear the proper equipment

Many team sports, such as football, require physical contact. Serious injuries can occur in physical contact sports. The right equipment can help reduce the number of injuries. Almost every team sport requires special equipment. You should have this equipment before playing. Make sure the equipment that you wear fits well. Poorly fitting equipment can also cause injuries.

### Know the rules of the game

Many injuries occur when players do not know the correct game rules. When you know the rules, you know what you cannot do. Players sometimes become injured because they or someone else did something they should not have done.

### Know your teammates' abilities

If you know how well your teammates play, you will know how to react. Suppose a person on your basketball team throws a quick pass. You need to be alert. If you do not expect a quick pass and the ball is thrown, it can hit your face.

### Think About It

10. Why might team sports be more dangerous than individual sports?
11. Why is it important to know the rules of a game?

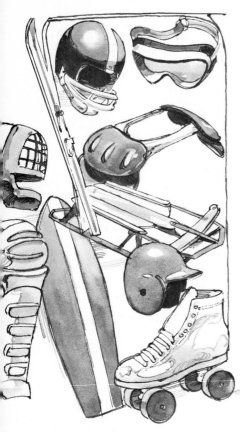

**FIGURE 18–7.**

*What are some examples of individual sports?*

*What are three things you can do to reduce the chances of becoming injured in a team sport?*

# Chapter 18

## Review

## Summary

18:1
1. Although a scrape is not a serious injury, it should be cleaned with soap and water.
18:2
2. Cuts are more dangerous than scrapes because they can hold dirt and germs.
18:3
3. Through proper training, sore muscles can be prevented.
18:4
4. When a bone is forced away from a place where it belongs, a dislocation occurs.
18:5
5. Wearing the right clothing, running on the proper surface, and proper training can prevent running injuries.
18:6
6. Wearing the proper equipment, knowing the rules of the game, and knowing your teammates' abilities will help prevent injuries in team sports.

## Words for Health

*Below are vocabulary words and incomplete sentences. Complete each sentence with the correct vocabulary word. DO NOT WRITE IN THIS BOOK.*

| | |
|---|---|
| dislocation | pus |
| infection | scab |
| joint | scrape |

1. Dried blood that forms a covering over an injured area is called a(n) _____.
2. A person has a(n) _____ when a bone is forced away from its joint.
3. The whitish material that forms around scrapes or cuts is called _____.
4. An injury which affects hands, elbows, and knees and that causes little bleeding is called a(n) _____.
5. The place where two bones meet is called a(n) _____.
6. Swelling and redness to an injured area is called a(n) _____.

## Look at Your Health

1. What parts of the body are usually affected most by scrapes?
2. What is one danger of a scrape?
3. How should a shallow cut be cleaned?

# Review

4. How can you stop the bleeding from a minor cut?
5. How can sore muscles be caused?
6. How can sore muscles be relieved?
7. What are three parts of the body where joints can become dislocated?
8. How can you treat a dislocated finger, other than a thumb?
9. What should a person wear while running in cold weather?
10. Name three things you can do to reduce the risk of becoming injured in a team sport.

## Actions for Health

*Think about the following situations. Then respond to the questions that follow.*

*Situation:* While playing baseball, your friend scrapes a leg sliding into a base. The scrape is bleeding slightly. Your friend says, "It's just a scrape. I'll continue to play. Besides, a scrape is not dangerous."

1. What would you suggest that your friend do after discovering the scrape?
2. Do you agree with your friend's statements? Why or why not?

*Situation:* Terry has noticed that Mark runs a mile each day. Terry says to Mark, "I could run a mile without any training." Mark responds by saying, "You don't know what you're talking about. If you ran a mile without training, you'd pay for it. Besides, I'll bet you cannot run a mile."

1. Do you think Terry should accept Mark's bet? Why?
2. If you were Mark, how would you respond to Terry's comment?

*Situation:* While playing basketball, your friend jams her thumb. The joint at the thumb hurts and is swelling. However, your friend continues to play. She tells you she will pull her thumb and it will feel better.

1. Would you recommend your friend continue to play? Why?
2. What would you tell your friend to do?

*Situation:* Your friend Pat has decided to begin to jog as a part of a new exercise program. Pat intends to make jogging a daily activity. Pat says, "Jogging should be great. I can wear any type of clothing and running shoes and run anywhere I please."

1. Do you agree with Pat's statements? Why?
2. What advice would you offer Pat?

## Individual Research

1. Interview a coach of a team. This coach can be from your school or another school in your community. Determine the injuries most common to the activities coached by this person.

2. Select any sport and describe how injuries in this sport can be prevented.

3. Write a report which describes an injury you suffered during sports or play. In this report, describe how you received the injury, how the injury was treated, and how the injury could have been prevented.

4. Name five parts of the body in which there are joints. For each joint, describe how it can become injured.

5. Visit an athletic trainer. Observe how this person helps others from becoming injured. You may find athletic trainers in a local high school or college.

6. Visit a store that sells different types of athletic shoes. You will notice that different shoes are made for different sports. Copy the following chart on a piece of paper. Select five sports. How do the shoes for each sport differ?

| Name of Sport | Description of Shoe Used |
|---|---|
| 1. | |
| 2. | |
| 3. | |
| 4. | |
| 5. | |

7. Report on a career in sports medicine. What training is necessary for this profession?

# LIFE MANAGEMENT SKILLS

- Wash all scrapes with soap and water.
- Follow behaviors to reduce your risk of suffering cuts when playing.
- Apply something cold to a dislocation.
- Do not run too far too soon.

# Your Environment

What are some types of pollution?

How can pollutants harm your health?

How can pollution be controlled?

Larry Hamill

# Types of Pollution

Washington Suburban Sanitary Commisssion

*The water tower is not really a globe. Did you notice that there is a map of the world painted on the tower? It reminds us that all living things in the whole world are affected by their environment. What is pollution? What causes pollution? What kinds of pollution affect you?*

Think about some of the things you need to be healthy. Some of these things are clean air to breathe, food to eat, and water to drink. Sometimes air, food, and water are affected by pollution. If so, your health may be harmed. This chapter will describe some of the types of pollution that can affect your health.

**GOAL:** *You will consider some of the pollutants in the environment that can affect your life.*

## Air Pollution

**Section**

**19:1**

Do you know how air, people, buildings, and plants are similar? They are some of the thousands of things that make up your environment. Your **environment** is everything that surrounds you.

Your environment affects your health. A clean environment can help to keep you healthy. A dirty environment can cause disease and illness. **Pollution** (puh LEW shun) is a term used to describe a dirty environment. Pollution is the presence in the environment of materials that are harmful to living things. Most pollution is caused by people.

*Define pollution.*

The air is an important part of your environment. Air is polluted from many sources. The burning of coal, gasoline, and trash contribute to air pollution. Burning these materials produces wastes that escape into the air. These wastes may be in the form of smoke, gases, or small pieces of dirt. Wastes in these forms are called **pollutants** (puh LEWT unts).

*What are pollutants?*

Rich Brommer

**FIGURE 19–1.** The combination of smoke and many different chemicals causes smog in a city.

Most air pollution comes from automobile engines. What do you think happens when a car's engine is running? The car uses gasoline and as gasoline burns, gases are produced. These gases pollute the air and are poisonous. You might not be able to see or smell these gases. Yet they enter your body when you breathe.

Other sources also pollute the air. Furnaces in homes and factories release smoke. Airplanes also burn gasoline. Industries sometimes release waste products into the air.

*In what way do mountains influence air pollution?*

In some cities, pollutants remain in the air longer than in other cities. For example, a city located in a valley may have more pollution than a city on the plains. A city in a valley is surrounded by mountains. Mountains may block winds from blowing over the city to blow pollutants away.

Polluted air can be trapped over any city. This can occur during warm weather when there is no wind. The upper warm layers of air may trap the air over the city. When this happens, pollutants are also trapped. As the amount of pollutants in the air increases, the air becomes hazy. This haziness which is made up of smoke and fog is known as **smog**.

## Think About It

1. Why do automobiles cause most air pollution?
2. Why might air over a city on a plain be cleaner than air over a city in a valley?

# Pesticides

Why do people wash fruits and vegetables before eating them? When people your age were asked this question, their response most often was, "To keep the food clean."

Most fruits and vegetables are sprayed with special chemicals called pesticides (PES tuh sides) while they are growing. A **pesticide** is a poison that kills insects and pests. Pesticides are sprayed on plants as they grow to protect the plants from being destroyed by insects, worms, and diseases. In this way, pesticides are helpful. But pesticides can be harmful if they are swallowed. Traces of pesticides can be removed by washing the fruit or vegetable.

*What is a pesticide?*

You might have pesticides in your home. Your parents might use pesticides to kill insects. This is another good use of pesticides.

Some people think that pesticides do more harm than good. They think that pesticides are dangerous to health. DDT is a pesticide that was found to be dangerous. It has been outlawed. Other pesticides are used instead.

*Why has DDT been outlawed?*

*How can pesticides drain into lakes and rivers?*

In the summer of 1981, fruitflies were found among the fruit crops in a small area in California. The crops were being destroyed by these insects. The crops were ordered to be sprayed with a pesticide called malathion (mal uh THI ahn). This pesticide would destroy the fruitflies. It also would prevent the fruitflies from entering other areas of the country. Many people did not want the crops sprayed. They felt that malathion was harmful. Government tests found malathion to be safe. Thus, the crops were sprayed.

**FIGURE 19–2.** Some foods can be made safe to eat if they are washed.

Larry Hamill

Pesticides can get into other foods besides those which have been sprayed. During heavy rains or flooding, pesticides can be washed off plants. Pesticides in the water can drain into lakes and rivers. Fish in these lakes and rivers can build up the chemicals in their bodies. If these fish are eaten by humans, traces of pesticides might also be eaten.

Pesticides are poisons. For this reason, the government regulates the use of pesticides to protect people from the effects of these chemicals.

**FIGURE 19–3.**

| Name of Pesticide | Purpose | Cautions or Warnings |
|---|---|---|
| 1. | | |
| 2. | | |
| 3. | | |

### Activity
**Pesticides in Your Home**

Many people keep pesticides in their home. When used properly, these pesticides can be helpful. You should be aware of the safe use of pesticides in your home. (1) Copy the chart on a separate sheet of paper. (2) In the left column, list the names of pesticides found in your home. (3) In the middle column, list the purposes of each pesticide. (4) In the right column, list the cautions or warnings for each pesticide.

## Think About It

3. How can pesticides be helpful to your health?
4. Why does the government test different types of pesticides?

## Section
## 19:3

# Water Pollution

Air, food, and water are important to you. You have read how the air is polluted and how pesticides can affect the food you eat. Now you will see how pollution can affect the water you use.

People get food from the water. Fish from rivers, oceans, and lakes are used for food. When water is polluted, fish can be killed.

Water pollution may be due to several reasons. Waste products from industries can be dumped into the water. Some of these products are poisons. These poisons kill plant and animal life in the water.

*What is one way water can be polluted?*

**FIGURE 19–4.** When water is not polluted, fishing is safe.

266

Many factories and industries use cool water from nearby rivers and lakes. While it is used, the water becomes hot and is often dumped back into the rivers and lakes. Hot water is a form of pollution because it increases the temperature of the river or lake. This type of pollution is known as **thermal pollution.** The change in temperature can injure the health of living things in the water. Hot water contains less oxygen than cool water. Fish die because of the high temperature and from the lack of oxygen.

Water that drains from land can also pollute rivers and lakes. The water from land may contain pesticides or other harmful chemicals. During a heavy rain, these pesticides and chemicals can be washed into the rivers and lakes.

Sometimes soil may wash away from land. Soil can muddy water and destroy living things in the water.

Sewage (SEW ihj) is another kind of pollutant. **Sewage** is wastewater from homes and industries. If untreated sewage is dumped into waterways, it pollutes the water. In many cities, sewage is carried in pipes to special treatment plants. In **sewage treatment plants,** germs and other substances in sewage are destroyed. A sewage system can overflow if it is overloaded. This causes wastes to be spilled into waterways. This results in pollution.

## Think About It

5. Why is thermal pollution dangerous to living things in oceans, rivers, and lakes?

6. In what ways can sewage pollute water?

**FIGURE 19–6.** Do you think trucks contribute to noise pollution?

## Section

## 19:4

*Why was noise pollution less of a problem many years ago?*

**FIGURE 19–7.**

| Types of Noise | Ranking | How to Avoid |
|---|---|---|
| 1) | | |
| 2) | | |
| 3) | | |
| 4) | | |

# Noise Pollution

Any loud sound that can harm a person's health is **noise pollution**. There are more people and more noise in our world to day than ever before. There are more machines and engines also. One hundred years ago, noise pollution was not as big a problem as it is today. Many of the products that make noise were not around then.

Many people are not aware of the many noises around them. Loud noises may be a part of everyday living. People may not think loud noises will hurt them. Yet noise can affect a person's health. See Chapter 20.

## Activity

### *Noises You Hear Each Day*

Each day you might hear loud noises. These noises might be harmful to your health. (1) Copy the chart on a sheet of paper. (2) In the left column, list five kinds of noises you hear each day. (3) In the middle column, rank the noises from loudest to quietest. The loudest noise should be ranked number 1 and the quietest ranked number 5. (4) In the right column, describe what you can do to help avoid each noise.

## Think About It

7. Why might some people not realize they are being affected by noise pollution?

# Radiation

Another form of pollution is radiation (rayd ee AY shun). One form of **radiation** is energy given off as light. Another form of radiation is particles given off by atoms.

Not all forms of radiation are pollutants. Radiation we receive from the sun can be helpful. It provides light and heat. You could not live without the energy from the sun.

X rays are another kind of helpful radiation. X-ray photos can be taken by a special machine to show pictures of the inside of your body. Doctors use these pictures to determine an injury or illness. Your dentist probably has taken X-ray photos of your teeth. These X-ray photos help your dentist discover problems inside your teeth and gums. Your dentist can then provide better treatment.

Radiation also treats cancer. **Cancer** is a disease in which harmful body cells multiply. Radiation can destroy some types of cancer cells.

Radiation is produced in **nuclear power plants** in the process of making electricity. Radiation from a nuclear power plant can be dangerous. If radiation escapes from such a plant, the environment around it would become polluted. Radiation can enter nearby air and water. When this happens, living things can be harmed. Contact with too much radiation can cause some kinds of cancer.

Nuclear explosions produce particle radiation. These particles may be carried thousands of miles by winds. When this happens, radiation can enter your body through the air you breathe and the food you eat.

Most countries now realize the dangers of pollution caused by radiation. As a result, the number of nuclear tests has been reduced. Nuclear power plants are also carefully regulated.

Gerard Photography

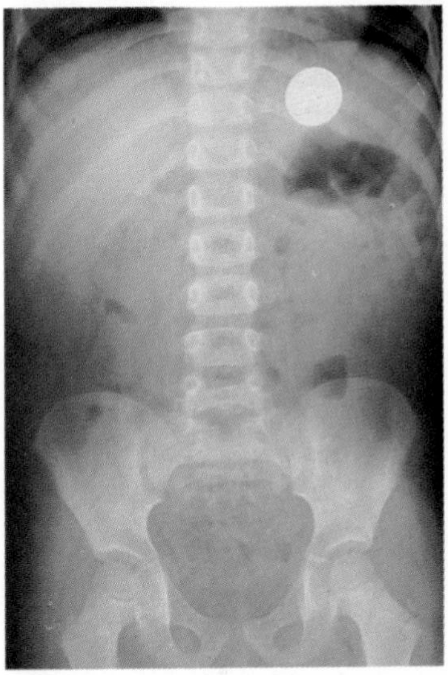

**FIGURE 19–8.** The coin in this little boy's stomach was located by using X rays.

*Define radiation.*

*How can X rays be helpful?*

*What is produced in a nuclear power plant?*

## Think About It

8. Why is the sun important to your health?
9. How can radiation in one part of the country affect a person who lives many kilometers away?

## Solid Wastes

*What are solid wastes?*

**Solid wastes** are the remains of products you throw away. These things do not include wastes carried away by air or water. Trash, garbage, and junk are among the materials called solid wastes.

Some pollution from solid waste is easy to see. Have you ever noticed garbage on streets or in parks? Have you ever seen garbage along the highways? These are examples of litter. **Litter** is garbage that is not disposed of properly outside of your homes.

Some people throw litter on streets and sidewalks to get rid of it. This can be a serious matter. If the amount of litter increases, it can attract rats, mosquitoes, and flies. These animals can be carriers of disease.

Besides the dangers of litter, many once-beautiful areas are unpleasant to see when they are covered by litter.

### Think About It

**10.** What is the relationship between litter and disease in people?

**FIGURE 19–9.** Roadside litter ruins the scenic beauty of America.

James Westwater

## The Silent Destroyer

Danny is eight years old. He cannot stand still. At home he wanders around the house, often stumbling. Sometimes he paces back and forth like a caged lion. Danny has trouble doing his homework. He cannot pay attention or think clearly. During recess at school he picks fights with his friends. He always seems tired, yet has trouble falling asleep at night.

Danny's mother took him to the doctor. She told the doctor about Danny's symptoms. She also said that Danny seemed all right just two weeks ago.

What is the matter with Danny? Is he just going through the "bad little boy" stage of life? Not quite!

The doctor took blood and urine samples from Danny. Tests on the blood and urine showed that Danny had lead poisoning. Lead poisoning results from the increased buildup of lead in a person's body.

Besides Danny's symptoms, there are other early signs of lead poisoning. Young victims may feel weak and suffer headaches and muscle pains. They may become clumsy and drop and break objects. As time goes by, the young person may have stomach pains and complain of a bad taste in the mouth. If the symptoms are ignored, the young victim may become blind and deaf. Many children die each year of lead poisoning.

This kind of poisoning affects very young children because they put just about anything in their mouths. The coating on toys may contain a material with lead in it. Putty placed around windows may also contain lead. Many children chew on objects and swallow pieces of them. An object that contains lead may even begin to taste good to a child. If the child swallows enough material containing lead, early symptoms of poisoning will occur in a few days. Lead poisoning is a silent destroyer of many children because most people do not recognize the symptoms.

Lead poisoning also is an environmental problem that can affect young people your age. Lead from the environment can enter your body. The exhaust fumes of many cars, trucks, and buses contain lead. This pollutant mixes with the air. During the winter months, lead mixes with water and snow in the atmosphere. Eating snow or icicles can be dangerous. Because of this, young people who live in cities are presented with a special health hazard.

Hickson-Bender Photography

## Summary

1. Air pollution is caused by exhaust from automobile engines as well as from the burning of coal, trash, and other products.
2. While pesticides can be helpful, they can also be harmful if they enter the human body.
3. Water pollution can be caused by products dumped into water from industry, heated water returned to oceans, rivers and lakes, and pesticides and soil washed into oceans, rivers, and lakes.
4. Loud sounds that can harm a person's health are known as noise pollution.
5. Exposure to large amounts of radiation can cause cancer.
6. Solid wastes, such as garbage and trash, can pollute the environment when not disposed of properly.

## Words for Health

*Below are vocabulary words and incomplete sentences. Complete each sentence with the correct vocabulary word. DO NOT WRITE IN THIS BOOK.*

| | | |
|---|---|---|
| environment | pollutants | sewage treatment plant |
| noise pollution | radiation | solid wastes |
| nuclear power plant | sewage | thermal pollution |
| pesticide | | |

1. A place where germs and substances in sewage are destroyed is a (n) _____.
2. Wastes that are in the form of smoke, gases, or small pieces of dirt are known as _____.
3. Hot or warm water that is dumped into rivers, oceans, and lakes is called _____.
4. Wastewater from homes, businesses, and industries is called _____.
5. Electricity can be produced at a (n) _____.
6. A poison that kills insects and pests is called a (n) _____.
7. Air, people, buildings, and plants are examples of things that make up your _____.
8. Products you throw away that are not carried in air or water are known as _____.
9. The form of energy given off from light and heat is called _____.
10. Loud sounds that can be harmful to a person's health are known as _____.

## Look at Your Health

1. What are two ways air can become polluted?
2. Why is air pollution more common in cities located in a valley?
3. Why should fruits and vegetables be washed before they are eaten?
4. Why might pesticides be used around the home?
5. What are two ways water can become polluted?
6. How can pesticides drain into rivers, oceans, and lakes?
7. What are two forms of radiation?
8. What are two ways radiation can be helpful?
9. What are two examples of solid wastes?
10. How can litter be dangerous?

## Actions for Health

*Think about the following situation. Then respond to the questions that follow.*

*Situation:* You and your friend Pat are walking home from school. After eating a candy bar, Pat throws the wrapper on the street. Pat says, "There's no litter basket around. I'm not going to carry trash."

1. Why might Pat's action be harmful to the environment?
2. If you were annoyed by Pat's action, what could you say to her?
3. What could you do if Pat disagrees with what you say?

## Individual Research

1. Write a report about the different products that cause air pollution. How does each product affect a person's health?
2. Write a report about two diseases that can be caused by drinking polluted water. What types of germs cause the diseases? What are the symptoms of the disease?

# LIFE MANAGEMENT SKILLS

- Do not swim in polluted water.
- Be aware of objects around you that produce loud noises.

# Pollution and Your Health

American Lung Association

*Your lungs are at work 24 hours a day. What conditions are best for the kind of work they do? How can you tell if the air you are breathing is clean? What happens to your body if your lungs cannot work as they should? How do you protect your lungs?*

To a great extent, your health is determined by your environment. People who live in clean environments are generally healthier than people who live in polluted environments. This chapter will describe how different types of pollution can affect your health.

**GOAL:** *You will investigate how different types of pollutants can affect your health.*

**Section**

## Air Pollution and Your Breathing

**20:1**

Air can contain many different pollutants. Each pollutant affects your body differently. However, when you breathe polluted air, you do not breathe only one pollutant. You usually breathe a mixture of several pollutants. The effects of these mixtures on your body can be dangerous.

Air pollution is known to damage statues made of marble or concrete. If air pollution can do this, it can also do great damage to parts of your body. Pollution affects the respiratory system and a person's ability to breathe. The air passages from the nose and mouth to the lungs are greatly affected.

*Which parts of the respiratory system are affected by air pollution?*

When wood, garbage, or other fuels are burned, millions of particles are released into the air. These particles enter the respiratory system. In the air passages, the particles become attached to and irritate the linings of the nose, throat, and lungs.

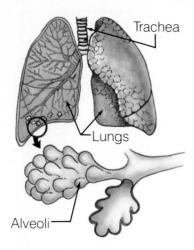

**FIGURE 20–1.** Lungs work best when you breathe in clean air.

*What is emphysema?*

Let us see what happens to these body parts affected by air pollution.

- Nose. A discharge from your nose causes you to sniffle.
- Throat. Soreness in your throat causes you to cough.
- Lungs. Diseases of the lungs become more common when people breathe polluted air. Emphysema (em fuh SEE muh) is a disease in which the air sacs in the lungs lose their ability to function.

Each of the above effects can make breathing difficult. They cause air passages to constrict. To constrict means to become smaller. When this happens, the lungs do not get enough oxygen. You would tire easily. Exercise and other physical tasks would become difficult.

## Think About It

1. Why should a person who has a cold stay out of polluted air?
2. Why is it difficult to exercise when air is polluted?

---

**Section**

**20:2**

*Name one form of air pollution.*

## Air Pollution and Illness

Air pollution can be dangerous to people who have lung diseases. The symptoms of lung disease increase when polluted air is inhaled. This often makes it difficult for people with lung disease to breathe. During periods of increased air pollution, many people die from lung diseases.

Cigarette smoke is a form of air pollution. Lung cancer is much more common among smokers than nonsmokers. When lungs are damaged from pollution, the body's ability to take in oxygen is decreased. This causes the heart to work harder to pump blood to all parts of the body. A diseased heart or a healthy heart that is overworked can be damaged. Air pollution increases the chances of heart attacks among elderly people.

## Think About It

3. What is the relationship between cigarette smoking and air pollution?
4. Why is it important to have healthy lungs?

Black Star/Fred Ward

**FIGURE 20–2.** People who work in large cities may need to take an oxygen break.

## Air Pollution and the Body Parts

Air pollution affects parts of the body other than the respiratory system and heart. The following story about Gail tells how.

Gail likes to jog. She often jogs in the park near her house. One day she decided to change her jogging route. She jogged on a path beside a highway. By the time Gail finished her jogging, she began to feel weak. She also had a headache. Yet, she ran the same distance she always ran in the park.

Gail's headache and weakness occurred because she jogged near a highway. The cars traveling on highways pollute the air. They produce a poisonous gas called **carbon monoxide.** Carbon monoxide is a gas that cannot be seen or smelled. Yet it causes headaches and weakness when breathed. When the air is highly polluted, it often contains large amounts of carbon monoxide. If Gail had jogged along her usual path in the park, she might not have had a headache or felt weak.

*How does carbon monoxide affect the body?*

**FIGURE 20–3.** Air quality is always being measured throughout the United States.

Air pollution can affect your body in other ways.
- Polluted air can burn your eyes and cause them to tear.
- Polluted air can make you feel dizzy.
- Particles from polluted air can be swallowed and enter your stomach and bloodstream.

Polluted air also makes everything around you dirty. This includes your body, your clothes, and your house.

 ## Activity

### Dirt in the Air

Often people do not realize that the air is dirty. The following experiment will help you become aware that dirt is in the air around you. (1) Take a short walk around your neighborhood. (2) Make a list of those things that you think are made dirty from the air. For example, you might run your finger down a car's hood and notice a streak. You might conclude this to be evidence that the air is dirty. (3) Present your evidence which shows that the air is dirty to your classmates. (4) There is a chance you may find little evidence to prove the air in your neighborhood is dirty. Why might this be so?

## Think About It

**5.** Why is it difficult for you to know if you are inhaling carbon monoxide?

**6.** How might you know whether or not your environment is polluted?

# Noise Pollution and Your Hearing

These things actually happened.
- A jet flying at high speeds caused windows to break.
- Windows broke when a gas tank that was seven kilometers away exploded.

Sound can be a powerful force. In the situations above, the windows broke because of loud noises made by the jet and the explosion. Loud noise has been known to crack metal. If noise can break glass and crack metal, what do you think it can do to the delicate parts of your ears?

Many people your age are suffering from hearing loss. Hearing loss may be caused by loud noises. When you hear loud noises, you might have a temporary loss of hearing. Sometimes you may experience a buzzing or humming after hearing a loud noise. These hums or buzzes are signs of hearing loss. They usually go away after a short time.

*What may cause hearing loss?*

If you are exposed to loud noises for a long time, hearing loss will occur. Nerve cells in your ears become damaged. Damaged nerve cells cannot be repaired.

*What parts of your ears can be damaged by noise?*

One of the major causes of hearing loss to people your age is listening to loud music. Loudness is measured by **decibels** (DES uh belz). A conversation is about 50 decibels. This loudness will not harm your ears. A jet moving overhead might be 100 decibels. This is loud and can harm your hearing.

*How is loudness measured?*

Dave Dennis

**FIGURE 20–4.** Earphones should be used wisely. Music close to the ear has a higher decibel level.

Many young people listen to music that is between 80 and 100 decibels. Unlike the sound of a jet overhead, listening to music extends over a period of time. This extended time exposed to noise is very harmful.

## Think About It

**7.** How might you tell whether or not you are suffering from hearing loss?

## Noise Pollution and Your Body

Suppose a person sneaked up behind you. This person made a loud noise and scared you. If this occurred, certain things would happen to your body. Your heartbeat rate would increase causing your blood pressure to rise. This is not healthy.

You do not have to be scared for your heartbeat to increase and your blood pressure to rise. Constant noise can produce stress. Stress also produces the above effects. Chapter 3 described the effects of stress on your body.

There is also a relationship between noise and disease. Noise can keep you from sleeping well. When you do not get enough sleep, your body becomes tired. A tired body is a poor defense against disease. Germs have an easy time affecting a tired body. If you can avoid loud noises, you will feel more relaxed. You will be able to sleep easier and your body will feel stronger.

*How can noise affect your health?*

Lee Balterman/fpg

**FIGURE 20–5.** Houses next to highways and train tracks receive a constant stream of noise.

Noise can also affect your study habits and your grades. If you try to do homework while a stereo is playing loud music, you might not be able to concentrate. You will make more mistakes. Research shows that a quiet environment helps people to learn.

## Think About It

8. How might loud noises affect your heartbeat rate?

9. What is the relationship between noise and study habits?

## Activity

### Noise and Your Concentration

Noise can affect your ability to concentrate. The following experiment will show you how. (1) In a quiet environment, slowly say the following words to five people: envelope, sky, airplane, light, watch, shirt, school, professor, pen, clerk. (2) Each of the five people is to repeat each word. If possible, these words should be repeated in order. (3) Conduct this experiment with five more people. This time, music should be playing loudly. (4) What were the differences between the responses of those in a quiet environment and those in a noisy environment? What can you conclude about noise and concentration?

FIGURE 20–6. Learning and concentrating can be done with greater ease in a quiet place.

## Pesticides and Your Health

Some pesticides are poisons and can be harmful. They can be accidentally swallowed by small children. All pesticides should be labeled and kept out of reach of small children.

*Why are pesticides dangerous to young children?*

Pesticides can also be breathed in accidentally. You might buy a pesticide to get rid of insects on a tree. If you spray the pesticide when a wind is blowing, the pesticide may blow toward your face. If you breathe in a large amount of the pesticide, you may get sick.

Do not spray a pesticide when the wind is blowing. Be sure you read the directions and warnings on all containers of pesticides.

# Water Pollution and Your Health

Most people assume that water that comes out of faucets is safe to drink. This may be true. But in many cities, public water contains many chemicals. Asbestos (as BES tus) fibers have been found in the drinking water in some major cities. **Asbestos** is a material that has been used in the construction of buildings. Asbestos is believed to cause cancer.

*Define asbestos.*

# Radiation and Your Health

Sometimes radiation can be harmful. In Chapter 17, you read about the effects of sunburn. Sunburn is caused by ultraviolet (ul truh VI uh lut) rays. **Ultraviolet rays** are a form of radiation. These rays can cause cancer.

X rays usually are helpful. Yet some people feel that too many unneeded X rays can be dangerous. They may cause cancer. Very few people receive too many X rays. However, to be safe, keep a record of the kinds of X rays you have. Also record the dates they are taken. You can show this list to a doctor or dentist before they give you more X rays. This can prevent unneeded X rays.

If you move, it is a good idea to have your X rays and other medical records transferred to your new doctor and dentist.

## Think About It

**10.** Why can being in the sunlight for too long a period of time be dangerous?

Doug Martin

**FIGURE 20–7.** Dental X rays in your dental file belong to you. If you move, your dentist will give you your dental file.

# HEALTH HIGHLIGHTS

## The Chernobyl Incident

The operation and building of nuclear power plants continue to create controversy throughout the world. A near-catastrophe occurred in Chernobyl, Russia, in 1986. An accident at a nuclear power plant released large amounts of radioactive materials into the environment. This had an impact on the entire world.

The accident at Chernobyl happened when safety features were turned off during a test of the power plant systems. When the leakage occurred, plant workers were not able to restart the safety equipment. Winds carried nuclear wastes around the world.

As a result of this accident, many people in Russia lost their lives to radiation sickness. Radiation sickness is an illness produced from overexposure to radiation. The signs and symptoms of radiation sickness include fatigue, nausea, weight loss, fever, bleeding from the mouth, and hair loss. Often the effects of overexposure to radiation do not show up until years later. Thus, many people in Russia may suffer the consequences of the Chernobyl incident in the years to come.

It is believed that people in other countries were not exposed to enough radiation to harm them. Fortunately, people in the United States and in other countries showed no signs of radiation sickness.

It is important to understand that it is impossible to avoid radiation completely. We are constantly exposed to radioactive materials produced in the environment. Cosmic rays from space give off radiation as do rocks and soil. Medical and dental X rays are used to promote health.

It is believed that an incident such as the one that occurred in Russia will not happen in the United States. The type of nuclear power plant used in Russia is different from those most used in the United States. Also, United States nuclear power plants are built with a second safety system to take over should a failure in the first system occur.

Will the explosion at Chernobyl cause countries to reconsider building nuclear power plants? Will countries begin to take steps toward building greater safeguards into nuclear power plants? Time holds the answers to these questions.

Tracy Borland

283

## Review

### Summary

20:1   **1.** The many pollutants in the air that mix together can harm the human body.

20:2   **2.** Air pollution can affect people with lung diseases and increase the chance of heart attacks in older people.

20:3   **3.** Air pollution can cause your eyes to burn, make you feel dizzy, and cause headaches and tiredness.

20:4   **4.** When you are around loud noises for an extended period of time, you might suffer some loss of hearing.

20:5   **5.** Loud noises can affect your heartbeat rate, blood pressure, and concentration.

20:6   **6.** Pesticides are dangerous if they are swallowed or inhaled.

20:7   **7.** Some water systems may be polluted from chemicals or asbestos fibers.

20:8   **8.** Too much radiation from the sun or from X rays can be unhealthy.

### Words for Health

*Below are vocabulary words and incomplete sentences. Complete each sentence with the correct vocabulary word. DO NOT WRITE IN THIS BOOK.*

asbestos    carbon monoxide    decibels    ultraviolet rays

**1.** A material used in the construction of buildings which is thought to cause cancer is _____.

**2.** The loudness of sound is measured by _____.

**3.** _____ are a form of radiation.

**4.** An odorless and colorless gas is _____.

### Look at Your Health

**1.** What body function does air pollution affect most?

**2.** List three parts of the respiratory system affected by air pollution.

**3.** Why does air pollution make breathing difficult?

**4.** How might air pollution affect you if you had a cold?

**5.** What are two lung diseases common among smokers?

**6.** What can happen to a diseased heart when it is overworked?

**7.** What can carbon monoxide do to your body?

**8.** How can air pollution affect your eyes?

**9.** What parts of the body, other than the respiratory system, can pollutants from the air enter?

10. What is the major cause of hearing loss?
11. What are two signs of hearing loss?
12. Why is it difficult for hearing loss to be regained?
13. What could happen to your body if you hear a loud, sudden noise?
14. What effect can noise have on your blood pressure?
15. What is the relationship between noise and disease?
16. What is the relationship between noise and study habits?
17. Why should pesticides be kept out of the reach of small children?
18. Why should pesticides be sprayed in the same direction as the wind is blowing?
19. What are two pollutants found in water?
20. How can ultraviolet rays be dangerous?

## Actions for Health

*Think about the following situation. Then respond to the questions that follow.*

*Situation:* You and your friend have decided to go jogging. Your friend says, "Let's go down near the highway. There is a 3-mile path that is great to run along."

1. What concern would you have about your friend's suggestion?
2. What suggestions can you give to your friend about where to jog?
3. What would your decision be in this situation? Why?

## Individual Research

1. Make a list of how different parts of your body can be affected by air pollution.
2. Write a report about how your life would change if you were no longer able to hear.

## LIFE MANAGEMENT SKILLS

- Be aware of the effects of air pollution on your body.
- Be aware that loud noises can be harmful.
- Be aware of the harmful effects of pesticides and radiation.

# Controlling Pollution

Signs give us directions and reminders. This reminder is about littering. Why is it necessary? Sometimes people do not pay attention to such signs. How else can we help to control pollution? What can you do to reduce the amount of pollution in your environment?

**M**any changes have taken place in the past century. New products are being made and used. But new products create other problems. They produce waste products which can be harmful to your health. This chapter will describe steps that can be taken to control these wastes so that your health will be protected.

**GOAL:** *You will learn how different types of pollution can be controlled.*

## Controlling Air Pollution Through Laws

In many large cities, the air has become cleaner over the past few years. This is the result of many new laws concerning automobile engines.

Cars are the greatest cause of air pollution. Cars built today pollute the air less than cars built 15 years ago. There are several reasons for this.

*What is the greatest cause of air pollution?*

- Cars built in recent years get better gas mileage than cars built years ago. They do not produce as many pollutants because they burn less gasoline.
- Almost all new cars use unleaded gasoline instead of regular gasoline. Regular gasoline contains lead. Lead gets into the air from the exhaust of engines that burn this kind of gasoline. Lead can be inhaled. Too much lead in a body can affect a person's stomach and brain. Unleaded gasoline does not contain lead. Thus, the exhaust of engines that use that kind of gasoline does not contain lead.
- New cars are built with pollution controls. These controls reduce the amount of pollutants from cars.

*What parts of the body can lead affect?*

In the 1960's the federal government passed many clean-air laws. These laws were to control the amount of pollutants produced by industries. As a result, industries are regulated and must show that they do not release harmful substances. Industries can be fined if they do not obey the laws. These regulations have helped to make the air cleaner.

## Think About It

1. Why might large cars pollute more than small cars?
2. Why is government important in the control of air pollution?

## 21:2

*What is the purpose of air pollution laws?*

*What is mass transit?*

*What is a car pool?*

**FIGURE 21–1.** Many people belong to a car pool to save money on gasoline and to reduce pollution.

CAR POOL
INFO
224-POOL

J. Kevin Fitzsimons

## Your Role in Air Pollution

You can help prevent and reduce air pollution. Air pollution laws are made to help protect you. You should be aware of the air pollution laws in your community. You can get information about pollution standards from local environmental agencies and organizations.

The way you live can affect air pollution. Could you get to places without being taken in a car? Since cars are the greatest cause of air pollution, people might find ways to reduce the use of cars. One way to travel and to help reduce air pollution is to use mass transit. **Mass transit** is a public transportation system which can include buses and trains. When you use mass transit, you help reduce the number of cars on the road.

Another way to reduce air pollution is to use a bicycle. Bicycles have no engines to pollute the air. When you cycle, you also exercise and improve your health.

You might also encourage your family to form car pools. A **car pool** is an arrangement in which two or more people are transported in one car. If you and your friends must travel someplace, you can suggest that you travel together in one car. This can help reduce air pollution. Today, many people form car pools to travel to work. They save money on gasoline and also reduce the wear on their cars. What are some other advantages of car pooling?

## Activity

### *Unnecessary Car Use*

Keep a log which describes the number of times in a week that members of your family drive a car to go places near your home. (1) How often could they have walked or used a bicycle? (2) How many kilometers would the walking or bicycling have totaled? (3) How much could have been saved in gasoline expenses?

## Avoiding Air Pollution

Air pollution cannot be completely erased, but you can avoid the effects.

- Reduce physical activity such as jogging and tennis during periods of heavy pollution. You breathe faster during physical activity. When you breathe faster, more pollutants enter your lungs.
- Avoid cigarette smoke. Cigarette smoke which is combined with other pollutants in the air is even more dangerous to your body.
- Stay indoors. Close all windows and circulate the indoor air by using a fan.
- Avoid areas where there are many cars. This is where air pollution is the greatest.

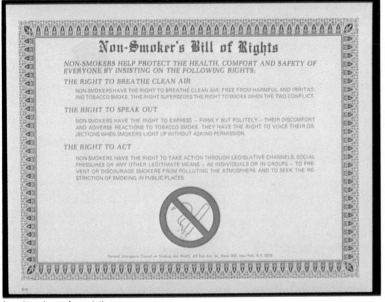

American Lung Association

**FIGURE 21–2.** Does the Non-Smoker's Bill of Rights make sense to you?

## Think About It

**3.** How can riding in a car pool help people save money?

**4.** Why is it a good idea to avoid playing near a highway?

## 21:4

*Why might you not be aware of slight increases in sound?*

*What can you do to control noise pollution?*

# Noise Pollution and the Law

Studies show that the noise level has increased one decibel each year for the past few years. The increase is so gradual, you may not be aware of it. However, your hearing is being affected all the time.

To help protect your hearing, noise laws have been passed by many local governments. Automobile horns are not allowed to be used in certain communities. Other laws might be concerned with noisy engines or playing music loudly.

The federal government also makes laws. For example, jet planes are less noisy now than in the past. Federal laws are concerned with wide-range problems of pollution.

## Section

## 21:5

**FIGURE 21–3.** Many home appliances contribute to noise pollution.

# Noise Pollution Indoors

A great deal of noise pollution occurs indoors. Stereos may be played at a high volume. Other machines may make loud noises when used. You can control indoor noises. Turn down the volume of TVs and stereos. Stay at a distance when someone is using a machine that makes a loud noise. If you must use such a machine, you can put earplugs in your ears to shut out much of the sounds.

Many people find that carpeting and drapes reduce noise. They absorb sound from both inside and outside the house.

## Think About It

**5.** Why might noise sound louder in a room without carpets than it would in a room with carpets?

**FIGURE 21-4.** These fruits were sprayed to destroy medflies. Inspectors constantly check for any signs of the flies.

# Avoiding Pesticide Pollution

Federal laws have helped to reduce the use of dangerous pesticides. Yet any pesticide can be dangerous if it is used the wrong way. For this reason, all pesticide containers must carry certain information on their labels. If someone accidentally swallows a pesticide, you should read the first aid directions on the container. A doctor or emergency squad should also be called immediately. Many communities have a poison control center that will offer assistance over the phone.

*What should you do if someone swallows a pesticide?*

The government also requires that fruits, vegetables, and meats be inspected for pesticides. If dangerous amounts of pesticides are found, these products are destroyed.

There are certain rules you should follow when using pesticides in your home.

- Some people spray pesticides along the floor to kill insects. A baby crawling on the floor can touch the pesticide. The pesticide can enter the baby's mouth from its hand. The baby can get sick.
- Do not spray pesticides near food or objects used to prepare or eat food. The pesticide can enter your body if you eat food covered by a pesticide.
- Store pesticides out of the reach of young children.

*What are two rules to follow in using pesticides in your home?*

FIGURE 21–5.

| Name of Pesticide | Where Used | Safety Concern |
|---|---|---|
| 1. | | |
| 2. | | |
| 3. | | |
| 4. | | |

## Activity

### *Pesticides In and Around Your Home*

Copy the chart on a sheet of paper. (1) In the left column, write the names of three pesticides that can be used inside or outside your home. (2) In the middle column, describe where the pesticide is used. (3) In the right column, describe one important safety concern you would have about the area in which the pesticide is used.

## Think About It

6. Why should you not use a pesticide that has no label on its container?

7. Why should pesticides not be sprayed in certain places?

## Section

## 21:7

## Controlling Water Pollution

Methods of reducing water pollution have been successful in some places. Some lakes and rivers which were once polluted have been cleaned. Fish can now live in these places. In addition, people can use these lakes and rivers for swimming.

FIGURE 21–6. Many people enjoy the fresh, clean lakes of New England for boating and fishing.

Frank Balthis

FIGURE 21–7. Flooding destroys property and creates several health hazards. One hazard is polluted drinking water.

If you live in a city the water you drink every day is safe. Your state government plays an important role in making sure drinking water is safe. It is checked daily.

Sometimes your drinking water may become polluted. This may result from large storms such as hurricanes. If you think your drinking water is polluted, call your local government. You can also listen to your radio for announcements about water conditions.

*What might cause drinking water to become polluted?*

Water that is not safe to drink contains germs. Germs can be killed if you boil water before drinking it. If you go hiking or camping, carry clean water with you. Sometimes clean water is difficult to find.

Some people get sick by swallowing water while swimming in a pool. The water in a pool might look clean, yet it might contain many germs. If you think a pool might have too many germs, try not to swallow any of its water. You might want to swim somewhere else.

## Think About It

**8.** Why do some people boil drinking water after a flood?

**Section**

## Getting Rid of Solid Wastes

**21:8**

Have you ever thought about what happens to garbage or where it goes? When garbage is picked up from your home or school, it can go to one of several places.

**FIGURE 21–8.** Recycling can help you earn money and save the environment.

*What is an open dump?*

One place garbage is taken is to an open dump. An **open dump** is a large open area where garbage is piled. This place is usually at the edge of a neighborhood. It is not near houses or people. Many cities get rid of garbage by using open dumps. Open dumps may create problems. Flies, mosquitoes, and rats may breed there. Sometimes the open dumps smell. This smell can travel and bother people living in nearby homes.

Some cities get rid of garbage at sanitary landfills. A **sanitary landfill** is a place where garbage is dumped. After it is dumped, the garbage is covered by layers of dirt. This prevents flies, mosquitoes, and rats from breeding. Parks and playgrounds are often built on sanitary landfills after they are completely filled and covered.

Some garbage is taken to city-owned **incinerators** (ihn SIHN uh rayt urz) where garbage is burned. The burning produces wastes that pollute the air. Many incinerators now have special filters to trap many pollutants before they enter the air.

## Think About It

**9.** Why might open dumps breed disease?

**Section**

**21:9**

## Recycling

Many things that are used can be reused. They do not have to be thrown away. Reusing wastes is called **recycling.**

Paper is one thing that can be recycled. It can be used to make more paper. Metals can be recycled. Some dumps use large magnets to separate metals from other products. These metals can be melted down and made into new products.

Many cities have recycling centers. They pay cash for things like newspapers, bottles, and aluminum cans. You can earn money by bringing things like these to recycling centers. At the same time, you will help keep your environment clean.

Name two materials that can be recycled.

## Avoiding Lead Poisoning

At the beginning of this chapter, you read about lead that enters the air from regular gasoline that is burned. But regular gasoline is not the only substance that contains lead. Tires and some paints contain lead. When tires and paint wear away, lead enters the air and can be inhaled. Some children might eat small chips of paint that contain lead. Too much lead in a person's body can produce lead poisoning. **Lead poisoning** is a condition in which the brain, stomach, and nervous system can be damaged by lead which is absorbed into the body.

What is lead poisoning?

To help prevent lead from affecting you,
- avoid playing near highways.
- do not use paint that contains lead.
- seek medical treatment if you think you might have lead poisoning. There are drugs that can treat this condition.

**FIGURE 21–9.** Information about poisonous materials are available from many sources.

## Review       Summary

21:1    **1.** Many large cities have clean air because of laws that control air pollution.

21:2    **2.** People can help to control air pollution by using car pools and mass transit.

21:3    **3.** People can avoid the effects of air pollution by reducing physical activities in areas where there are many cars.

21:4    **4.** Laws established by local communities and the federal government can help protect people from noise pollution.

21:5    **5.** Stereos and some kinds of machines that are used indoors can produce noise pollution.

21:6    **6.** Pesticides should be used properly to avoid any harmful effects to the body.

21:7    **7.** Many rivers and lakes that were once polluted have been cleaned and made safe for use.

21:8    **8.** Open dumps and sanitary landfills are two places at which solid wastes can be disposed.

21:9    **9.** Used paper, bottles, and aluminum cans are examples of items that can be recycled.

21:10   **10.** Among some of the items that can produce lead poisoning are tires and some kinds of paints.

## Words for Health

*Below are vocabulary words and incomplete sentences. Complete each sentence with the correct vocabulary word. DO NOT WRITE IN THIS BOOK.*

car pool          open dump
incinerator       recycling
lead poisoning    sanitary landfill
mass transit

**1.** Garbage is burned in a(n) _____.

**2.** A place where garbage is dumped and covered with dirt is a(n) _____.

**3.** Injury and damage to the brain, stomach, and nervous system can be due to _____.

**4.** Public transportation, such as buses and trains, is known as _____.

**5.** Reusing solid wastes is called _____.

6. A large, open area where garbage is piled but not covered by dirt is known as a(n) _____.
7. An arrangement whereby two or more people are transported in one car to reduce air pollution is called a(n) _____.

## Look at Your Health

1. Name one reason why cars today pollute the air less than cars built 15 years ago.
2. How are federal pollution standards enforced?
3. What is the purpose of air pollution laws?
4. Name two ways to help reduce air pollution.
5. Why should physical activity be reduced during heavy air pollution?
6. In times of heavy air pollution, why should you avoid being near many cars?
7. How is noise pollution more and more of a problem each year?
8. What is one example of how the federal government controls noise pollution?
9. What is one cause of noise pollution indoors?
10. How can indoor noise pollution be reduced?
11. Why must pesticide containers carry certain information on labels?
12. What is one rule to follow when using pesticides in your home?
13. What may cause your drinking water to become polluted?
14. How can you kill germs in drinking water?
15. How can an open dump be a problem?
16. How are incinerators made safe?
17. Name two things that can be recycled.
18. Why can recycling be profitable for you?
19. Name two products that contain lead.
20. What parts of the body does lead poisoning affect?

## Actions for Health

*Think about the following situations. Then respond to the questions that follow.*
*Situation:* A neighbor on your street owns a very old car that produces a great deal of smoke every time it is driven. You find the exhaust to be annoying.

## Review

1. What three things can you do?
2. Which one thing would be the best to do? Why?

*Situation:* The air pollution in your area is very high. An announcement on the radio says that people should remain indoors. Your grandfather who has heart disease decides to go outside for his daily walk.

1. What concern might you have?
2. What would you say to your grandfather?
3. What could your grandfather do instead of walking outdoors?

*Situation:* Your school needs ideas about how to raise money for new uniforms for its athletic teams.

1. What suggestion can you offer that at the same time will help fight pollution?
2. How could you go about carrying out your suggestion?

## Individual Research

1. Try to bring a copy of some local pollution control laws to your class.
2. Make a list of the things you have thrown away during the past week. Of these things, which ones could have been reused?
3. Write a report about a disease caused by polluted water.
4. A sanitarian is a person who checks the quality of the food you eat and of the water you drink in your environment. This person may also have other tasks. Write a report about the various tasks performed by a sanitarian.

## LIFE MANAGEMENT SKILLS

- Follow laws that serve to protect you from the effects of pollution.
- Reduce physical activity during times of heavy air pollution.
- Try to avoid areas where there are many cars.
- Try to control the sources of noise in your home.
- Use pesticides in a safe way.
- Save materials for recycling.

# Glossary

# A

**adjustment:** a change to make something better

**administrator:** person who runs the hospital and plans the budget

**adolescence** (ad ul ES unts): state or process of growing up physically, emotionally, and socially; the time period when a person's body changes from that of a child to that of an adult

**adolescent:** name that a person is called during adolescence; the name for a person who is no longer a child and not yet an adult

**adrenal** (uh DREEN ul) **glands:** glands located on top of each kidney; secrete a hormone called adrenaline

**adrenaline** (uh DREN ul un): hormone secreted by adrenal glands; raises blood pressure and increases the amount of sugar in the blood

**aerobic** (er ROH bihk) **exercise:** exercise that uses a lot of oxygen, is continued for an extended length of time, and improves cardio-respiratory fitness

**agility** (uh JIHL ut ee): ability to be agile, to make quick and easy movements with your body; one of the areas of physical fitness

**aging:** to experience changes that occur after physical growth ends

**alcohol:** depressant drug found in beer, wine, whiskey, and some other drinks

**allergy** (AL ur jee): unusual reaction from something breathed in, eaten, or worn

**alveoli** (al VEE uh li): tiny air sacs in the lungs

**anaerobic** (an uh ROH bihk) **exercise:** exercise that is done for a short time, uses a lot of oxygen, helps develop speed, and does not develop overall fitness

**anosmia** (a NAHZ mee uh): partial or complete loss of smell

**appendicitis** (uh pen duh SITE us): inflammation of the appendix

**arteries:** blood vessels that carry blood away from the heart

**asbestos** (as BES tus): material used in the construction of buildings; this material is thought to cause cancer

**aspirin:** chemical compound in many prescription medicines

**asthma** (AZ muh): disease that affects the parts of the body used in breathing; person will usually wheeze

**auscultation** (aw skul TAY shun): method of using a stethoscope to hear body sounds

# B

**bicuspids** (bi KUS pudz): teeth in back of the cuspids; these teeth have two cusps that are used to tear and crush food

**blood:** liquid that circulates nutrients and oxygen to the body cells

**blood alcohol level:** the level of alcohol in a person's blood

**blood pressure:** the force of blood against the walls of the blood vessels

**blood vessels:** tubes in the body through which blood circulates

**bowel movement:** process in which solid waste is removed from the body

**Braille** (BRAYL) **system:** method of touch reading and writing used by a person who is blind; raised dots that represent letters of the alphabet are grouped together in different ways

**brain:** mass of nerve cells inside the skull

# C

**caffeine:** stimulant in coffee and some cola drinks

**calculus** (KAL kyuh lus): substance on the teeth that is formed when plaque becomes hard; must be removed by the dentist or dental hygienist when teeth are cleaned

**cancer:** disease in which harmful body cells multiply and attack healthy cells

**capillaries** (KAP uh ler eez): tiny vessels that connect arteries to veins

**carbohydrate:** nutrient such as sugar or starch that is a source of energy for the body

**carbohydrate loading:** eating extra amounts of carbohydrates to make the body ready for exercise that requires endurance

**carbon monoxide:** gas that cannot be seen or smelled; can cause headaches and weakness when breathed

**cardio-respiratory** (KARD ee oh·RES pruh tor ee) **fitness:** ability to do exercises which require oxygen for a certain period of time; one of the areas of physical fitness that strengthens the heart and lungs

**car pool:** arrangement in which two or more people are transported in one car

**cavity:** hole in the enamel that covers the tooth

**cementum** (sih MENT um): bonelike tissue that covers the root of the tooth

**circulatory system:** a transport system made up of blood, blood vessels, and the heart

**cocaine:** an illegal stimulant drug obtained from the leaves of the coca plant

**communicable disease:** an illness caused by a pathogen that enters the body

**communication:** exchange of information among people; the forms of exchange may include reading, writing, talking, listening, using sign language or the Braille system

**cooling down:** 10-minute period after exercise when you do moderate exercise that gives your heart a chance to slow down and lowers the body temperature

**CPR:** stands for cardiopulmonary resuscitation; first aid procedure to help circulation and breathing start again if they have stopped

**crack:** an illegal and harmful drug made from cocaine

**crown:** the part of the tooth that can be seen

**cusp:** pointed part on the crown of the tooth

**cuspids** (KUS pudz): teeth in the corners of the mouth; they have a very pointed cusp to tear food

# D

**deaf:** not being able to hear most sounds

**deaf-mute** (MYEWT): a person who cannot hear or speak

**decibel** (DES uh bel): unit used to measure the loudness of sound

**decision:** act of choosing or making up your mind

**decision making:** deciding which of two or more choices to make

**dental hygienist** (HI jeen ust): person who has the special training needed to clean and floss your teeth and to assist the dentist

**dentin:** hard tissue that forms the body of a tooth

**dentist:** person who has the training needed to examine and treat the teeth, mouth, and gums

**depressant** (dih PRES unt): drug that slows the rate of body activities

**designer drug:** drug that is made in homemade labs and imitates the effects of other kinds of drugs

**diabetes** (di uh BEET us): condition in which the body cannot produce enough insulin

**diabetic** (di uh BET ihk) **coma:** occurs when a person's body does not have enough insulin; signs include a flushed face, cherry-color lips, and dry skin

**diagnosis** (di ihg NOH sus): process of identifying a disease or disorder based on a person's symptoms

**dietitian** (di uh TIHSH un): person who has the special training needed to help others plan balanced, healthy meals, and special diets

**digestive system:** the parts of the body that make food usable to the body

**disability** (dihs uh BIHL ut ee): physical or mental defect in a person that may occur at birth or as a result of an accident, injury, or disease

**dislocation** (dihs loh KAY shun): forcing of a bone away from a joint

**dissolution** (dihs uh LEW shun): a legal way to end a marriage

**distress:** stress that harms the body; a physical or mental demand that harms the body

**divorce:** a legal way to end a marriage

**doctor:** person who is trained to diagnose, study, and treat sickness

**drug:** chemical put in the body which changes the way a person thinks or feels

**drug-free:** to do things without the misuse of drugs

# E

**eardrum:** thin membrane in the ear that vibrates when sound waves hit it

**emergency:** unexpected illness or injury that requires immediate medical attention

**emergency room:** special place in the hospital that handles unexpected illnesses or injuries

**emotional growth:** progress that you make in learning to control your emotions

**emotions:** feelings that you have inside you

**enamel:** the very hard tissue that covers the crown of a tooth

**endocrine** (EN duh krun) **system:** glands in the body that produce hormones

**environment:** everything that surrounds you

**ethyl** (ETH ul) **alcohol:** kind of alcohol found in alcoholic beverages; also called grain alcohol

**eustress** (YOO stress): stress that improves how your body works; a physical or mental demand that helps you to perform at your best

# F

**fast food:** a food that is ready to eat when you buy it

**fat:** nutrient that provides your body with a source of energy and helps your body store vitamins

**fermentation** (fur mun TAY shun): action of yeast cells upon grains, vegetables, or fruit sugars

**fever:** increase in body temperature due to illness or injury

**filling:** material that repairs a cavity in a tooth; placed into the tooth by a dentist

**first aid:** quick care given to an injured or ill person

**flexibility** (flek suh BIHL ut ee): ability to bend and move your body in different ways; one of the areas of physical fitness

**floss:** the stringlike material that is placed between teeth for flossing

**flossing:** scraping the teeth with floss to remove plaque and bits of food from between the teeth

**fluoride** (FLOOR ide): a chemical that helps to prevent tooth decay; a chemical that may be added to drinking water, or may be applied by the dentist, or comes in tablets or toothpaste

**food group:** foods that contain the same nutrients

**friend:** someone you know well and like

**frostbite:** injury to a part of the body due to freezing temperatures

# G

**gingivitis** (jihn juh VITE us): condition in which gums are sore and bleed easily

**glands:** organs in the body that secrete hormones

**goal:** something toward which you work

**grateful:** being thankful for what you have; showing that you appreciate others

**growth hormone:** a hormone secreted by the pituitary gland; causes bones and muscles to grow

# H

**habit:** something that is repeated again and again until it becomes automatic; a usual way of doing something

**hallucinogen:** drug that affects a person's senses

**handicap:** limit that results from having a disability

**health consumer:** person who buys health products and health services

**health educator:** person who has the special training needed to improve the knowledge, attitude, and behavior of people

**health history:** facts about a person's past health and past habits and those of the person's family

**health inspector:** person with special training who has the job of checking that health services meet health standards

**health knowledge:** an awareness of facts which affect your health

**health product:** something that you use to be at your best

**health record:** special file in which the doctor records information about a person's health

**health service:** a place or person that helps others to be healthy

**health standard:** a rule or a way of doing things that protects your health

**healthy:** living life at your best; involves good physical, mental, and social health

**heart:** muscle that pumps blood throughout the body

**heart attack:** damage that occurs to a part of the heart; caused by a blocked blood vessel

**heat cramps:** muscle pains that result from extended physical activity; the muscle becomes hard and tight

**heat exhaustion** (ihg ZAWS chun): physical reaction to being in a warm temperature for too long a time; usually due to extreme physical activity and sweating while in the warm temperature

**heatstroke:** condition in which the body temperature is very high because of being in the sun or heat; sometimes called sunstroke

**hormone** (HOR mohn): chemical messenger produced by a gland; controls and regulates growth and development during adolescence

**hospital:** special place where people receive medical care, diagnosis, and treatment

**hospital attendant:** person who helps hospital patients with daily activities

**hypothermia** (hi poh THUR mee uh): condition in which the body temperature is lowered due to cold dampness, and wind

# I

**incinerator** (ihn SIHN uh rayt ur): place or building in which garbage is burned

**incisors** (ihn SI zurz): teeth in the front and center of the mouth; teeth with a flat, sharp edge that cut up the food that is eaten

**infection:** swelling and redness to an injured area

**informed decision:** choice that is made after considering the facts

**inherit:** to obtain the genes for a trait or disorder from your parents

**insulin** (IHN suh lin): chemical which controls the use of sugar in the body

**insulin shock:** condition in which the body has too much insulin; person may look pale and have cold and moist skin

**intern:** doctor who has finished medical school and is completing a year of further study at a hospital

**internship:** extra year of study performed by an intern

**iris:** part of the eye that contains muscles that control the size of the pupil

**isometric** (i suh MET rihk) **exercise:** exercise that tightens muscles for five to eight seconds without making a movement

**isotonic** (i suh TAHN ihk) **exercise:** exercise that contracts the muscles to produce a movement; an exercise that improves muscular strength not cardio-respiratory fitness

# J

**joint:** place where two bones meet

# K

**kidneys:** organs which remove waste products and excess water from the blood

# L

**large intestine:** receives undigested food from the small intestine

**lead poisoning:** condition in which the brain, stomach, and nervous system are damaged from lead absorbed in the body

**legally blind:** having 20/200 vision after correction in the better eye; a person who has 20/200 vision can see no more at 20 feet than a person with normal vision can see at 200 feet

**lens:** part of the eye that causes light rays to bend and focus on the retina

**licensed practical nurse (LPN):** person who assists the registered nurse

**life expectancy** (ihk SPEK tun see): prediction of how long you can expect to live

**litter:** garbage that is not disposed of properly outside of the home

**lungs:** two large sacs in the chest area in which the exchange of oxygen and carbon dioxide occur

# M

**mainstreaming:** law which allows children with handicaps to attend public schools

**marijuana** (mer uh WAHN uh): mild hallucinogen that is usually smoked; it comes from the leaves, stems, and flowering tops of an Indian hemp plant

**mass transit:** public transportation system which can include buses and trains

**medical doctor:** person who has the special training needed to prevent, diagnose, and treat illness

**medical emergency:** illness or injury that requires quick treatment

**medical technologist** (tek NAHL uh just): person with special training who helps the doctor by doing certain tests in the laboratory

**mental health:** well-being of your mind, thoughts, and feelings; mental well-being

**methyl** (METH uhl) **alcohol:** made from fermentation of wood products; poisonous

**minerals:** nutrients that direct many of the activities in the body

**molars:** teeth in the back of a person's mouth; have several cusps that are used to grind food

**mucous** (MYEW kus) **membranes:** protective lining of the body organs

**muscular endurance:** ability to last or to continue doing something that requires muscular strength; one of the areas of physical fitness

**muscular strength:** use of strong muscles to help a person lift, pull, and push; one of the areas of physical fitness

**muscular system:** all of the muscles in the body

# N

**nasal speculum** (SPEK yuh lum): instrument used by a doctor to spread the nostrils apart; used to check if there is anything that blocks breathing

**nerve cells:** cells that form fibers in the body and carry messages

**nervous system:** organs of the body that act as a message center

**neurological** (noor uh LAHJ ih kil) **disorder:** disorder in which messages between the brain and nerves are not clear; occurs when cells in a person's brain, spinal cord, or nerves become damaged

**nicotine:** stimulant drug in tobacco

**noise pollution:** loud sounds that can harm a person's health

**noncommunicable disease:** an illness that is not caused by a pathogen

**nuclear power plant:** place where radiation is used in the process of producing electricity

**nurse:** person who has the special training needed to care for the sick and injured

**nursing assistant:** person who helps a nurse care for patients

**nutrient** (NEW tree unt): substance in foods that is used by the body for growth, for repair of body cells, and to provide energy

**nutrition** (new TRISH un): the study of what a person eats, eating habits, and how these affect health

# O

**occupational therapist** (THER uh pust): person who teaches patients to eat, dress, and work

**open dump:** large open area where garbage is piled

**operating room:** separate place in a hospital where surgery is done

**operation:** procedure in which the body is made healthier by surgery

**ophthalmoscope** (ahf THAL muh skohp): instrument used by a doctor to see the blood vessels and internal parts of the eye

**optic nerve:** part of the eye that carries nerve messages from the retina to the brain

**orthodontist:** a dentist who is trained to fit braces on people's teeth

**OTC drug:** drug that can be bought without a doctor's prescription

**otoscope** (OHT uh skohp): instrument used by a doctor to look inside a person's ear to examine the ear canal and the eardrum

# P

**PABA:** chemical that screens out the sun's ultraviolet rays which cause tanning

**palpation** (pal PAY shun): method of touching or feeling a person's body to learn how it is functioning

**paralyzed** (PER uh lized): loss of use of a part of the body

**patient:** person who is in the hospital for medical care or treatment

**peer pressure:** influence on a person by people of his/her age group

**percussion** (per KUSH un): method of tapping on a person's chest, abdomen, or back by a doctor with his/her fingers to produce sounds that tell what is going on inside the body

**periodontal** (per ee oh DAHNT uhl) **disease:** a disease of the gums and other tissues that support the teeth

**periodontal membrane:** layer of tissue between the cementum and the jawbone that helps to hold a tooth in place

**pesticide** (PES tuh side): poison that kills insects or pests; often used in the home

**pharmacist** (FAR muh sust): person with special training who reads a doctor's prescription and fills the order

**physical dependence:** bodily need for a drug

**physical examination:** process of having a doctor check a person's body and gather information about the person and his/her family to assess and plan for the person's health

**physical fitness:** includes physical exercises that get your body in the best possible physical condition for you

**physical health:** how well the body works; the well-being of the body

**physical therapist** (THER uh pust): person who helps patients move; may work with exercises, heat, light, crutches, and braces

**pituitary** (puh TEW uh ter ee) **gland:** pea-sized gland at the base of the brain; sometimes called the "master gland" because it regulates the activities of the other glands; secretes growth hormone during adolescence

**plaque** (PLAK): sticky substance that contains bacteria; forms near the gumline and in between teeth; sticks to the grooves and curves on your teeth

**platelets** (PLAYT luts): cells in the blood which help to form clots

**pollutants** (puh LEWT unts): wastes in the environment in the form of smoke, gases, or small pieces of dirt

**pollution** (puh LEW shun): presence in the environment of materials that are harmful to living things

**postnasal** (pohst NAY zul) **drip:** heavy discharge that drains from the nose to the throat

**prescription** (prih SKRIHP shun): written order from a doctor that allows a person to get a special medicine

**prescription drug:** special medicine a person can get with a prescription

**prickly heat:** skin rash that occurs in hot weather; caused by sweat glands that do not work well

**protein:** nutrient which is needed for growth and repair of body cells

**psychiatrist** (suh KI uh trust): medical doctor who helps persons adjust to problems; may prescribe drugs

**psychological dependence:** emotional need for a drug

**psychologist** (si KAHL uh just): person who has the special training needed to assist persons in problems of daily living

**puberty:** the period of life when body changes take place; a boy begins to look more like a man; a girl begins to look more like a woman

**pulp:** the center of the tooth that contains nerves and blood vessels; enters the tooth through an opening at the tip of the root

**pupil:** small dark hole that looks like a circle in the middle of the eye; the size of the pupil changes to control the amount of light that enters the eye

**pus:** whitish material that forms around scrapes or cuts

# Q

**quack** (KWAK): person who tries to sell you useless products and services

**quackery:** the method a quack uses to sell useless products or services

# R

**radiation** (rayd ee AY shun): particles given off by atoms or energy given off as light

**recovering:** returning to normal health after surgery or illness

**recovery room:** special room where a person's body functions are checked after surgery

**recycling:** processing waste materials for reuse

**red blood cells:** carry oxygen from the air in the lungs to all cells in the body

**reflex action:** movement of a body part without direction from the brain

**reflex test:** test a doctor uses to check if a person's nerves will cause him/her to have certain movements or reflex actions

**registered nurse (RN):** person who cares for patients under the orders and instructions of a doctor

**reproductive system:** parts of the body involved with producing offspring

**residency:** the period a medical doctor spends on getting advanced training

**resident:** doctor who gets advanced training in special areas of medical care or surgery

**respiratory system:** body parts which function in the exchange of gases between the air you breathe and your body

**retainer:** plastic device to keep teeth in place

**retina** (RET nuh): inner lining of the eye that has many nerves sensitive to light

**root:** part of a tooth that holds it in the jawbone

# S

**sanitary landfill:** place where garbage is dumped and then covered by layers of dirt

**scab:** dried blood that forms over a cut or injury

**scrape:** a wearing away of the outer layers of skin against a hard surface

**scrub room:** room in a hospital in which everyone scrubs hands, wrists, and arms thoroughly before performing surgery

**sewage** (SEW ihj): wastewater from homes and industries

**sewage treatment plant:** place where sewage is treated to remove harmful substances

**side effect:** unwanted result after taking a drug

**sidestream smoke:** smoke you inhale from other people's cigarettes

**sign language:** form of communication which involves fingers and hands in different ways; the signs are used instead of words

**skeletal system:** composed of all the bones in the skeleton

**skeleton:** body's frame which consists of all the bones

**small intestine:** part of the body in which digestion is completed; receives food from the stomach

**smog:** haziness that is made up of smoke and fog

**social growth:** progress that you make in relating well with other people

**social health:** way you relate to other people; social well-being

**social worker:** person who has the special training to find resources that help people with a variety of needs

**solid wastes:** remains of products that are thrown away

**soybean:** high-protein plant food

**specialist:** doctor who works in one special area of medicine

**speech pathologist** (puh THAL uh just): person with special training who studies and treats speech problems

**sphygmomanometer** (sfihg moh muh NAHM ut ur): instrument or blood pressure cuff that is used to measure the two blood pressure readings

**spinal cord:** nerve fibers that run through the spinal column; these fibers extend from the brain through most of the backbone

**sports medicine:** specialized study of all things that happen to a person's body during exercise

**stepfather:** someone who marries a person's mother

**stepmother:** someone who marries a person's father

**stethoscope** (STETH uh skohp): instrument a doctor uses to hear body sounds

**stimulant** (STIHM yuh lunt): drug which speeds up the body's activities

**stress:** body's reaction to any demand made upon it; a physical or mental demand made upon the body

**stretcher:** a table upon which a person is moved; sometimes on wheels

**stroke:** clogged or burst blood vessel in the brain; damage to parts of the brain will occur

**symptom:** change in bodily function from a normal pattern

# T

**tamper-resistant package:** a sealed container that shows whether or not a drug container has been opened before purchase

**tar:** brown, sticky substance in cigarette smoke

**thermal pollution:** hot water that is dumped back into rivers and lakes; raises the temperatures of the rivers and lakes

**thyroid** (THI royd) **gland:** gland located at the front of the neck near the voice box; secretes a hormone that controls how fast a person will grow

**tolerance:** a need for larger and larger amounts of a drug to get the effect a person was once able to get

**tongue depressor** (dih PRES ur): a wooden stick used by a doctor to hold down a person's tongue during a physical examination

**toothbrushing:** movements with a toothbrush to remove plaque from the exposed surfaces of teeth

**trachea** (TRAY kee uh): tube which leads from the throat to the lungs; another name for the windpipe

# U

**ulcer** (UL sur): sore that forms in the stomach lining

**ultraviolet** (ul truh VI uh lut) **rays:** rays from the sun that are a form of radiation

**Universal Product Code:** computer code symbols which contain information about the name, manufacturer, and size of a product

**urinary bladder:** muscular sac that stores urine

**urinary** (YOOR uh ner ee) **system:** parts of the body involved in removing liquid wastes

**urine:** liquid waste that is stored in the urinary bladder before being removed from the body

# V

**veins:** blood vessels that carry blood to the heart

**veterinarian** (veh trun ER ee un): a person with special training who prevents and treats disease in animals

**vitamins:** nutrients which help your body use proteins, fats, and carbohydrates

# W

**warming up:** ten to twenty minutes of getting muscles ready to do more work; prevents injury and soreness to muscles

**water:** liquid that is a part of all cells, helps the body digest food, and is part of blood and urine

**wheeze** (WEEZ): whistling sound made when a person breathes; occurs during asthma attacks

**white blood cells:** blood cells that help protect you from germs

**withdrawal:** illness that occurs when a drug upon which a person is dependent is taken away

# Z

**zinc oxide:** cream put on the skin to block all the sun's rays from your skin

# Index

## A

**Acne,** 239
**Addiction,** 181
**Administrator, 168**
**Adolescence, 27**–32
**Adolescent, 27**
**Adrenal glands, 33, 111;** act., 111
**Adrenaline, 33**
**Aerobic exercise, 49;** act., 50; illus., 49
**Agility,** 46, **47,** 53; illus., 47
**Aging,** 38
**Air pollution,** 263, 264, 275–278, 287–289; act., 278, 289; illus., 264
**Alcohol,** 82, **193**–197
**Alcoholic drinks,** 194, 195
**Alcohol-related problems,** 196, 197
**Allergy, 226**
**Alveoli, 107,** 108; illus., 109
**Ambulance service,** 173
**American Cancer Society,** 240
**American Dental Association (ADA),** 64–66
**Amphetamines,** 183
**Anaerobic exercise, 49;** act., 50; illus., 49
**Anosmia,** 96
**Appendicitis, 226** 227; illus., 227
**Appendix,** 226, 227; illus., 227
**Arteries, 106;** illus., 106
**Asbestos, 282**
**Aspirin,** 186
**Asthma, 226,** 239; inhaler, illus., 226
**Athletic trainers,** 230
**Auscultation, 157**

## B

**Backbone,** 103
**Bacteria,** 62
**Balanced diet,** 81, 107
**Beer,** 193, 194
**Bicuspids, 61;** illus., 61
**Bitter,** 95; illus., 95
**Bleeding,** 251
**Blindness,** 91, 121, 122; act., 122
**Blood,** 75, **105**–107; composed of, 105; functions of, 105, 106
**Blood alcohol level, 195**
**Blood cells,** 105
**Blood pressure, 158,** 159, 280
**Blood sample,** 159
**Bloodstream,** 106, 194
**Blood vessels, 106**
**Body movements,** 155
**Body senses,** 89
**Body systems,** 103–112
**Body temperature,** 152; act., 152
**Bones,** 27, 105, 253
**Bowel movement, 108**
**Braces,** 68
**Braille system,** 97, **121;** illus., 122
**Brain,** 89, 93, 95, 97, **103,** 104, 123, 125, 194
**Brain disorder,** 125, 126
**Breakfast,** 78
**Breathing rate,** 33, 108; act., 108

## C

**Caffeine, 182;** illus., 182
**Calculus, 62,** 63

## C (continued)

**Cancer, 160, 269,** 282
**Capillaries, 106;** illus., 106
**Carbohydrate loading, 81**
**Carbohydrates, 74,** 81
**Carbon monoxide, 277**
**cardiopulmonary resuscitation (CPR), 224,** 225; illus., 224
**Cardio-respiratory fitness,** 46, **47,** 48, 53; illus., 47
**Car pool, 288**
**Cavities,** 62, 67; illus., 62
**Cavity filling,** 62, 63
**Celsius,** 152
**Cementum, 59;** act., 60; illus., 60
**Cigarette smoking,** 107, 108, 197–200, 276, 289; chart, 199
**Circulatory system, 105**–107; illus., 106
**Clean air laws,** 288
**Clerical helper, 168**
**Cocaine, 214**
**Cold,** 97, 235, 241, 243
**Common cold,** 62, 160
**Communicable disease, 160**
**Communication,** 19, 98, **123**
**Cooling down, 54**
**Crack, 214**
**Crown, 59,** 61; act., 60; illus., 60
**Cusp, 59,** 61; act., 60; illus., 60
**Cuspids, 61;** illus., 61
**Cuts,** 250, 251

## D

**DDT,** 265
**Deaf, 123**–125; act., 125
**Deaf-mute, 124**
**Decibels, 279**

**Decision, 8,** 205–212; steps in making a, 210, 211; act., 209, 212

**Decision making, 205**–212

**Deep-freeze surgery,** 244

**Dental health,** 9, 59–67

**Dental hygienist,** 62, **141**

**Dentin, 59,** 63; act., 60; illus., 60

**Dentist,** 9, 62, 63, 66, **141;** illus., 66

**Depressant, 180**–182, 193

**Designer drugs, 214**

**Diabetes, 228,** 229

**Diabetic coma, 228,** 229

**Diagnosis, 150,** 165

**Dietitian, 141, 168**

**Digestion,** 35

**Digestive juices,** 108

**Digestive system, 108,** 194; illus., 109

**Disability,** 117–127

**Dislocation, 253**

**Distress, 34**–37; illus., 34, 35

**Divorce,** 22

**Dizzy,** 78, 185, 237

**Doctor,** 165–172, **168;** illus., 172

**Drug, 179**–187, 198, 207, 214

**Drug-free, 212,** 213

**E**

**Ear,** 89, 93, 94, 123, 153; illus., 93

**Ear canal,** 153

**Eardrum, 93,** 153; illus., 93

**Ear specialist,** 153

**Ear wax,** 123, 153

**Eating habits,** 73, 75; act., 80

**Emergency, 165**

**Emergency care,** 173, 222, 223

**Emergency room, 172,** 173; illus., 173

**Emotional growth, 29**–31

**Emotions,** 27, **29**–31; act., 31

**Emphysema,** 276

**Enamel, 59,** 62, 66; act., 60; illus., 60, 62

**Endocrine system, 110**–112; act., 111; illus., 111

**Energy,** 73, 74, 78

**Environment, 263,** 269, 281

**Ethyl alcohol, 193**

**Eustress, 34,** 35; illus., 34

**Eye examinations,** 153

**Eyeglasses,** 7

**Eyeguards,** 91; illus., 91

**Eyes,** 91, 92, 153

**F**

**Fahrenheit,** 152

**Family,** 9, 20, 208, 209

**Fast food, 79**

**Fats,** 74, 80

**Fermentation, 193**

**Fever, 152**

**Filling,** 62, 63

**First aid, 221**–226

**Five senses,** 89–97

**Flexibility,** 46, **47,** 53; illus., 47

**Floss,** 65

**Flossing, 65,** 67; illus., 65

**Fluoride,** 66

**Fluoride pill,** 66

**Food group, 75,** 76, 80; chart, 76

**Friend,** 15, **16,** 17, 20, 32; act., 17, 18; chart, 16

**Frostbite, 241;** act., 242; illus., 241

**G**

**Garbage,** 270, 293, 294

**Gingivitis,** 63

**Glands, 27,** 28, 33, 110–112

**Goals,** 80, **213**

**Grain alcohol, 193**

**Grateful,** 21

**Growth hormone, 27**

**Growth spurt,** 27, 28

**Guide dog,** 121

**Gums,** 63–65, 155

**H**

**Habit,** 73, 75, **181,** 198

**Hallucinogen,** 184

**Handicap,** 117–127, **118,** 128

**Headache,** 186

**Health consumer, 135**–138

**Health decision,** 8, 10

**Health educator, 141,** 161

**Health history, 150;** illus., 150

**Health inspectors, 139;** illus., 291

**Health knowledge, 6**–10; act., 8, 10

**Health products, 135**–138; act., 137

**Health record, 150**

**Health services, 135,** 138–142; act., 141; chart, 140, 141

**Health standard, 139**

**Healthy, 5**

**Hearing,** 89, 93, 94

**Hearing aid,** 123

**Hearing disabilities,** 124

**Hearing loss,** 93, 94, 123, 124, 279

**Heart,** 33, 104, **106**–108; illus., 106

**Heart attack,** 221, **223,** 224, 276

**Heartbeat,** 158

**Heart disease,** 160, 198

**Heat,** 97, 235

**Heat cramps, 235,** 236

**Heat exhaustion, 237;** act., 239

**Heatstroke, 237,** 238; act., 239

**Height-weight chart,** 151

**Heroin,** 181

**High blood pressure,** 159

**Hormones, 27,** 28, 110-112

**Hospital, 165**–173

**Hospital attendant, 141**

**Hospital careers,** act., 168; chart, 168

**Hospital pamphlet,** act., 171
**Hypothermia, 243,** 244

**I**

**Incinerators, 294**
**Incisors, 60;** illus., 61
**Infection, 250**
**Informed decision, 207**
**Inherit, 126**
**Inner membrane seal,** 188
**Insect bites, 226**
**Insulin, 228,** 229; illus., 228
**Insulin shock, 229**
**Intern, 167**
**Internship, 167**
**Iris, 90;** illus., 90
**Isometric exercise, 48,** act., 50; illus., 48
**Isotonic exercise, 48;** act., 50; illus., 48

**J**

**Joint, 253**

**K**

**Kidneys, 110;** illus., 110

**L**

**Large intestine, 108;** illus., 109
**Lead bands,** 188
**Lead poisoning,** 271, 295
**Legally blind, 121**
**Lens, 90;** illus., 90
**Licensed practical nurse (LPN), 168**
**Life expectancy, 149**
**Litter, 270;** illus., 270
**Lung cancer,** 198, 199, 276
**Lungs,** 104, **107,** 156, 157, 198–200, 276; illus., 106, 109

**M**

**Mainstreaming,** 128
**Malathion,** 265
**Malnutrition,** 126
**Marijuana, 184;** illus., 184
**Mass transit, 288**
**Medical care,** 165
**Medical doctor, 141**
**Medical emergency, 221**–229
**Medical technologist, 141, 168,** 169
**Medicine,** 179
**Mental defect,** 117
**Mental health, 6,** 7, 135, 137, 142, 143
**Mental health clinic,** 142
**Mental health service,** 142
**Methyl alcohol, 193**
**Minerals, 74;** chart, 74
**Molars, 61;** illus., 61
**Morphine,** 181
**Mouth,** 59–61, 108
**Mucous membranes, 154**
**Mucus,** 154
**Muscle cramps,** 81
**Muscles,** 27, 74
**Muscular endurance,** 46, **47,** 53, 81; illus., 47
**Muscular-skeletal systems,** 104, 105; illus., 104
**Muscular strength,** 46, **47,** 48, 53; illus., 47
**Muscular system, 105**

**N**

**Nails,** 74
**Nasal speculum,** 154
**Neck,** 28
**Needs,** 15, 16
**Nerve cells, 103**
**Nerves,** 74, 90, 125, 155; illus., 125
**Nervous system, 103,** 104, 125
**Neurological disorder, 125,** 126

**Nicotine, 198**
**Noise pollution, 268;** hearing and, 279, 280; indoor, 290; law and, 290; your body and, 280, 281; act., 268, 281; illus., 290
**Noncommunicable disease, 160**
**Nose,** 95, 154, 276
**Nostrils,** 154
**Nuclear power plant, 269,** 283
**Nurse, 141**
**Nursing assistant, 168**
**Nutrients, 73**–81, 107
**Nutrition, 73**–81

**O**

**Occupational therapist, 168**
**Open dump, 294**
**Operating room, 172**
**Operation,** 172
**Ophthalmoscope, 153**
**Optic nerve, 90;** illus., 90
**Orthodontist,** 68
**Otoscope, 153**
**Overeating,** 77
**Over-the-counter (OTC) drug, 186,** 187, 212; act., 187; chart, 187
**Overweight,** 151, 159

**P**

**PABA, 241**
**Pain,** 97
**Palpation, 156;** illus., 156
**Paralyzed, 225**
**Patients,** 165–173
**Peer pressure, 207,** 208, 213; illus., 207
**Percussion, 156;** act., 157; illus., 157
**Periodontal disease, 63,** 64
**Periodontal membrane, 59;** act., 60; illus., 60
**Perspiration,** 81, 236

Pesticide, **265,** 281, 291; act., 266, 292
Pharmacist, **141, 185**
Physical defect, **117**
Physical dependence, **181,** 182
Physical examination, **149**–159; illus., 153, 154, 156, 157, 158, 159
Physical exercise, 9, 37, 46, 48, 80, 81, 107; act., 50, 54; illus., 46, 48, 49, 52–54
Physical fitness, **45**–54; program for, 52, 53
Physical growth, **28**
Physical health, **5,** 135, 136, 143; act., 137; chart, 140, 141
Physical therapist, **168,** 230
Pituitary gland, **27,** 111, 112; illus., 111
Plaque, **62**–65, 67
Plasma, **105**
Platelets, **106**
Poison control center, 291
Poisoning, 126
Polio, 118
Pollutants, **263,** 264, 275, 287, 288
Pollution, **263**–270, 275–282, 287–295
Pollution controls, 287
Postnasal drip, **154**
Prescription, **185,** 186
Prescription drug, **185,** 186, 212; chart, 185
President's Council on Physical Fitness, 45
Pressure, 97
Prickly heat, **239**
Proteins, **74,** 78, 80
Psychiatrist, 142
Psychological dependence, **181,** 182, 183, 198
Psychologist, 142
Puberty, 112
Pulp, **59;** act., 60; illus., 60
Pulse, 158, 159

Pupil, **90;** act., 90; illus., 90
Pus, 153, **250**

**Q**

Quack, **143**
Quackery, **143**

**R**

Radiation, **269,** 282, 283
Recovering, **82**
Recovery room, **172**
Recycling, **294,** 295; illus., 294
Red blood cells, **105,** 106, 159; illus., 107
Reflex actions, 155
Reflex tests, 155, 156
Registered nurse (RN), **168**
Reproductive system, **112**
Residency, **167**
Resident, **167**
Respiratory system, **107,** 108, 275; illus., 109
Retainer, 68
Retina, **90;** illus., 90
Ribs, 104, 105; illus., 104
Root, **59,** 61; act., 60; illus., 60
Running (jogging), 254, 255

**S**

Salt, 81, 82, 95, 236; illus., 95
Sanitary landfill, **294**
Scab, **250**
Scar, **250**
Scrape, **249,** 250
Scrub room, **172;** illus., 172
Sense organs, 89, 93, 95, 97
Sewage, **267**
Sewage treatment plants, **267**
Shrink bands, **188**
Side effect, **185**
Sidestream smoke, **200;** illus., 200

Sight, 89–92
Sign language, **124;** act., 125; illus., 124
Skeletal system, **104,** 105
Skeleton, **104**
Skin, 74, 97
Skin cancer, 160, 239–241
Skull, 104, 105
Small intestine, **108,** 194; illus., 109
Smell, 89, 95, 96; act., 96
Smog, **264;** illus., 264
Smokeless tobacco, 200
Smoking, 197–200; act., 200
Snuff, 200
Social growth, **32**
Social health, 6, 7, 135, 138
Social health service, 142–143
Social health service consumer, chart, 142
Social workers, **142**
Solid wastes, **270,** 293–294
Sore muscles, **251,** 252; act., 252
Sound waves, 93
Sour, 95; illus., 95
Soybeans, 82
Specialist, **167**
Speech pathologist, **141**
Sphygmomanometer, **158**
Spinal cord, **103,** 125; illus., 125
Sports injuries, **249**–256; act., 255
Sports medicine, 230
Starches, 74
Stepfather, 22
Stepmother, 22
Stethoscope, 157
Stimulants, **182**–183, 198
Stomach, 108, 194; illus., 109
Stress, **33**–37, 280; act., 37
Stretcher, **170**
Stroke, **225**
Sugars, 67, 74, 79, 82; act., 67

**Sunburn,** 239–241, 282; illus., 240

**Surgery,** 172, 227

**Sweet,** 95; illus., 95

**Symptom, 150**

## T

**Tamper-resistant packaging,** 188

**Tar, 199**

**Taste,** 89, 95; act., 96

**Taste buds,** 95; illus., 95

**Team sports,** 256

**Teeth,** 59–67, 155; kinds of, 60, 61; structure of, 59, 60; act., 60

**Thermal pollution, 267**

**Thermometer,** 152; act., 152; illus., 152

**Throat,** 276

**Thyroid gland, 28,** 112, 153; illus., 111

**Tobacco,** 198

**Tolerance, 181,** 182

**Tongue,** 95, 154, 155

**Tongue depressor, 154**

**Tonsils,** 155

**Toothbrushing,** 64, 67; illus., 64

**Tooth decay,** 62, 63, 79; illus., 62

**Toothpaste,** 66

**Touch,** 89, 97

**Trachea,** 107

**Tranquilizer,** 180

**TV,** 98

## U

**Ulcer,** 35

**Ultraviolet rays, 282**

**Underweight,** 151

**Unit dose packaging,** 188

**Universal Product Code,** 144

**Urinary bladder, 110;** illus., 110

**Urinary system, 110;** illus., 110

**Urine,** 75, **110,** 169

## V

**Veins, 106;** illus., 106

**Vending machines,** 79; illus., 79

**Veterinarian, 141;** illus., 140

**Vision,** 121

**Vitamins, 74,** 81; chart, 74

## W

**Warming up, 54**

**Waste materials,** 105–110

**Water,** 75, 266, 267, 282, 293

**Water pollution,** 266, 267, 282, 292, 293; illus., 267, 293

**Weight,** 151

**Wheeze, 226**

**Whiskey,** 193–195

**White blood cells, 106,** 159

**Windpipe,** 107; illus., 109

**Wine,** 193–195

**Withdrawal,** 181, 182

**Wood alcohol,** 193

## X

**X rays,** 126, 170, 269, 282; illus., 63, 269

## Z

**Zinc oxide,** 241